DEEP TRIVEDI

Deep Trivedi is a renowned author, speaker and master of psychology. He writes and conducts workshops with an all-pervasive perspective, guiding individuals towards the achievement of their full potential. To date, he has led millions of people onto the path of success and happiness through his works.

In his voluminous works, Deep Trivedi has extensively explained Nature, its laws, its behaviour, its psychology and the effect it has on human life. No aspect of life and human psychology has been left untouched by him. He states that lack of psychological knowledge and understanding is the sole reason for all the sorrows and failures that pervade human life.

He has authored the bestsellers 'I am The Mind', 'I am Krishna', 'I am Gita', 'Everything is Psychology', '101 All Time Great Stories', 'The Black Book of Soul', '3 Easy Steps To Win At Life' and many more. His bestseller 'I am The Mind' has been published in several national and international languages. He has been awarded the Times Power Men Award 2018 for his immense contribution to society.

His command over the biggest psychologies of life can be gauged by the fact that he holds the record for 'Maximum Workshops on Human Life', 'Maximum Workshops on Psychological Aspects of Tao Te Ching', 'Maximum Workshops on Ashtavakra Gita' and 'Maximum Workshops on Bhagavad Gita', spanning 168 hours, 28 minutes, 50 seconds in 58 days in different National and International record books. He also holds the record for 'Maximum Number of Quotations on Human Life' (about 12038) on subjects such as Soul, Human Life, Psychology, Laws of Nature, Destiny and many more. He has also been awarded an Honorary Doctorate for his works on the psychology of Bhagavad Gita. His interactive workshops have brought about a revolutionary transformation in people's lives by addressing their day-to-day concerns. These workshops have been conducted in front of live audiences across India.

He is known for his special ability to touch upon the deepest aspects of life and explain them in a lucid language, leaving no scope for ambiguity. The distinct spiritual-psychological language and expression in his writings and workshops begin to have an instant effect on the mind of the reader or listener, which makes Deep Trivedi a pioneer in this field.

To know more about Deep Trivedi, visit www.deeptrivedi.com

DEEP TRIVEDI

The Speaker

Deep Trivedi uses a unique combination of psycho-spiritual content, voice, language and expression, which effectuates an instantaneous transformation in his viewers and listeners. Millions of lives have been transformed just by listening to him.

His interactive workshops have brought about a revolutionary transformation in people's lives by addressing their day-to-day concerns. Deep Trivedi sheds light on every aspect of human life and mind and he has extensively spoken on the Bhagavad Gita, Tao Te Ching, Ashtavakra Gita, Secrets of Nature, Mind, Soul, Time, Destiny, and numerous other topics such as:

- **Ego**
- **God**
- **Guilt**
- **Love**
- **Anger**
- **Future**
- **Wealth**
- **Phobias**
- **Religion**
- **Complex**
- **Marriage**
- **Freedom**
- **Partiality**
- **Day-Sleep**
- **DNA-Genes**
- **Path of Life**
- **Personality**
- **Expectation**
- **Acceptance**
- **Hypocrisy**
- **Creativity**
- **Confusion**
- **Good-Bad**
- **Involvement**
- **Concentration**
- **Laws of Nature**
- **Time and Space**
- **Mind and Brain**
- **Self-Confidence**
- **Joy and Happiness**
- **Natural Intelligence**
- **Power of Transformation**

MONEY & ITS SMART PSYCHOLOGY

Stop Chasing Money... Let Money Chase You!

DEEP TRIVEDI

Author of the Bestsellers 'I am The Mind', 'I am Gita' & 'Everything is Psychology'

Also available in Hindi, Marathi and Gujarati

First Edition: 2024

Printed in India

Concept, Illustration and Design:

www.aatmaninnovations.com

Publisher: Aatman Innovations Pvt. Ltd.
Place of Publication: Mumbai

ISBN 978-81-19685-92-9

Money...money...money! What is it about money that makes the world go round? Money sparks joy in your life but also makes you cry tears of frustration. Money brings people together but also holds the power to break them apart. Money is the reason behind man's phenomenal progress but is also the cause of his downfall. What makes money so contradictory in nature? Have we, as a human race, failed to understand the contradictory nature of money? Is it possible to have money in abundance and still live a life of peace and bliss? The answers to these questions can only be found by delving into the depths of two words—money and psychology.

Surely, in this regard, it is inessential to explain what money is. For, is there anyone in this world who is not acquainted with the concept of 'money'? If presented with an opportunity, you could even pen a reasonably good essay on the subject. Therefore, money is certainly not an entity that is completely alien to anyone. Now, let us take a look at the word 'psychology'—what is psychology? Once again, I'm certain you will be able to jot down a few thoughts on this subject as well. This implies, you are acquainted with both money as well as psychology. So, the question naturally follows: is there any connection between the two? In all probability, this question may silence you, plunge you into contemplation, or you may even reject the very idea of a connection between the two. Whatever be the case, through this book, we will not only delve into the subject of money but also gain a profound understanding of psychology. Moreover, we will discuss in depth the relationship between 'money' and 'psychology' and also explore whether or not a connection between the two truly exists.

We will endeavour to grasp the concept of money in all its profundity because 'money' is the biggest nuisance in today's

> "To **gain control** over **money,** first **gain** an **insight** into its **psychology**

times. Similarly, we will discuss psychology in depth because a profound psychological understanding is crucial to navigate the complex circumstances of the modern era. And since the primary focus of this book is money and its psychology, we will also keenly explore the relationship between the two. Most importantly, we will endeavour to expand the horizons of our 'psychological understanding' whenever such an opportunity presents itself. For, ultimately, psychology is at the root of everything!

Well, you are already familiar with money, as you deal with it frequently on a daily basis. So, you are not completely oblivious to it. Therefore, we will first comprehend the meaning of psychology. Simply stated, psychology is the art of understanding the 'mind'. And based on the present disposition of the 'mind', to grasp its past and future, i.e. to determine the causes (past) and implications (future) is the range of psychology. At this point, let me clarify a common misconception that the mind is present only in human beings, which is yet another grave misunderstanding about the mind! The fact is, there is not a single living or non-living entity in the universe that is devoid of a 'mind'. The only distinguishing factor is, the mind is present in its entirety in human beings. This is precisely why it is only the human mind that is discussed, and also why comprehending the human mind is far more challenging. But, honestly speaking, it is never easy to fathom the mind, irrespective of whose mind it is.

Gaining an understanding of anything apart from the mind is not so daunting, but when it comes to fathoming the mind, usually, everyone's mental faculties fall short. Neither are they able to comprehend their own mind, nor of others. They continue to remain deluded not just about themselves but regarding others as well. Tell me, you have spent an entire lifetime with yourself, but if someone were to ask you to define yourself, what would your response be? You would be rendered speechless. Words will elude you. Even after journeying a life spanning fifty years, you will not be able to state anything about yourself with certainty. And if someone were to pose the same question about your life partner, you will exclaim, "Don't even ask! I've been trying to solve this mystery since the day I got married, but I'm still clueless!"

The point worth pondering here is, when you are unable to state anything with conviction about your own mind or that of your life partner, then how on earth can you ever fathom the minds of other living or non-living entities? And the truth is, you are unable to do so! No matter whose 'mind' it is, the human being invariably remains confused about it. Whereas, comprehending the mind is crucial for any kind of interaction. Indeed, if you interact with anyone without understanding their mind, you are bound to commit blunders and fall flat on your face. And this is precisely the state of affairs all around us.

Well, the most significant point in this discussion is that comprehending the 'mind' and explaining it to others falls under the purview of psychology. And this is precisely why developing one's "psychological understanding" is of paramount importance so that it eases our interactions with others, be it with an object or a person. In fact, even as we explore and try to fathom the "psychology of money", we will seize every opportunity to enhance our "psychological understanding". For, it is due to the

Money never creates any nuisance for kings

lack of psychological knowledge that everyone's interactions have become cumbersome, be it with fellow human beings or inanimate objects.

The crux of the matter is, regardless of who or what you are dealing with, comprehending their mind—in other words, their psychology—is of utmost importance. Dealing with anyone without a thorough grasp of their psychology is a challenging task, even if it is your most persistent problem—'money'. And since this book deals with the subject of money, let us dive right into comprehending the reasons behind the problems triggered by money. The first question that arises is, does money truly possess a psychology of its own? The question is pertinent because if money has a psychology, then money must also possess a 'mind' of its own. For, it is only the mind that has a psychology. Therefore, let me make it clear that money does possess a 'mind' as well as a 'psychology' of its own. As a matter of fact, why just money, there is no visible or invisible entity in this entire universe that is devoid of its own mind and psychology. For example, providing light, energy and vitamin D is the psychology of the sun. Similarly, flowing, cleansing and quenching thirst is the psychology of water. Likewise, hunting is the psychology of a lion, tiger or cheetah, while grazing is the psychology of a cow or buffalo. In essence, whether it is a living or non-living entity, everyone and everything undoubtedly possesses its own unique psychology. With this explanation, I'm sure you must have grasped this point.

Now, everything you have comprehended so far is based on my explanation, but it is my earnest desire to see you develop your psychological understanding—and how will that happen? It can only happen by expanding your knowledge of psychology. And for that purpose, it is essential to comprehend what psychology truly is. So, the function of psychology is to unravel things, that is, to bring to the fore all the hidden aspects. And how can something be unravelled? By gauging its past and future—in other words—the causes behind it and its implications. And this is precisely what I wish to teach you—how to perceive the causes and implications of everything. Generally speaking, most people are able to grasp what is being said or what is apparent to them, but the one who is adept at psychology grasps even the past events that have led to that statement as well as the implications of that statement. And you too must develop this quality and become adept at it. So, tell me, based on my explanation thus far, were you able to grasp any point that was over and above my explanation? Ideally, you should have grasped one additional point. If you haven't, take some time to mull over it. Close your eyes and ponder deeply on it. If you wish, read the aforementioned explanation once again; and to that end, I will allow you some more time. Just think; what could be that unspoken aspect that you should have grasped without it being spelled out? If you really want to learn psychology, take a pause and refrain from reading any further.

To give you an analogy, just as X-rays and MRI reveal the internal functioning of the 'body', psychology delves into the depths of every person's mind. And it is imperative for you to learn the art of delving into the minds of others, because understanding the mind eases one's interaction with others, be it with people or objects. In fact, dealing with others without comprehending their mind is the very reason problems are plaguing one's life. Therefore, you must revisit what has been explained so far to increase your psychological understanding. Whatever you do, strive to glean the unspoken psychological truth stated in the aforementioned explanation. And discovering this is not an arduous task at all. For, psychology unfolds progressively, much like peeling away the layers of an onion. As you grasp one aspect of a subject and continue to peel away its layers, you will automatically delve deeper and deeper into its core. And this descent into the depths of a subject is what we call 'psychology'. Indeed, a few insights about you will suffice for a master of psychology to gain a complete understanding of you. They will then delve deeper into those insights and discern your personality in its entirety.

Essentially, while everyone is able to grasp the spoken words, psychologists grasp everything that precedes and follows those words as well, capturing the unsaid. And it is my ardent desire to transform you into such a master of psychology. It is for this reason that I have presented you with the aforementioned test, hoping that you succeed in it.

Well, I am sure you must have made an effort and some of you must have even grasped what I have been referring to. Nonetheless, I will still go ahead and explain. So, as I had mentioned earlier, providing light is the psychology of the sun, flowing is the psychology of water, hunting is the psychology of a lion and grazing is the psychology of a buffalo. The unspoken aspect that needed to be grasped from this is that the psychology of these entities is not a new phenomenon. The sun has been emitting light since millions of years. Similarly, the lion has been hunting its prey since prehistoric times, just like it does today. Neither has an herbivorous lion ever existed nor has the sun ever stopped emitting light. So, what does this imply? It signifies that each entity possesses its unique, original psychology, which remains unaltered. I wanted you to reflect on this very facet so that you could comprehend this point on your own. Besides, grasping this truth was not very challenging either; the only reason an exercise like this can prove to be difficult in the initial stages is because there is no training available to help one delve into psychological contemplation. However, rest assured, as you progressively grasp the causes and implications of all the things that you see and hear, you will continue to evolve into a master of psychology. On my part, I will not miss out on any opportunity to transform you into a 'Master of Psychology'. I shall

"**Money** is **quite similar** to a **wife**. It is actually the **wife who controls you**, but you **believe** it is you **who holds** the **reins**

repeatedly offer you the chance to comprehend the causes and implications of every matter.

Alright, let me pose another question. What could be the reason behind all my explanations so far? Why do you think I am stating all this? Take some time to ponder over this. In fact, I would suggest, don't read any further. This is essential because in today's competitive era, it is imperative to learn to delve into the depths of every subject. Grasping the causes and implications of everything is crucial—and this very art is called psychology. And the reason why I wish to transform you into a master of this art is because the entire game of life hinges upon a person's psychological power. The more layers one can peel away in a psychological sense—in other words—the more one delves deeper, the more effortlessly one will be able to deal with people and situations. For, whether it is an object, person or situation, a comprehensive understanding of each one of them is essential to deal with them perfectly. Grasp well that it is precisely this inability to deal with others without a proper understanding of them that causes all kinds of troubles. And in order to carve a splendid life for ourselves, it is necessary that we tackle everything effectively—be it objects, people or situations—and triumph over them. And for this purpose, it is crucial to develop within ourselves a virtual 'X-ray machine of psychology'. Remember, without a proper psychological understanding, it is impossible to emerge victorious in the battle of life. That is precisely why I am placing so much emphasis on increasing your psychological understanding.

Coming back to the key point of this discussion, everything has its own psychology, and this psychology is primordial. The takeaway is, money is not an exception to this either. Money too possesses a psychology of its own and it exists since time immemorial. So, do not wrongly assume that money's psychology is a new phenomenon or that money has only recently learnt to create nuisance in our lives. Money's psychology remains unaltered and it has always been what it is today. And after this detailed explanation, it is needless to state that if you wish to gain the desired control over money, a thorough comprehension of its psychology is a must. If money is causing you distress or if you are unable to acquire the desired amount of money, it is solely due to your ignorance of its psychology. And when you are ignorant of the psychology of something, you invariably tackle it in a wrong manner. For example, since you are well aware of the psychology of the sun, you know when to deal with it and for what purpose. You will think of the sun only when you need light or vitamin D. Similarly, it is a psychological truth that dealing with wives requires utmost humility, but being ignorant of this rule, if someone attempts to deal with their wife in a high-handed manner, pray tell, what would the consequence be? He will suffer both mentally as well as physically. Hopefully, you have grasped what I am trying to convey with the aforementioned examples. If not, let me re-emphasise that "dealing with anything without understanding its psychology will only harm you". Consider this an immutable principle of life. At this point, I need not reiterate that money has become a bane for everyone simply because of their ignorance of its psychology. This implies that a thorough comprehension of the psychology of money is absolutely essential. Therefore, let us straightaway dive into grasping the psychology of money and the various points one needs to keep in mind in order to comprehend its psychology. Our aim behind this exercise is to equip ourselves well to tackle 'money' effectively.

Before we proceed further, let us quickly recap our discussion so far. The takeaway of the previous chapter is that if one has to deal with anything effectively, it is essential to comprehend its psychology. However, many of you may also question the necessity of why we should even deal with anyone in the first place. Why should we pointlessly tax our brain in first comprehending the psychology and then engaging in interactions? Is dealing with anyone even necessary? These questions can definitely cross your mind because entities like the sun, water and earth have existed for aeons without really engaging in interactions. In such a scenario, one may surely question as to why we should unnecessarily cudgel our brains, and that too for the sake of a life spanning a mere 80–100 years. The question is not misplaced, but the predicament is, you are neither the earth nor the sun. You are a human being. Moreover, there is a fundamental difference between the basic structure of humans and inanimate objects. While it is true that inanimate objects engage in minimal interactions, one must also acknowledge the fact that plants engage with a wider range of elements such as 'air, water and minerals'. Speaking of animals, they are engaging with a greater number of things when compared to plants. And when we consider human beings, they obviously deal with countless objects, people and situations.

I'm sure this was easy to grasp, but tell me, why is there a difference in interactions? Everything from inanimate objects to human beings coexists in the same universe, so why is someone engaging in minimal deals, while others are engaging in countless interactions? What could be the underlying reason for such a stark contrast? It would still be comprehensible if only a few people were engaged in numerous interactions; however, when every person is engaged in countless interactions, it becomes essential to understand the reason behind it. Obviously, if only a few people were engaged thus, we could call them insane, but we certainly cannot label everyone insane. This implies, it is perhaps necessary for humans to engage in numerous interactions. But this once again prompts the question: why is this the case? I want you to make an earnest effort to find the answer to this 'why'. If you wish, take some time to reflect upon it. Be assured that these contemplations, no matter how minuscule, will increase your psychological power manifold. Hence, it is my ardent wish that you spare some time to think over it.

Now that you have mulled over this question, I'm sure you must have arrived at an answer too. So, as explained earlier, every entity in the universe possesses a 'mind' of its own. And now, let me make it emphatically clear that any disparity which is apparent in dealings and interactions is based solely on the 'mind'. The truth is, there is a vast difference between the fickleness of the minds of inanimate objects and that of human beings. Honestly speaking, the difference is as vast as the distance between the earth and the sky. And it goes without saying that the more fickle or volatile the mind, the greater will be the needs. Since the mind of inanimate objects is more or less devoid of volatility, their needs are almost non-existent. The minds of plants and animals are more volatile than inanimate objects, hence their needs exceed those of inanimate objects. Taking this premise into account, I do not need to state separately that the human mind is extremely fickle, and therefore, its needs are also limitless. This is simple arithmetic: the greater the number of one's needs, the more one will have to deal with others; in other words, one's dealings increase in direct proportion to one's needs. And since the needs of human beings are boundless, engaging in deals becomes a compulsion for them. The human being has all

> **Money** is the cause of **man's** **'degradation'** but money is also the **reason behind** **'development'**

kinds of needs, right from food, clothing and shelter to myriad other things, and surviving without them is impossible. Therefore, questioning why we must engage in dealings or why human beings are engaging in so many interactions is pointless. Simply grasp the fact that one has to engage in dealings in order to fulfil one's needs. And if you seek favourable outcomes from your dealings, then it is essential to enhance your psychological understanding. Therefore, never question why you must augment your psychological understanding either.

Well, you must have surely grasped why engaging in deals is essential and also the fact that augmenting your psychological understanding is crucial to engage in deals effectively. So, I will now present another opportunity to you to enhance your psychological understanding. If you reflect upon our discussions so far and deepen your psychological understanding a little, you will gain insight into the very 'foundation of Nature's design'. If you wish, take some time to revisit all the points explained so far, but do not let this opportunity to increase your psychological understanding slip by.

By now, you must have certainly tried to comprehend the basis of Nature's design and many of you must have grasped it as well. Nevertheless, I will still expound on it. The foundation of Nature's design is such that the entire Nature is balanced on the basis of the 'mind'. To state an example, the more fickle one's mind is, the greater are its needs. In other words, the fickleness of the mind is balanced by 'needs'. Continuing in the same vein, the more needs one has, the more one is dependent on interactions or dealings. That is, needs are balanced by the 'dependency on interactions and dealings'. And as far as engaging in deals is concerned, grasp well that Nature has bestowed 'intelligence' upon everyone in the exact proportion to one's dependency on dealings. And in revealing this, I have disclosed a profound secret of Nature's supreme intelligence. With this, you can gauge the height of Nature's supreme intelligence.

Just think about it: an inconceivably vast universe brimming with countless entities, and yet, Nature has maintained such a marvellous balance! Dependence is based on the fickleness of the mind, and intelligence is bestowed in direct proportion to the dependency. The dependence of trees and plants exceeds that of inanimate objects, hence they have been granted greater intelligence. And since the human being's dependence is boundless, he has been granted limitless intelligence. Astonishingly, this extraordinary balance of Nature is established on the basis of the 'mind'. This in itself can help you gauge the significance of the mind as well as the importance of augmenting one's psychological understanding. I hope you realise that opportunities to explore and learn such profound mysteries of Nature do not come by easily, whereas we have managed to fathom a significant secret of Nature in the course of this simple discussion. In fact, I want you to think upon and fathom all the mysteries of the mind, life and cosmos on your own; all you need to do is deepen your interest in profound psychology.

Well, it has now been established that human beings have to necessarily deal with countless objects, people and situations in their lives. And for that purpose, they are also equipped with the requisite intelligence. However, it is crucial to keep in mind that human beings have been granted this intelligence solely for the 'purpose of engaging in deals'. This is an extremely significant hint I have given you. Read this sentence a few times if you wish, but do grasp the underlying message—employing one's intelligence for any purpose apart from engaging in deals efficaciously is akin to misusing the intelligence bestowed upon us by Nature. Regrettably, most people are wasting their precious intelligence in strange, misguided pursuits, and this is the reason why a multitude of troubles have afflicted the world. Indeed, there are very few people who can impart valuable and meaningful teachings, while there is an abundance of those who impart futile and unproductive teachings. Consequently, everyone's precious intelligence is being depleted in the course of acquiring such futile knowledge. Reflect upon your own life if you wish. Surely, you must have expended a significant amount of intelligence to learn and understand things. But the question remains—has all that 'knowledge and understanding' proven useful in carving a splendid life? Doesn't this prove that you have squandered away your intelligence? This is why I am strongly emphasising the point that Nature has granted us intelligence solely 'for the purpose of engaging in deals'. Comprehend the fact that whether it's God or religion, adversities of life or business, money or family, the ability to deal with a plethora of things is the biggest necessity of life. So, I hope you will remain cognisant of this fact and from today onwards, utilise your precious intelligence only for the purpose of dealing.

Well, you must have surely grasped by now that Nature has bestowed intelligence upon us solely for the purpose of dealing. Now, tell me, what should be the basis of dealing with anyone? Undoubtedly, the fulfilment of needs. It goes without saying that any person would want to engage in a deal or transaction only when his needs stand to be fulfilled. This being the case, what is the most crucial aspect you need to be aware of when engaging in a deal? Well, it's important to grasp who or what you are dealing with, its utility and your own needs. If the utility of that object fails to align with your need, then the deal could prove to be detrimental. This is basic psychology and everyone must certainly be aware of it; but unfortunately, very few people are cognisant of these fundamental truths. That is why I keep reiterating that it is psychological ignorance that has created complications in everyone's lives. Otherwise, it is a straightforward psychological truth that human needs are boundless because the human mind is fickle. And naturally, with needs comes dependency, which in turn necessitates engaging in deals to fulfil those dependencies. And intelligence is a prerequisite for engaging in deals, an abundance of which Nature has bestowed upon human beings. Hence, human beings should utilise their intelligence only for engaging in deals and nowhere else; and every person should do it solely for fulfilling their needs. Therefore, while engaging in a deal, it is crucial to be aware of one's needs and the utility of the object or person in question. Certainly, if even this fundamental psychological sequence needs to be explained in the present scientific age, it is not a good sign. For, this exposes both the standard of the psychological knowledge of human beings and the current level of their education.

Essentially, if you have to deal even with God, it is imperative that you are absolutely clear about the usefulness of God and what need you are trying to fulfil through God. And this 'rule' of engaging in deals applies to everyone and everything, including money. Once again, I have given you a significant hint. Now, ask yourself—after gaining so much clarity, do you conduct your dealings mindfully or do you engage in a deal mindlessly, without giving it a thought? The hints I am providing you are profound, so try to grasp them in their entirety. Of course, elaborating on these matters extensively will not be possible here as the subject of this book is 'money and its psychology', not the psychology of dealing.

So, henceforth, prior to engaging in any kind of deal, pay close attention to the usefulness of the object and your own needs. Refrain from needlessly engaging in any deal without comprehending its utility. First, comprehend the utility of the entity you are dealing with and then evaluate its usefulness based on your needs. Proceed with the deal only if the two aspects are in alignment with each other. For instance, one does not need an air conditioner in freezing weather. Yet, if someone 'engages in a deal' with an air conditioner to cool such an environment, what would you call that person? This is precisely the point I am trying to convey through these subtle hints.

Basically, a thorough comprehension of the utility and usefulness of everything is highly essential in order to make a deal beneficial. And very often, you do try to engage in a deal on the basis of utility. I am not saying that you blindly engage in deals all the time. For instance, when someone mentions water, you associate it with quenching thirst, cleaning the house and washing clothes. And verily, you deal with water to fulfil such needs. In a similar vein, if someone mentions a car, you know it serves the purpose of transportation. In the case of bread and vegetables, you are aware that they satiate hunger. Likewise, a bed serves the purpose of providing restful sleep and a home provides you with a roof over your head. You are cognisant of the fact that there is joy in living with family, while friends bring cheer and camaraderie in your life. In essence, you are aware that each object has its own specific utility. And by identifying your needs based on your understanding, you even deal with them accordingly.

So, it is not that you are totally ignorant about how to engage in deals. You certainly know how to deal, but there are many crucial dealings and interactions that you engage in without a proper understanding. In such instances, neither do you evaluate the utility of the object or entity involved, nor do you take into account your own needs. And it is precisely in these situations that you find yourself trapped. In other words, although you know how to engage in deals, you are not an expert at it. You know how to navigate dealings that are unimportant or insignificant, but when it comes to engaging in the significant deals of life, you falter. And the key point is, dealing with 'money' is one of those significant deals. Very few people are able to deal with money effectively. Most people are neither cognisant of their monetary requirements nor do they really comprehend the utility of money. This is precisely the reason why everyone is troubled by 'money' the most, and the comprehension of money's psychology therefore becomes crucial. And now that

> "There is a vast **difference** between the **actual scarcity** of **money** and the **feeling** that **money** is **scarce**

we have established a solid background, we can straightaway commence a discussion on the psychology of money.

The foremost question that springs to mind about money's psychology is—what is the utility of 'money'? You deal with money day in and day out, so you must surely be cognisant of its utility. However, considering the extent to which money has troubled everyone, I don't think anyone has a fair idea of its utility. For, there is bound to be some or the other reason behind the mental distress that money has caused everyone. Well, if we try to grasp the utility of money, it is obvious that one cannot eat or consume money. Similarly, you cannot build a home or a bed by simply stacking currency notes. Fashioning a vehicle out of banknotes and adding wheels to it, you cannot embark on a journey. In essence, money does not seem to have a direct, specific and tangible utility. Then what makes money so enigmatic that everyone yearns for it? What is it about money that despite possessing no direct utility, it is everyone's prime necessity? Truth be told, it is because money encompasses everything despite having no discernible utility that it is termed 'maya' or 'illusion'.

Well, let us return to our primary question—what is the utility of money? To arrive at the answer, it is essential to delve into the psychology of money, and to that end, we will have to sift through the pages of history. For, as I have mentioned earlier, both money and its psychology are ancient. Therefore, to comprehend the psychology of money, we will have to delve into its history. Without doing so, we can neither grasp the psychology of money nor gain an insight into its utility. Therefore, in the next chapter, we will strive to fathom the psychology of money by perusing its history.

◉

Before we proceed with delving into the history of money, it is essential to first peruse the history of 'humankind', as it is the human being himself who is directly connected with money. And in this context, it is abundantly clear that all claims about the human being's origins are speculative at best. However, if the universe is approximately 13.8 billion years old and the Earth is around 4.5 billion years old, the human race must have been in existence for a minimum of twenty-five thousand years. Well, irrespective of the time when the human race came into existence, it is certain that during the primitive times, humans must have had a limited comprehension of their basic needs of hunger, thirst and shelter. The growling pangs in their stomachs must have given them the indication of being hungry and tiredness would have prompted them to sleep. Similarly, changes in weather must have stoked the necessity for shelter. This is a basic psychoanalysis which does not require much contemplation.

So, let us directly dive into the history of human development. In this context, it is certain that as human beings began to recognise their needs, they started becoming more and more organised. Of course, progress was not achieved overnight, but there was a gradual advancement with time. In the nascent stages of their organised existence, humans adopted a nomadic lifestyle, which meant that their groups would form settlements in one location, domesticate animals, and subsist on the flora and fauna available in close proximity. And when the resources in one settlement depleted, the entire group would migrate to another location that was favourable for establishing a new settlement. However, a point worth pondering is, how can it be called the fickle 'human mind' if it continued to live in such a primitive state, satiating itself with limited resources?! I have already emphasised that the human mind is extremely fickle and it constantly seeks new and better things. So, soon enough, humans were fed up with eating the food that grew in their settlement. Indeed, if the same kind of food is consumed daily, wouldn't the mind be bored? So, in its quest for excitement, the fickle human mind was bound to conjure up ever-new needs.

Now, as I have mentioned earlier, human beings have received intelligence from Nature to fulfil their needs. So, on the strength of their intelligence and with the aim of keeping the excitement in life alive, they initiated transactions with neighbouring settlements. This was perhaps the first significant application of human intelligence. To illustrate this, imagine a scenario wherein one settlement cultivated bananas and rice, while the neighbouring settlement grew wheat and apples. So, the residents of the first settlement began exchanging their rice and bananas for wheat and apples from the second settlement. Naturally, this led to both settlements experiencing a variety of food items, and needless to say, this culinary diversity added more spice to their lives as well. The point worth noting is, the fickle human mind craves variety in order to maintain a sense of excitement in life. A single object cannot sustain excitement for too long. Another aspect that needs to be grasped is, it is human intelligence that fulfils the ever-escalating needs of the mind. And undoubtedly, human intelligence has performed remarkable feats, especially in the field of science. There is absolutely no doubt that it has ably and abundantly catered to each and every one of the ever-increasing needs of the mind.

Well, moving on from the subject of human mind and intelligence, let us discuss the mutual transactions that had initiated between settlements. In that era, the concept of 'inexpensive' bananas and 'expensive' apples did not exist. In

Just like air and water, money has also become a prime necessity of life

other words, those were the times when a bunch of vegetables held an equivalent value to a bunch of delicacies, which means that every commodity was traded based on the barter system.

Then, approximately 4,000 years ago, humans settled down to some extent, and during this period they also acquired farming skills. The settlements grew in size and developed further; and once humans became adept at farming, the need to frequently relocate to newer areas also reduced considerably. In fact, the very reason they had to relocate was due to the consumption and subsequent depletion of edibles such as vegetables and fruits. However, now that they had learnt to cultivate crops on their own, the paucity of flowers, fruits and grains was no longer a concern. Nevertheless, in order to establish settlements, it was imperative for the environment to be conducive for farming. Hence, settlements predominantly thrived near rivers and lakes.

Acquiring farming skills had a two-fold benefit for human beings. First, it granted them the freedom to grow crops of their choice, resulting in them becoming self-reliant to the extent that they could now grow a variety of fruits, flowers and vegetables, which in turn helped them retain interest and excitement in their life. Second, it provided them with a permanent home; for, once they mastered the art of cultivating fruits, flowers and vegetables, they no longer felt the need to relocate frequently. In essence, it was only because of their farming skills that humans settled down to a considerable extent. However, can a human being truly settle down? Can the mind stop conjuring ever-new desires and needs? So, with shelter and sustenance no longer being a concern, humans invented new needs such as comfortable homes, clothing, jewellery, utensils, beds and so on. In other words, humans now took a step towards the concept of convenience and adornment.

On the whole, the human race was continuously progressing towards an increasingly stable existence. On one hand, the mind was conjuring up brand-new needs to sustain its excitement, and on the other, human intelligence was busy inventing novel objects, catering to the ever-growing needs of the mind. In other words, intelligence was effectively supporting the rapidly soaring needs of the mind, which is verily the duty of human intelligence. Here, I have given you a major psychological hint, which implies that if one's intelligence fails to keep pace, but the mind still persists in growing its desires, the 'mind' will undoubtedly fall into trouble. And in this world, it is verily such minds that are restless and distressed. I have once again stated a profound psychological truth. Pay heed to it, as it will save you from quite a few troubles in life.

Mainly, to fulfil the escalating needs of the mind, humans had now begun to construct lavish homes, carts and chariots, fashion exquisite clothing, concoct delicious food and delicacies, and manufacture numerous items for their comfort and convenience. Most significantly, the exchange value of goods had also modified based on their utility and demand. In other words, the system of exchanging a bunch of vegetables for a bunch of delicacies became obsolete. Indeed, with the continuous progress and development of the human race, the erstwhile system gradually waned. In other words, the earlier system of exchanging one apple for one banana was now replaced with exchanging one apple for multiple bananas. And in exchange for carts, chariots and jewellery, one could now obtain a year's worth of food. Essentially, farming was no longer necessary to meet food requirements, as food could be acquired in exchange of building carts and chariots and crafting jewellery.

Viewed from this perspective, new avenues of employment were continuously emerging in tandem with the advancement of the human race. The most significant aspect was, surviving without engaging in work had now become impossible. Similarly, the consumption of flowers and fruits no longer appealed to man, for, an array of commodities was now available to suffuse the mind with pleasure and joy. And to acquire all those commodities, both physical labour and intelligence had become prerequisites; manual labour by itself did not suffice. Basically, it had now become imperative to take up employment if one wished to lead a better life. In short, this marked the advent of a structured economy.

Well, the key point is, the human race was continuously progressing with time, and due to the ever-increasing variety of goods, markets had begun to emerge as well. However, despite these advancements, the barter system was still prevalent in the market. In other words, one commodity was still being exchanged for another. Although, there was one major shift—art and creativity had now begun to be appreciated and valued. And since artistic and creative objects such as carts and jewellery carried a higher value, those who crafted these commodities were able to

> Just like a **wife, money** too tries every possible trick to **grab your attention**

purchase more goods; and this was simply because the era in which vegetables and delicacies were considered of equal value had passed.

With the passage of time, gold gradually started emerging as a precious metal, and naturally, it gained recognition and acceptability as a highly valuable commodity. And within a short span of time, its worth skyrocketed to the point where one could acquire a substantial amount of goods in exchange for a nugget of gold. Meanwhile, settlements had also begun to grow into organised kingdoms, implying that the era of kings had dawned as well. In short, there was an all-round transformation in the standard of living of human beings. However, the most significant change took place when gold attained the status of a priceless commodity. For, in a sense, gold had assumed the form of 'money'. And this was bound to happen because with a single nugget of gold, one could acquire a massive quantity of goods. In essence, 'money' had taken birth in the form of gold.

Well, gold had surely become invaluable but a new problem had emerged with the discovery of its pricelessness. As gold gained immeasurable value, it became a catalyst for corrupting people's minds. Incidents of gold theft became rampant and even wars erupted over the possession of this precious metal. It is worth noting here that with the emergence of 'money' in the form of gold dawned the era of 'theft and plundering'. Moreover, the advent of money in the form of gold also marked the beginning of the great divide between the rich and the poor. For, the more gold one possessed, the more affluent one was considered, and in the same vein, those who did not possess gold were deemed paupers. Most significantly, it was no longer essential to earn gold in order to become wealthy, because the path to riches by way of wielding power, that is, through looting and plundering, had been discovered too. And needless to mention, in order to increase one's power and might, the manufacture of weapons for the purpose of plundering and waging wars had also begun in full swing. Essentially, it can be said that the adage, 'Necessity is the mother of invention' was proven in that era itself.

Quite notably, once humans embarked on the path of progress, their advancement continued unabated. And verily, it shouldn't cease either! For, this is what distinguishes humans from animals. In the case of animals, a lion hunted in the ancient times and it continues to hunt in the present day too. The point worth noting is that whether it is a lion or a human being, both started off by consuming raw meat in the initial stages of their life, but observe how far humans have advanced while the lion still feeds on raw flesh. And herein lies the glory of the human race. So, development should not cease at all, because the day development comes to a halt, it will not take long for humans to downgrade to the level of animals.

Well, with the passage of time, as human needs were escalating, new inventions were also being birthed in view of those ever-increasing needs. Everyone was now striving to become rich, which in turn saw an escalation in conflicts and disputes over wealth. And it is worth noting that as progress and development gained momentum, vices such as theft and deceit did not lag behind either. One could say that alongside progress, vices were also on an upward swing.

But despite all these developments, gold continued to be recognised as money for the next two thousand years. Of course, to some extent, diamonds and gemstones had also begun to gain popularity. But whether it was gold or precious gemstones, with the passage of time, they had outlived their purpose and were no longer considered the basis for transactions. With the ever-increasing progress, one could feel a strong need for a stable object for exchange purposes. Although humans were progressing steadily, an organised base or structure for transactions still eluded them despite their best efforts. And necessity is anyway the mother of invention; the day needs come to an end, discoveries and inventions will also cease. Thus, around 700 BCE, this need was fulfilled for the first time in Lydia, Turkey, where coins were minted to facilitate transactions. Indeed, the invention of coins in Turkey will be considered the most concrete step taken in the direction of 'lending money its modern form'. However, these coins were still made of gold and their value was still based on exchange. In other words, the basis of transactions remained the same, whereby one coin fetched a specific quantity of wheat or iron. So, even though coins had been invented, the basis of their exchange was not fully scientific as yet. Nonetheless, it was surely more convenient than the system prevalent in the erstwhile eras.

However, before long, another problem reared its ugly head as these gold coins became an easy target for unrestrained plundering. Consequently, those who possessed these coins were no longer safe; in fact, the lives of those carrying such coins to and fro were now in jeopardy. And verily, what can be more precious than human life? So, this paved the way for the advent of copper coins; in other words, gold coins gave way to the minting of copper coins. Then, around 118 BCE, China introduced leather-based promissory notes, which obviously turned out to be far more convenient. However, in the initial stage, this system was confined to China alone.

Subsequently, in the seventh century, China created paper, and within a short span of time, promissory notes made of paper came into circulation. This system continued in China for the next five hundred years, but even during this period, this arrangement remained confined to China alone. In the same era, the Song dynasty of China officially began to produce banknotes. Notably, China was the only country at the helm of all these endeavours to lend a modern form to money. As for Europe, the circulation of banknotes began only after 1650, and that too almost 400 years after the renowned explorer Marco Polo brought banknotes from China to Europe. And it was only after this point that this system gradually transformed into the modern money market.

In the present age, every country has its own currency with innumerable banks, and due to the advancement in the field of science, we now have access to countless goods, ranging from essentials to those providing comfort and convenience. This, in a nutshell, is the history of money. To grasp the complete psychology of money, delving into its history was imperative, which is why we have discussed the topic in brief. And if you truly wish to delve into the psychological depths of money, do remember its history. For, every secret surrounding the psychology of money will be revealed only through its history.

In the preceding chapter, we delved into the history of money and grasped how money has evolved into its present form. And as for the 'significance of money', it does not require an explanation in this modern era. Everyone is cognisant of its utility, as people's very lives are steered by money. Frankly speaking, in this day and age, the only mantra that resounds across the world is "money, money, money". Irrespective of one's religion or nationality, everyone is invariably chanting the money mantra. Hence, a pertinent question arises—from where has money acquired such immense power that everyone is chanting the money mantra day in and day out? Well, to arrive at an answer to any question regarding money, it becomes imperative to first understand what money is. Obviously, it is currency that we term as money, whether it is in the form of dollars, pounds, rupees or euros. The question that arises then is, what is the utility of money? In this context, tell me, if someone were to place ten thousand dollars on a plate and serve it to you saying, "This is your dinner," how would you respond? You will obviously wonder if that person is insane, and instead tell him to fetch you food that is edible. "Will I eat dollars?" you will ask in exasperation. Similarly, if someone were to fashion a bed out of stacks of millions of pounds and ask you to sleep on it, you would surely become ill at ease. In other words, money does not seem to have any direct utility. This then raises the question as to why money is so important. Well, it is undoubtedly due to its 'exchange value'. You may not be able to feast on money, but you can certainly splurge it to host a meal for thousands of people. You certainly cannot stack dollars to make a bed, but in exchange for the dollars, you can buy any bed your heart desires. Therefore, it is amply clear that despite a lack of direct utility, it is the 'exchange value' of money that lends it such immense importance.

Now that you have grasped the reason behind the importance of money, tell me, how did it acquire such immense power? Interestingly, the answer to this question was hidden in the chapter describing the history of money. And I have already explained that a profound contemplation of the psychology of anything leads to a better comprehension of its causes and implications. And this comprehension of cause and effect is precisely what psychology is all about. Let us suppose that someone expresses anger, an event that has occurred in the present moment. However, a deep contemplation on the person's anger can reveal the cause behind it. It can also reveal what that person is likely to do once he is enraged. In other words, with the help of a thorough contemplation, one can ascertain both the cause of the anger expressed in the present as well as its outcome that is likely to occur in the future. In a similar manner, by perusing the history of money discussed in the previous pages, one can surely arrive at the answer to the question 'how has money acquired such immense power'. And if you wish to augment your psychological power, you must definitely revisit the chapter on the history of money and seek the answer to this question. This will greatly assist you in improving your 'psychological understanding'.

Well, you might wonder why I am placing so much emphasis on augmenting your psychological understanding. It is because psychology is not confined merely to the knowledge of the 'present'. Of course, perceiving the present as it truly exists and even comprehending it is psychology; unfortunately, however, everyone's knowledge of psychology is so limited that they cannot comprehend even the events occurring in the present moment. And this is the very reason why a multitude of complexities are rearing their ugly heads in everyone's lives. The person who is

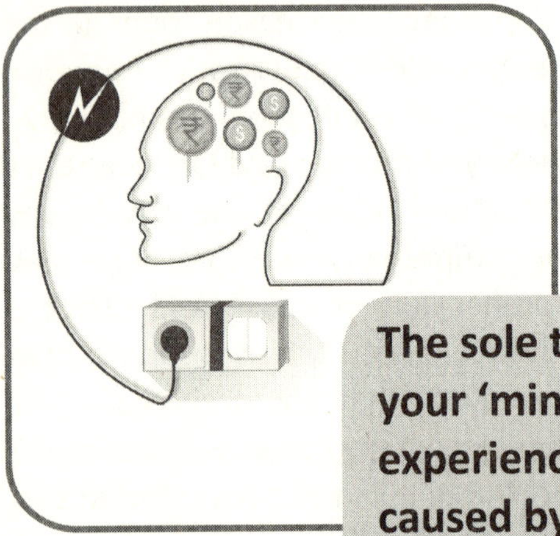

> **The sole target of money is your 'mind'. It is the mind that experiences the desperation caused by shortage of money, and it is the mind alone that is gripped by madness resulting from excess money**

perceived as virtuous often turns out to be wicked. Similarly, the very object that is perceived to be a source of happiness ends up becoming the cause of distress. Why does this happen? It is only because of psychological ignorance. Just think; if discerning the present itself is so challenging for you, how will you ever be able to comprehend the causes (past) and consequences (future)? Imagine how easy navigating your life could become if, along with the present, you could also comprehend the causes and consequences of everything! My sole aim in explaining all this is to kindle your interest in improving your psychological understanding. And that is why, while discussing the psychology of money, I am also trying to enhance your psychological power.

Since we are discussing this subject, let us also comprehend in brief what psychology is all about. The first stage of psychology is to be aware of just about everything that lies within and outside you as it truly exists in the present moment. Then, based on that understanding, grasping its cause(s) and consequence(s) is the peak of psychology. Apart from this, all other discussions on psychology should be considered as the childish prattle of kindergarten students. Psychology, in its truest sense, gives you the insight to comprehend the 'past, present and future' of every object, person and situation. Once you awaken this understanding within yourself, life will become effortless, beyond your wildest imagination! Well, for now, can you explain why the Bhagavad Gita is considered the greatest and most profound psychological scripture? That is because in the Gita, Krishna reveals the past, present and future of not only the Mahabharata war but also that of Arjuna. Moreover, he reveals what the consequences will be if Arjuna engages in battle in the present, and also what the outcome will be if he chooses to retreat from the battle. And it is due to this profundity that the Gita is revered as a text that expounds supreme psychology.

But let us now focus on our main topic—money and its psychology—and reflect on the question: from where has money acquired such tremendous power? Hopefully, in perusing the history of money, you would have already arrived at the answer. And indeed, you must seek these answers, no matter how trivial they may seem, to enhance your psychological power. For, it is a person's psychological power alone that determines the quality of his life. There is nothing else apart from this that has a direct bearing on one's life. Therefore, paying heed to things that do not help increase one's 'psychological power' as opposed to those that do is just another form of ignorance. Indeed, what could be a better learning than being able to comprehend the 'past, present and future' of every object, individual and situation? That is why, I am repeatedly urging you to kindle your interest in improving your psychological understanding. Profound psychological discussions are a rarity anyway, so when a worthwhile opportunity has presented itself, why squander it? Therefore, I urge you once again to make an effort on your own to arrive at the answer to this question by perusing the history of money.

Honestly speaking, it is my ardent desire that you yourself should discover the answer to 'where money derives its power from' so that your psychological understanding is improved manifold. And improving this understanding is crucial because currently, you are not able to perceive things as they are—you perceive a 'diamond' as a worthless stone and vice versa. And by mistaking worthless stones for diamonds, you have accumulated stones. On numerous occasions, you have even rejected diamonds, considering them to be mere stones. Upon closer reflection, you will certainly recall numerous such instances in your life. Even the root cause of all your sorrows is that your house is teeming with valueless stones, while the market is abundant with precious diamonds. But remember, those who must have recognised diamonds for their true worth must be having nothing but priceless diamonds in their lives. And it is needless to say that the lives brimming with diamonds would obviously be flourishing. And it is my heartfelt wish to see everyone flourish in their lives. Hence, at every opportunity, I am trying to awaken your psychological power. Of course, this book does not deal with general psychology; nevertheless, there is no harm in increasing your psychological power by leveraging these small opportunities. The ultimate goal, after all, is to carve a magnificent life, isn't it?

Taking a step in that direction, let us now address the main question and try to comprehend how money has acquired such immense power. Undoubtedly, many amongst you must have already analysed this. In fact, on delving into the history of money, we had discovered that in the primitive times, humans lived in isolated settlements and sustained themselves by consuming whatever supply of fruits and flowers they would find. As a result, humans did not really require money, or in other words, an exchange system, because they were sustaining themselves with the supplies that were readily available. Essentially, they were content with whatever resources were available to them in close proximity. However, over time, a sense of monotony crept in due to consuming the same type of food repeatedly and adhering to the same lifestyle. Gradually, the fickleness of the mind took over, and with that, humans began to 'crave' variety. From this need for variety emerged the process of 'mutual exchange' of goods amongst settlements. In due course, the fickle human mind began to crave homes, jewellery and household items, and these ever-increasing needs led to the production of novel commodities. This led to the emergence of markets, or in other words, a structured system for the exchange of goods. Basically, new products for comfort, luxury and adornment began to be fashioned in tandem with the escalating needs of the human being. And the growing range of commodities led to the establishment of markets as well.

This, however, is just one aspect of the situation. One must also grasp that earlier, as long as the need was limited to food alone, one type of food grain could be exchanged for another. In other words, the barter system sufficed. However, as the needs extended beyond food, humans felt it necessary to adopt a new process for exchange purposes. Obviously, how could houses, chariots, bullock carts, jewellery and other items be exchanged for 'grains' of equivalent value? So, this led to the process of assessing the value of individual goods and assigning prices to them. Then, gradually, the interplay of demand and supply also came into existence; and thereafter, as the requirement for essential goods continued to escalate, one began to feel the need for a means that could have a 'constant exchange power'. And it was gold that first shouldered this responsibility, emerging as a universally accepted option for exchange.

Well, this was all about the universally accepted exchange option; meanwhile, science had also entered the scene. And it goes without saying that the advent of science transcended human needs to the skies. Science, in its own way, did not disappoint, as it offered an abundance of commodities that provided comfort and convenience. Human needs that were so far confined to food grains expanded further, ranging from exquisite clothing and sumptuous cuisine to a vast range of products designed to increase comfort and convenience. On the other hand, human life that was once confined to the boundaries of a settlement expanded to far-off states and even distant countries. Consequently, one felt the need for an 'organised, stable currency' as relying solely on gold was no longer feasible. It was in this manner that currency was introduced. Beginning with China, it then spread to Europe; and now, currency, in some form or the other, is the basis of exchange in all countries of the world.

In the course of this entire history, it is worth noting that along with human development, the 'exchange process', that is, money has also advanced simultaneously. In other words, human advancement and the exchange process have progressed hand in hand, which implies that they not only complement each other, but also support one another. And this was inevitable, as development and exchange both stem from the same root— 'need'. The escalating needs of humans ensured their continued advancement, and this continuous development, in turn, led to the strengthening of the exchange process. Therefore, you must grasp that 'need' lies at the very foundation of the advancement of the exchange process, that is, money. It is human need itself that has engendered the exchange process, and it is need alone that has augmented its power over time. Always remember that it is human 'need' itself that has propelled 'money' to its present form. Therefore, never forget the word 'need'!

Well, I'm sure you have grasped that needs have driven money to its present form, but our primary question remains—from where did money acquire such immense power? So, in this context, you must comprehend the psychological principle that whatever lies at the root of the 'development' of an object also lies at the root of its 'power'. Indeed, if need has spurred the evolution of money, then it is this 'need' alone that has given money its current power. In essence, money came into existence on account of needs and it also derives its power from needs. So, naturally, the entire psychology of money will revolve around 'needs'. Therefore, firmly etch the word 'need' in your mind. For, it is 'need' itself that will step by step

> "The **money earned** from 8–10 hours of hard work must be used to buy **happiness** and **peace** for the remaining 16 hours

unveil the enigma of money and its psychological power. Thus, from this point onwards, we shall delve into all the aspects of money and its psychology in a step-by-step manner. All you need to do is focus on the word 'need'.

This leads to the question: did this exchange system hold as much importance at its outset as the currency used presently called 'money'? The answer is, currency certainly did not enjoy as much importance in the initial stages. In fact, its power increased in accordance with escalating human needs. This further gives rise to the question—what is the basis of the relationship between the 'power of money' and 'needs'? Comprehending this point is imperative because as human needs continue to escalate, money is also becoming increasingly powerful. Thus, grasping the basis of their relationship assumes paramount importance. So, in answer to the question above, grasp clearly that the relationship between the power of money and needs is based on 'the exchangeability of money'. In other words, money is powerful for the very fact that human needs are being fulfilled through its exchange. It is worth grasping here that no matter which angle you perceive it from, the power of money is directly connected with 'needs'. And it is through the ever-escalating human needs alone that money continues to derive its power.

While describing the history of money, I was repeatedly asking you to focus on the word 'need'. And this was precisely my question—where is money deriving such tremendous power from? And it is now crystal clear that 'money is deriving its power' from the escalating needs of human beings. And all those who have grasped the word 'need' while perusing the history of money can undoubtedly take pride in their psychological acumen. After all, gleaning the implicit, that is, the unsaid from the explicit is verily the power of psychology. And I wish to awaken this power in everyone.

Well, we have now clearly grasped that the 'escalating needs of human beings' have lent money its power. Therefore, let me reiterate that as we proceed with comprehending the entire psychology of money, you must never forget the word 'need', as it will ease your understanding of the psychology of money.

Based on our discussion thus far, you may well ask, why is the comprehension of money and its psychology crucial? Well, it is crucial because money possesses certain powers that impact the lives of human beings. And in today's era, there is no need to re-emphasise the fact that money possesses power, for, everyone is well acquainted with those powers. However, the question is, how much power does money actually possess? Finding the answer to this question is essential because money has been creating utter havoc in everyone's lives. That being the case, if we are able to gauge the extent of money's power, it can give us an insight into how important it is to grasp its psychology. But how can the power of money be measured? The answer is simple—by comparing it with other powerful entities. So, this leads to the question: which entity in today's time possesses greater power than money? If you claim that weapons are powerful, then you must realise that it is impossible to manufacture weapons without money! All the materials required to manufacture weapons can be purchased only with money. Even purchasing readymade weapons requires money. Therefore, weapons certainly cannot be more powerful than money. If you consider a country's Prime Minister and President to be the most powerful, then that is a misconception too. For, without the power of money, they can neither win elections nor retain their power. In other words, nothing in this world seems to hold as much power as money. That being the case, we are left with just one possible entity—'God'. Of course, everyone's perception of the extent of God's power is subjective, but one cannot deny that temples, mosques and churches wield an overpowering influence over the world. For this reason, one should at least not have any reservations about accepting God as powerful.

This raises another pertinent question—is money so powerful that its power needs to be compared to that of God? And if that is the case, then one must ascertain who wields more power in the present day and age—God or money? And I have raised this question for good reason. Actually, everyone must attempt to find the answer to this question because it is directly connected to their lives. I'm sure you would exclaim, 'This question concerns our lives and we are not even aware of it?!' Well, how often should I reiterate that this is nothing but a dearth of psychological understanding!

At present, however, simply comprehend that in this day and age, a vast majority of people consider both money and God to be powerful, and surely, there is no harm in it either. However, the problem is, everyone is confused about who amongst the two reigns supreme. A slight reflection on this will reveal that you too are perplexed about the same, and that is the reason why this question bears a direct relation to your life. Albeit unconsciously, the truth is that the lives of most people are revolving around this very question. So, it is futile to even wonder why this question has been raised. Grasp the fact that in your confusion about who is more powerful—money or God—you end up expending your energies and putting in efforts in both, earning money as well as pleasing God. A simple introspection will reveal to you this truth about your life. The question is, why does this confusion exist? Why should both be worshipped equally? Why do people strive relentlessly for the sake of both? What is the significance of the competition between the two? These questions are a reality of your life. And yet, you ask me whether money can really be compared to God. My response is, if you can live with this comparison, then why can't I even pose the question? Raising this question was necessary because its psychological effects are quite profound. And in any case, confusion of any kind is always destructive. For this reason too, it is essential to delve into the very core of this question.

In light of the premise stated above, it is crucial to decide whether God and money should be pursued with equal fervour. And if both are vital, then who amongst the two is more powerful? The answer to this question could very well change the course of one's life, which is why it is important to seek a psychological answer to it. It should be decided once and for all who is more powerful amongst the two. Indeed, all confusions regarding this should be eliminated forever. Now, for an ordinary person, both are obviously powerful, and this is verily the reason he spends his entire life in a frantic pursuit of both. Indeed, no one expends their precious time and energy on anyone or anything without reason. So, if you are expending your valuable time and energy on God as well as money, then there must be something worthwhile that you perceive in both. Although, you must grasp that there is a fundamental difference in their powers. The power of money is real, while the power of God is imaginary. Having said that, there is also a similarity between the two—and that is 'need' which forms the very source of their power. Money fulfils present needs, while God instils hope towards the fulfilment of future needs. Whatever the reason be, never forget the fact that 'need' lies at the core of both.

Well, there is no denying the fact that fundamentally, 'need' lies at the root of the power of both, God as well as money. However, to fathom who is more powerful, we need to comprehend the reality of the present times. And the ground reality is that money is required even to please God! Without money, neither can one procure flowers and garlands to present as offerings to God, nor is it possible to find means of transport

to visit places of worship. Moreover, without money, even the construction of temples, mosques, churches and other abodes of God is impossible, so much so that even the blessings of God are received based on the amount of money one can spend for it. Indeed, the one who offers the largest sum of money gets to be the first one to perform *aarti*, a ritual performed to worship God. In other words, in today's times, 'money' can exist without God, but it is impossible for 'God' to exist without money. Viewed from this perspective, in this first test of power between God and money, money certainly appears to have the upper hand.

Well, now that we have established this point, let us move on to the next one. Everyone has surely grasped that whether it is God or money, both derive their power from needs. Now, on the face of it, most people have faith in the power of both, but it is worth noting that more often than not, people's faith in the power of God fails them at the crucial moment. And that is because this power is imaginary, not real. This implies that even though you truly believe that God is powerful, you cannot rely solely on God's power to achieve anything substantial. For instance, you may believe that by wearing a charmed ring, you will attract wealth, but you do not sit twiddling your thumbs relying solely on the ring, do you? You inaugurate a shop at an astrologically auspicious hour, but you rely only on the business to bring in the money. Why is this so? It is because in the real world, a six-hour long prayer session cannot even buy you a cup of tea! However, when it comes to money, it never fails to deliver. By paying the right price, you can even get your hands on an airplane at the snap of a finger. And in today's times, this is verily the self-evident power of 'money' that no one can deny. And deep down, everyone is also keenly aware of this truth. They may very well claim that money is not important to them and that God holds greater significance, but in reality, they are well aware that even their efforts to please God are aimed only to acquire money.

In such a scenario, it is better for you to accept for once that 'money' holds far greater significance as compared to God. Accepting this is crucial because psychology is nothing but the truth, and it is impossible to grasp psychology without accepting the truth. Hence, I urge everyone to comprehend and acknowledge the 'ultimate power' of money. Because the fact is, in today's times, the larger majority perceives money to be the biggest power, holding the greatest significance. And if that is the case, well, that is how it is! All I am urging you to do is realise this fact and accept it with complete honesty. And I am suggesting this only to ensure that your confusion regarding who is more powerful is resolved once and for all. Otherwise, you will continue taking two steps towards money and two towards

God, and ultimately reach nowhere; whereas, it is my heartfelt desire to guide you towards your destination. It is worth noting that whether it is God or money, attaining both requires time and energy, and no one possesses an infinite reservoir of time and energy. Therefore, one must at least have a definite clarity on which of the two entities deserves eminence. And it is precisely to bring this clarity that I have broached this subject. Moreover, it is also my earnest desire to hold the mirror to the truth that resides within you—the one which makes you run to God only for seeking monetary gains.

In other words, if you truly wish to comprehend the psychology of money and its power, you will have to accept the reality of your mind. Problems will not be resolved by remaining mired in confusion. Money is indisputably the most powerful entity in the present times and verily, it is everyone's foremost priority too. And this truth is etched in everyone's mind—all I am doing is merely holding the mirror to you.

Alright, moving further, let me present you with a test to bring you face to face with this reality. Remember, you have to take this test yourself and introspect thoroughly. Let's say you are given a choice to live in a world that will either be replete with only temples, churches and mosques, or a world that will only have television, electricity, mobile phones, cars and airplanes. Which of these worlds would you prefer to spend the remaining days of your life in? Which option will make your life easier? Do not dismiss this question as being hypothetical, and nor should you claim that both have their own rightful place. Both may have their own place, but one of them definitely holds more significance in your life; my only question is, which one is that? And this being the case, the question of my premise being hypothetical simply does not arise.

> “The **only principle** behind **earning** more money is **‘Whatever you do, do it wholeheartedly’**

Well, whether you accept it or not, the truth remains that it is money and its power that hold greater significance for you. Consider this: on failing to visit a place of worship for a couple of days, you do not become as restless as you do when there is a five-minute power outage. Not offering prayers for a week does not trouble you as much as losing your mobile network for a minute does. Therefore, one must realise the truth and accept it. For, one can arrive at solutions to problems only with the help of truth. Confusion only breeds misconceptions, which creates further problems; and money is obviously the primary problem in today’s times. Therefore, if you truly wish to triumph over money and its psychology, then you have no choice but to first accept the reality that in today's times, money holds the greatest importance for you. In the present era, even God is being worshipped only for the sake of 'money'. All I am saying is, if you accept this fact, it will ease your journey ahead. Otherwise, you will end up squandering your life entertaining misconceptions and hypocrisy and gain nothing—neither God nor money.

Basically, everyone must accept that 'money' has become more powerful than God in the present day and age. But the question that naturally arises is, why is it so? Well, it is solely due to 'needs'. Evidently, God doesn’t guarantee the fulfilment of 'needs' whereas money does. Every kind of 'need' in this world can be fulfilled on the strength of money; and naturally, in the present era, everyone needs a decent home, car, mobile phone and comfortable lifestyle. Today, everyone aspires for good health while also wanting access to good-quality medical treatment in times of illness. Today, everyone wishes to splurge on indulgences and dine in prestigious restaurants. The truth is, in the present era, the list of needs is endless. And being born as a human being, there is nothing wrong in harbouring needs and fulfilling them. However, this brings us back to the same question—of what consequence are needs if they cannot be fulfilled? Without money, not a single need can be fulfilled. And this is precisely why the modern-day man approaches even God, directly or indirectly, only to seek money. Moreover, the ground reality is, even the construction of temples or mosques is impossible without money. In such a scenario, one obviously cannot deny the self-evident power of money.

In fact, underestimating this ultimate power of money can be quite dangerous, for, victory will always elude those who underestimate the strength of their enemy. Therefore, if you wish to triumph over money, it is imperative to acknowledge its power. And it has been proven that the exponentially increasing needs of human beings have elevated money to a position that is far more powerful than God. At this point, let me also clarify that neither is this God's fault nor his weakness. In the present times, if money appears to be more powerful than God, then it is solely on account of the massive increase in everyone's 'needs'. And the reason behind this surge in 'needs' is that the commodities which can fulfil those needs are available in abundance. Moreover, the exchange power of money is such that everything that the heart desires can be obtained in exchange for it. It is precisely for these reasons that presently, the power of money has surpassed that of God. Well, so be it! I am merely urging you to fathom this truth and accept it. If you wish to comprehend the psychology of money and leverage it, you will have to first accept this reality and then move ahead. Otherwise, you will suffer on both counts, as both money and God will punish you. And honestly speaking, this is precisely what everyone is experiencing. Due to their confusion about who is more powerful, they are not able to attract money, while worshipping God no longer seems appealing. But as far as you are concerned, kindly break free of this vicious cycle. Accept the reality that money is your mind's first and foremost priority. If you are wise, grasp the hint I have given, as this single truth will give your life a focussed direction.

The kind of power that money wields has now been demonstrated unequivocally. In fact, in this day and age, one's relationship with God is also directly or indirectly based on acquiring money. Whether one worships God to pass an exam or to build a career, monetary gain is the ultimate aspiration. Whether one pays obeisance to God to attain power or acquire fame, man's ultimate yearning is for money itself. Moreover, as mentioned earlier, one cannot deny that the construction of places of worship is also impossible without money. So, basically, the power that money wields is a self-evident reality.

Well, if money possesses power, so be it! How is it a matter of concern for us? Why should we even bother comprehending its psychology? These questions can certainly arise in the minds of many, and if you too are thinking on similar lines, then it would be prudent to comprehend the principle of power. And the principle of power states—'that which possesses power will surely have its own impact'. There is no such power that is devoid of some or the other impact. And this is verily a psychological principle. So, the power of money may or may not concern you, but the effect it has on you is certainly your concern; and that is why comprehension of money's psychology is imperative. Incidentally, apart from discussing the psychology of money, I am also explaining other principles of psychology at every available opportunity so that understanding them can help you live a seamless life. Indeed, opportunities to learn such profound psychological principles do not come by so readily. Therefore, refrain from asking why I am sharing psychological principles at almost every instance.

The key point is, if power exists, then it surely must produce some 'effect' too. Since the sun has power, its effect ensues in the form of sunlight and heat. Floods and tsunamis wield their own power, hence they too definitely have their own effect. Similarly, whether it's an ailment like headache or a disease like cancer, both have their own power and respective effects. As you can see, nothing is free from this 'play of power and its effect'. In fact, every person in this world possesses his own power and its corresponding effect. To put it simply, anyone who wishes to increase his impact will have to augment his power too. Grasp well that whether it is an organisation, belief, thought or anything else, it will produce an effect corresponding to the power it possesses. For instance, the more powerful an organisation is, the greater is its effect or influence. Likewise, the influence exerted by any belief system is directly proportional to the power it wields. At this point, I don't think this principle of psychology requires a more elaborate explanation.

So, let us head straight to the main point of this discussion. And the point is, since money wields unlimited power, its effect on people is bound to be in proportion to its power; and this is verily the case too. With that in mind, it is crucial to comprehend the effect of money on people, because a profound understanding of this effect can help us find ways to deal with it.

There is no denying the fact that in the current age, money has established absolute dominion over a vast majority of people. The pervasive effect of money can be gauged from the fact that even a newborn child in today's world is burdened with just one expectation—to earn a fortune when he grows up. Here, you must also grasp that usually, even the encouraging words spoken to a child such as "You will earn great fame" or "You will become great" carry an implicit expectation that the child will earn well in due course. One's aspiration to see their child grow up to become a doctor or an engineer also has money at its root. Even when one wishes to see their child become a scientist or an artist, one's eyes are more or less set on money

Despite being nothing, money is everything—this is why money is termed 'maya' (illusory)

itself. Therefore, in the present era, it is impossible to deny the unparalleled influence that money exerts on our lives. In this day and age, maxims such as 'What did you bring to this world and what will you take with you?' carry no significance whatsoever. They are mere hollow words that have lost their relevance. It is said that when Alexander the Great departed from this world, he left empty-handed. Well, so what? At least his hands were full till the time of death, weren't they? In other words, he enjoyed the benefits of money till his last breath. And this is the reality of the human being's mindset in this era, which is a stark proof of the 'effect of money'.

Well, tell me, what determines a person's status in this day and age? Undoubtedly, it is money. The greater the amount of money one possesses, the higher is his status. Money is akin to a double-edged sword for the modern-day man, for, it is not just a bane but a boon as well. It is money that holds utmost importance in interpersonal relationships. On one hand, money forms the basis for building relationships, and on the other, it is money that is responsible for marring relationships too. Often, money drives a wedge amongst siblings and strains the bond between a parent and child. In fact, losing a relative does not cause as much anguish as monetary loss does. That being the case, how can one turn a blind eye to the impact of money on everyone's lives? These days, even professionals practising medicine and law, who should principally treat everyone equally, provide their services on the basis of financial considerations. Well, when even God's blessings are received based on how much money one can spend for it, how can these people be blamed?

In our discussion thus far, we have become well acquainted with the limitless power of money and its effect. You too must be surely experiencing this pervasive effect of money on a daily basis. However, the influence of money on today's human being is not limited to this alone. The truth is, money has now assumed the form of 'pressure', making it even more dangerous. There is constant pressure to acquire money for everything, right from securing a child's education to establishing him in life, from keeping one's spouse happy to maintaining social status for oneself and one's family, from pursuing simple hobbies and interests to executing numerous responsibilities. Moreover, these days, one also endures the pressure of paying Equated Monthly Installments (EMIs). The state of affairs is such that a person wakes up in the morning groaning under the pressure of acquiring money and then spends the entire day reeling under that pressure. Moreover, the paucity of money compels the modern-day man to suppress a number of desires in the course of a single day. He weaves sweet dreams at night and also witnesses those dreams being shattered in the morning due to scarcity of money. He suffers the taunts of his family members and is subjected to ridicule by the society at large. Indeed, the poor man wakes up at the break of dawn hoping to earn money, only to retire to bed at night agonising over the paucity of money. In a way, money has established absolute dominion over humans, stripping them of their very joy of living. And this effect of money is an indisputable truth that requires no further evidence, as most people are living proof of all the experiences described above. In short, the pervasive effect of money cannot be denied at all.

Hence, you must correctly assess the effect of money on your personal life. Considering the magnitude of money's impact on you, it is important to fathom its influence on your life. Besides, this assessment will also aid you significantly in comprehending the psychology of money and effectively dealing with the effects of money. Therefore, if you wish, note down the 'effect of money' on your life. Alternatively, you can jot down concise pointers outlining its effect. Since money has been exerting such a massive influence on your life, you must at least undertake this short exercise to deal with its effect.

Indubitably, the human being has been affected by money, but it is not as if money has established absolute dominance over his life alone. Had that been the case, the human being would have perhaps dealt with it in some way or the other. In all probability, he would have rid himself of the pressure of money on the strength of hard toil. Regrettably, however, money has seized control of the human 'mind' too—and this poses a grave danger. An even more serious matter is that very few people are cognisant of this truth. Indeed, they are totally ignorant of the fact that money has overpowered their minds.

If you do not believe me, take a peek within and introspect. The state of affairs is such that your mind finds solace on acquiring money and slips into despondency when there is a paucity of it. If money becomes a bone of contention in interpersonal relationships, conflicts emerge. Love flourishes within relationships only if there is enough money, otherwise they become pointless. A sudden and substantial financial gain inflates a person's ego, while loss of money shatters the mind. A day spent without the scarcity of money is considered a day well spent, else it is deemed ruined. The mind puffs up with conceit because of money and also begs and grovels due to money. Money plunges the mind into desolation and also elevates it to the zenith of joy. In other words, it is money that determines the state of your mood. Whether the day will turn out to be favourable or not is also dictated solely by money. In such a scenario, it is needless to say that the quality of one's life is also being determined by money.

In fact, the joys and sorrows that a mind experiences are also now being determined by money. In other words, the human 'mind' is no longer independent, for, money is now reigning supreme over it. Pay heed to what I have just stated, for, it is your mind that is being discussed here. Therefore, it is imperative for you to reflect upon the escalating power of money, because the manner in which money's power is escalating is truly alarming. Indeed, if money has turned man into a puppet, pulling the strings to control even the smiles and frowns on his face, then of what consequence is his existence? What is his worth as a human being?

It is, therefore, necessary to engage in a profound contemplation on the absolute domination of money over the human 'mind'. For, there exists nothing more beautiful in this universe than the human mind. The mind is the only entity that can take pride in its independence. It is the human mind alone that can revel in unbridled joy and dance and sing with delight. Unlike the sun, it is not bound to just one activity—provide sunlight and heat—for as long as it exists, nor is it compelled to just continue flowing like water. The human mind is under no compulsion to stand rock solid and immovable like a mountain, nor is it forced to stand rooted to a spot like a statue at a road junction. It is, in fact, so independent that it can shower joy in one moment and spew rage in the very next. The mind is capable of plunging into the love of a beloved just as ardently as it can immerse itself into an activity of interest. It is the human mind alone that can cherish the beauty of sprawling landscapes and also enjoy the simple environs of his home. In a universe as vast as this, it is the human mind alone that can laugh heartily, dance gracefully, sing melodiously, rejoice with abandon, soar to heights of joy, experience delight, remain immersed in peace and bask in tranquillity. Verily, if money begins to reign over such a beautiful mind, then this definitely begs contemplation.

In essence, it is the human mind alone that is capable of revelling in countless forms of joy. That being the case, if money begins to govern this 'mind', the most beautiful and independent entity in the universe, then it is certainly a matter of grave concern. Therefore, analysing the psychological effects of money becomes crucial in such a scenario. Indeed, such overpowering dominance of money over human mind and life simply cannot be tolerated. In my view, the overbearing influence of money on human mind and life is verily the biggest problem plaguing the world today. Without resolving this issue, the possibility of human life blooming with happiness and peace seems a distant dream. I assert that irrespective of the great strides made in the world, all progress shall remain futile unless we resolve the issue of money's escalating power. Therefore, while you may still strive to establish settlements on the moon and Mars, closer home, you must pay heed to the burgeoning power of money. Now, whether the world pays attention to this issue or not, we will certainly unravel the multi-layered intricacies of the psychology of 'money and its power' through this book. We will take into consideration the impact of money on the mind and life with the sincerity it deserves; because life will flourish in the present age only when 'money's burgeoning power and its impact on people' is taken seriously. Therefore, through this book, we will now conduct a thorough psychoanalysis of the power of money and its impact. And this is both imperative and unavoidable because money has assumed an absolute and overarching dominance over the 'mind and life' of human beings.

Before we move forward with our discussion, let us first answer the question: what is a human being? Is he merely a creature that walks on two legs? And if that is so, would you call any two-legged creature a human being? Absolutely not! For, a human being's identity is not confined to his physical structure alone; he is, in fact, much more. Upon visualising a human being, what comes to mind is a decent, civilised being who is creative, joyful, merciful, compassionate, affectionate and cooperative. However, all of these qualities now seem fanciful, because in the real world, you will find that the human being is vile and brazen. He is distressed and destructive; he is a thief and a charlatan, and evil and violent too.

This prompts the question—is this how a human being ought to be—and whether this is even acceptable? No, absolutely not! For, the human being is the ultimate creation of Nature and the most exquisite one at that. The mind and heart of a human being should be nothing but pure and blissful. His life should always soar high. However, in reality, this is not the case. Barring a few, no one's life resembles what a human being's life ought to be. To describe the current state of the world in the words of the celebrated Indian poet Sahir Ludhianvi, "Each human is wounded and each soul is thirsty; their eyes are welled up, riddled with restlessness, and hearts are depressed, plunged in agony."

Considering the present state of affairs, it's comprehensible that everyone is distressed, for, life entails toil and struggle. In a cut-throat world, a few problems and difficulties are bound to rear their ugly heads. In fact, this level of strife is quite the norm in the current age which is fraught with competition and struggle. However, if the human being becomes the very embodiment of vices, then it is utterly shameful indeed. Just think about it; the one who was meant to share love is spreading hatred. The one who was supposed to be trustworthy has become deceitful. In the words of the eminent poet Neeraj, "The state of affairs is such that even animals have become more loyal than humans." The question is, would you call this entity a human being or merely a creature that walks on two legs? The language I have used is harsh and the issue is upsetting too, but this is the stark reality. And, in any case, the truth never changes just because it's unpalatable, does it?

I'm sure everyone is well aware of this ground reality, but yes, I leave it to their prudence whether they want to accept it or not. The key question is: what has triggered this deterioration in the minds and lives of human beings? Well, it is the burgeoning influence of 'money' that is solely responsible for the continuous deterioration of the mind and life of human beings. In other words, this degradation is the ultimate effect of the escalating power of money. This is why, as money tightens its grip on human beings, their degradation continues. A quick glance at the history of humankind will reveal this truth in all its starkness. In fact, the way the human being is conducting himself today is definitely not how Nature had intended when it sent him on this earth. It was his needs that fuelled the power of money, and money, in turn, drove him insane. If selfishness has pervaded humankind today, it is solely on account of money. In fact, a great number of people are so obsessed with money that in its quest, they even stoop down to murdering their own family members. Every day, news of such incidents keeps filtering in from around the world. Really, does such conduct befit the human being? It certainly does not, but the harsh reality is, humans have degraded to this level. In their selfishness, they do not even consider the other person a fellow human being. This is truly tragic! And let me make it clear that the growing influence of money is entirely responsible for this. We have no choice but to admit the truth that today, the ever-increasing influence of money has made it difficult for the human being to be 'human' in the truest sense.

An even more alarming fact is, this downward spiral is showing no sign of abating. Honestly, there is no end to the degradation of the human race on account of money. Today, the entire world is tormented by the vice-like grip of corruption. Leaders or officials whose primary duty is to serve the people, have now become the embodiments of corruption. There is nothing worth commending about the justice system either. In the corridors of justice, who is truly concerned about ripping off the mask of falsehood and finding out who is honest and who isn't? Is anyone really interested in investigating who is a criminal and who is innocent? Who has the time to determine what is legal or illegal? Today, the only rule prevailing in these corridors is that those who can afford to spend huge amounts of money on lawyers are on the right side of law. It is only the activities of such people that are legal, and they alone have the right to live.

> "**Money** is **valuable** only if it brings **pleasure** to the **mind** and **imbues** the **heart** with **contentment**

The point to deduce from this is, on the strength of your affluence, you can roam around freely despite committing a multitude of crimes; conversely, if your pockets are empty, you can be framed in false cases and condemned to languish in prison.

Such is the extent of corruption that even a poor hawker has to shell out money from his meagre earnings to pay extortionists for allowing him to conduct his business. The truth is, those who have the power of money have stripped the poor of their very right to live! And needless to say, if the system has crumbled to such an extent, then it is the ever-burgeoning 'power' of money that is responsible for it.

In fact, the repercussions of 'money-power' seem to be endless, so much so that the power of money has spawned a whole new world of crime. And the nature of these crimes is such that they can put the entire human race to shame—theft, murder, kidnapping, extortion, bloodbath, plundering and many other countless offences! As a matter of fact, the world's prisons are bursting at the seams with criminals, while a far greater number of offenders are roaming freely outside in the world. Millions of cases are pending in courts, and as for cybercrime, it has escalated to epic proportions. And if this isn't enough, one can find a horde of fraudsters peddling false assurances and miraculous charms and amulets to the poor. People's conduct as well as their business dealings are underscored by deception, and even one's word and deals cannot be trusted anymore. Truth, honesty and integrity have vanished without a trace. Almost every commodity sold in the market is a counterfeit, while the people themselves are nothing but impostors and tricksters.

In short, the degradation of the human race has truly crossed all limits due to the escalating power of money. And I don't think I need to provide further clarity on this matter. The burgeoning power of money has, indeed, turned the human being into a creature worse than a beast. And this cannot be tolerated at all. I am hereby issuing a warning that if a solution to deal with the escalating power of money is not sought soon enough, the matter will truly spiral out of control. This will lay to waste not just human life but also every milestone of progress achieved thus far. For, today, even an attack launched by one country on another is driven solely by money. In other words, humans are being dragged into wars because of money. This has given rise to an urgent need to seriously deliberate upon the inhuman behaviours prompted by the escalating power of money and also seek ways to curb them. For, money has really put 'humankind' in grave danger.

We have so far explored in detail the problems emerging from the rising power of money and also delved into the degradation of the human race on account of this power. You have also grasped the extent to which money has assumed dominion over your life...and even your mind. We have also discussed how bitterness has made inroads into interpersonal relationships and how crimes have escalated manifold due to money. This being the state of affairs, one must contemplate whether one really wishes to live a life that has degraded to such levels. Do you really wish to live in a befouled environment fraught with negativity? Do you wish to be smothered by the problems spawned by money? Do you wish to languish and wither day by day in a world teeming with deceitful people? Now is the time to ponder upon these questions with the gravity they deserve, and you must begin by asking these questions to yourself. It is imperative to do so because human life is a wonderful opportunity bestowed upon us to live joyfully and accomplish magnificent feats. Therefore, ask yourself every day whether you wish to squander this beautiful opportunity by harbouring money-related stress. Being born as a human being, do you wish to live in a world rife with selfish, deceitful and self-centred people?

Today, you will have to take a good look at yourself and ask in all earnestness whether you will accept the 'you', in other words, the person that the pressure of money has turned you into. Let me ask you this: are you not aware of the significance of being born as a human being? Do you not comprehend the value of this precious human life? Do you not realise that this beautiful life, spanning eighty to hundred years, will soon come to an end? Are you oblivious to any of the above-mentioned things? Despite being cognisant of all this, are you willing to spend your entire life succumbing to the pressure brought on by money? Is living in constant anxiety and fear due to the pressure of money acceptable to you? Today, the opportunity to question yourself is available to you, so bombard yourself with a plethora of such questions. Grill yourself with these questions and rouse yourself back into conscious awareness! Awaken from the slumber that money has lulled you into. Resolve that as a human being, you shall never degrade yourself to living the life of a 'beast'. Decide that come what may, you will no longer fritter away your life amidst such extreme levels of tension, stress, scramble, pressure and negativity.

Since the opportunity has presented itself today, I urge you to use it to rouse yourself and transform yourself too. Otherwise, you will gain nothing and life will just fade into oblivion. You will miss the bus and won't even be left with the chance to express regret. So, consider this the most crucial question of today: going forward, what kind of a life do you wish to live? Be mindful that if you miss this opportunity, you will miss out on the best version of your life. Therefore, I urge you and also give a fair warning to you to awaken yourself. Life is a golden opportunity to 'live' blissfully; therefore, in every respect, carve a beautiful life for yourself. This is also your sole duty towards yourself, so perform this duty to the best of your ability, and to that end, repeatedly ask yourself the aforementioned questions.

I am confident that after my persistent urging, you will surely spend some time to introspect about yourself and your life. I am also confident that thereafter, you will make a fresh start. Criticising others or cursing the world will yield nothing, for, the change will have to be initiated within yourself first. And once you decide to change the course of your life, you can focus on others too. You can then ask them whether they wish to live in

> "The **nuisance created** by the **shortage** of **money** far exceeds the **nuisance** of **money** itself

such a corrupt world, where the innocent are being crushed and the guilty are flourishing. You can ask them whether they wish to conduct business deals in an environment where cheating is rampant. Then, pose the question to everyone in this world about whether they are really so helpless and devoid of choice that they must exist in a society where everything is determined solely by 'money power'. Do human beings have to live in a world where money is the be-all and end-all of everything? Are humans condemned to live in an environment befouled by deviousness and wickedness? Awaken yourself first and then endeavour to awaken the world. Before humanity gets hopelessly mired in the maelstrom of problems, embark on a profound contemplation of these questions. In fact, I have penned this book on the psychology of money with the sole aim of urging the entire world to seriously contemplate on all these issues. For, I cannot bear to see 'humankind' being destroyed to such an extent merely on account of 'money'.

Today, it is crucial for the entire world to collectively decide whether there shall be eight billion human beings living on this earth or a horde of strange creatures that resemble humans. The time has come to contemplate on this issue in depth, and if you fail to do so, everything will be ruined. And each and every one of you will have to begin this process by rousing yourself and becoming aware of this problem. Commence this exercise now itself by asking yourself scores of such questions. Take the initiative today, and tomorrow the entire world will follow you.

Admittedly, the world is brimming with intellectuals who are deeply concerned about both, human beings and the human race as a whole. They even undertake numerous endeavours to improve human life, holding discussions day and night on several topics. Whether it is the television channels or the newspapers, the media consistently brings to light various pressing issues. In other words, tireless endeavours are afoot to improve and enhance human life. And such endeavours should definitely continue. After all, no entity is more significant than the human being in this entire universe. However, all these discussions and endeavours are of no use if the 'power' of money continues to weigh down heavily. I state with absolute conviction that the burgeoning power of money and the vices it spawns are collectively the biggest problem in the present times. Unless this problem is reined in, everything will be rendered futile. The situation will become so pitiable that no new endeavour or even the progress made by science will be of any use. The human being will continue to wither under the ruthless onslaught of money, and every person will be rendered helpless. Therefore, I appeal to all the intellectuals of the world to continue with their endeavours to improve human life, but at the same time, comprehend the gravity of the most pressing problem that humans are facing and tackle it on priority.

Indubitably, the entire world needs to contemplate on the ever-escalating power of money before it is too late. I'm sure, you too must be engaging in debates on various topics in your office and at home. So, initiate a discussion on the rising impact of money as well. I assert that once humans are liberated from the pressure of money, they will actually emerge as 'human beings' in the truest sense of the word. Otherwise, the day is not far when they will be reduced to beasts that once resembled human beings. And obviously, nobody would ever wish to live such a life. Therefore, it would be wise for the entire world to initiate a discussion on the rapidly increasing influence of money before it is too late. Through this book, I have anyway laid down the foundation for this 'discussion' and I am confident that my endeavour will not go in vain.

The time is now ripe to determine what kind of a world we wish to create for ourselves. What kind of people do we wish to co-exist with? What kind of social structure and governance system do we desire? Do we aspire for an atmosphere of amicability or do we want vileness to prevail in the world we live in? Do we wish to live in a world where humanity thrives or do we want to establish the law of the jungle? Now is the time to deliberate upon how one can possibly live in a world where everyone is hell-bent on deceiving each other. How can one live in a world where justice is delivered on the basis of money? How can a place where billions of lives are wilting away under the pressure of money be considered 'a world of human beings'? Verily, a world such as this cannot be called 'a world of humans' by any stretch of imagination. The world of humans should be characterised by justice, with absolutely no scope for oppression, atrocity and wickedness. In fact, everlasting peace and tranquillity should permeate its atmosphere and an environment of brotherhood, love and trust must necessarily prevail in such a world.

Tell me, don't you aspire to live in such an Elysian and beautiful world? Think about it; after billions of years, the human being has finally arrived on Earth. Surely, he has not arrived here to live in a place where the dreadful law of the jungle prevails. You too must be longing to live in such a beautiful world, don't you? But the question is, is it possible to create such a world? Of course, it is and it can be created with great ease. For, is there anything that is impossible for the human being? If humans can conquer the moon and Mars, they can certainly turn their own planet into a realm of enchanting beauty. And to that end, what do they need to do? Triumph over the problems spawned by money—that's it!

Well, that is all fine, but is it really possible to liberate oneself from the clutches of money—the very object that has taken control of our minds and lives? Can we truly overcome the power of money that has surpassed even that of God? These questions are justified, but you must grasp that this world inhabited by humans was naturally not like this at all. When humans arrived on Earth, they were not afflicted by such extreme levels of stress and tension. It is indeed the burgeoning power of money that has led to this situation. Simply stated, when money was not as powerful as it is today, the evils spawned by money did not exist either. In other words, the world was not supposed to be an awful place as designed by Nature. If we comprehend this from a psychological viewpoint, this problem is not a natural phenomenon, but created entirely by man himself. And in any case, there is no third power that is active in this universe; whatever exists is either naturally created or has been invented by humans. This is verily a significant point that I have made. Grasp clearly that whatever exists is either the creation of Nature or that of human beings.

Based on the psychological truth stated above, comprehend another fact that whatever has been naturally created cannot be altered by humans. The moon, stars, rivers, mountains and the Earth itself have all come into existence naturally. Nature maintains complete control over air and water too. Therefore, humans cannot wield much influence over these elements. Humans cannot transform the moon into the sun or a mountain into a river. Making the moon, sun, mountains or rivers disappear at will is beyond their capability, and neither can they control the onslaught of tsunamis or floods. In essence, humans cannot exercise any significant influence over what is naturally designed and controlled. Similarly, it is Nature itself that has equipped human beings with two hands and two feet. Even if he wishes, the human being cannot metamorphose himself into

Even a newborn child in today's world is burdened with just one expectation—to make a fortune when he grows up

having fifty hands and feet. Besides, no one wishes for fifty hands and feet either! And even if such a desire exists, it would not materialise, for, one has no choice but to live with what has been determined by Nature.

Coming back to the main point, how can the world of humans be transformed into a beautiful realm? To answer this question, tell me, who has ruined it in the first place? Undoubtedly, the culprit is none other than the escalating power of money. And who has created money? Obviously, it is the human being himself who has created as well as lent power to 'money'. So, it is now clear that humans themselves are the sole creators of all the evils resulting out of money. It is, therefore, needless to mention that it is humans alone who can eliminate what they themselves have created. Had this issue originated naturally, we would have been powerless. But since the problem has been created by humans, a glimmer of hope certainly exists. And all my previous discussions were aimed at conveying this very point—if human life has become hellish, it is only because of money. And money has been created by human beings. Therefore, if humans earnestly wish, they can definitely rein in money and all the problems spawned by it. This is the ultimate principle of psychology. For instance, cars have been invented by human beings; therefore, if humans so desire, they can cease the manufacture of cars and eliminate them from the world altogether. In essence, humans possess the power to eliminate or improve whatever they have created.

In conclusion, the power of money and the evils it has engendered can very well be eradicated from the world. Indeed, there are no obstacles in this, as the human being himself is its creator. Therefore, henceforth, refrain from questioning whether the world can be turned into a realm of wonder, whether the pressure of money can be reduced, whether we can overcome the power of money, or whether we can triumph over the evils spawned by money. In this context, I have already presented a profound psychological principle which states that whoever has created something also possesses the ability to eliminate it. If Nature can eliminate its creations such as the rivers, mountains, Earth and the universe, then why can't humans eradicate what they have created? Therefore, do not harbour the misconception that humans cannot triumph over the problems engendered by money.

Well, having established this fact, it is reassuring to know that by overcoming all the problems generated by money, the world can be transformed into a beautiful realm. This begs the question: How can this be achieved? Well, this can be done by conducting a profound psychoanalysis of the entire issue. For, not only are all human-engendered problems psychological in nature, but to resolve every problem, there exist predetermined psychological principles too. That is the reason why discovering solutions to any human-engendered problem without engaging in a profound psychoanalysis is impossible. Every statement I make is psychologically accurate and profound discussions such as this are quite rare, so continue to assimilate every profound statement as we move forward. Do not assume that the stated psychological principles are confined to a single book or subject. The very meaning of a principle is that it can be applied in multiple situations. For now, we can conclude that liberation from all the problems engendered by money can be achieved since money is man-made. And as for how this can be accomplished, well, we will have to conduct a thorough psychoanalysis of the matter. And that is precisely what we shall do as we proceed further.

We have thoroughly grasped the truth that 'money' has seized absolute control over the human mind and life. Everything from family, society, religion, governance to the world at large are victims of the 'nuisance of money', and this nuisance has turned life into a living hell. It is solely due to money that stress and scramble, conflicts, crimes and many other problems have become an inseparable part of human existence. Surely, leading such a life is futile. And you too must be wanting to liberate yourself from the nuisance of money; you too must be nursing a desire to live in a beautiful world, don't you?

The question, however is, how should the ever-growing nuisance of money be restrained? How can the world be transformed into a beautiful place? For that purpose, comprehend this principle of psychology clearly—if the cause behind a particular entity's existence is eliminated, that entity will vanish automatically. In other words, the ultimate principle of psychology states that if the root cause behind the world's current hellish condition is eradicated, the world will be transformed into a paradise. And this psychological principle is universally applicable. You can apply this principle to any problem and a solution will surely emerge, as this is an irrevocable principle for ridding oneself of problems. Therefore, kindly take maximum advantage of this principle.

To sum it up, though we yearn to transform the world into a beautiful realm, 'money' poses the biggest hindrance in achieving this goal. So, if we were to apply the principle of psychology, then the most effective method to eliminate the nuisance of money is to eradicate money itself. In other words, eliminate the cause and the problem will vanish on its own. Since money is the root cause of this problem, the simple solution is to eliminate 'money' itself from the world. When money ceases to

As important as it is to earn money, it is equally crucial to spend money

exist, the nuisance of money will be wiped out as well. For, the principle of psychology states that the problem will be resolved the moment its root cause is eliminated.

Well, the principles of psychology stand true, but money is completely unlike the other problems where eliminating the 'cause' resolves the issue. Here, I have once again made a significant observation. The principle of psychology which states that eliminating the cause of the issue will eradicate the problem, can be readily applied to every other problem in the world, but this is just not possible in the case of money. For, in today's times, money has become so formidable that if eliminated, it would generate a multitude of new problems. In fact, it would take us back to the era when human beings wore leaves to cover their modesty and survived on raw meat! In other words, we would regress terribly! For, the 'evolution of money and the development of humans' go hand in hand. In such a scenario, the moment money is wiped out, it would instantly jeopardise human progress as well. So, all said and done, the issue of money is a complex one. On one hand, money is the 'cause' of degradation in human beings, but on the other, this money is also the ‘reason’ behind human development and progress. And development is our foremost desire, which we all know is impossible without 'money'. This in itself should help you gauge the status that money has attained.

At present, however, let us grasp the fact that eliminating money does not seem to be a viable option. In fact, it has become so formidable that it has outsmarted even the psychological principle of problems. So, does this mean that it is impossible to find liberation from the problems engendered by money? Well, it is possible, but the matter is complicated. To liberate ourselves from the problems triggered by money, we will have to delve deeper into psychology. In fact, you will have to first comprehend the 'special psychology' of problems. Just as there is a general and a special theory of relativity, there exists a special as well as a general psychology of problems too. However, the subject of our book is not the psychology of problems; therefore, we will explore the nature of problems only to the extent that it aids our comprehension of the psychology of money.

Pay close attention to everything I am about to elucidate. Although the subject is deep, assimilating it will transform your life. For, what I am about to explain next are the principles of 'the psychology of problems'. And we are well aware that everyone is troubled in life only because of problems. If life was devoid of problems, there would be no cause for distress. Therefore, carefully read the principles explained here. Once grasped in entirety, you will not only triumph over money-related problems, but also learn to resolve all the other problems in your life.

Opportunities to learn from such profound discussions on psychology will not come by so easily, hence I would suggest that you take notes.

Comprehending the psychology of problems is crucial because the world is rife with problems. Every person is plagued with a multitude of problems and the most challenging part of this situation is, not even a single 'problem' is reaching a resolution. So, why aren't problems getting resolved? For centuries, people have been demanding that corruption must be eradicated, so why isn't corruption being rooted out? Everyone wants to alleviate tension, but why isn't tension being eliminated? And this is not just about tension or corruption; irrespective of the problem in question, the resolution to all problems continues to elude us. And this is a universal experience. You too must be grappling with numerous problems and even making extensive efforts to overcome them. But ultimately, all your endeavours must be yielding nothing but despair. And interestingly, most of the problems of the human being are centuries-old, which implies that even the attempts made to resolve them over the ages have proven futile.

This brings us back to the same question: why is this the case? Why do these problems refuse to end? Everyone yearns for a problem-free life and no one wants to be besieged by problems. So, why is there a dearth of profound contemplations aimed at resolving problems? Why hasn't a profound psychoanalysis of problems ever been conducted? Why is there a lack of seriousness in eradicating the problems plaguing the human being? Alright, let's put that aside, for, these questions will only result in a long-drawn-out discussion. Let us return to the main point which remains that most problems have persisted through the ages. It is also a reality that even the collective efforts of governments, society, religion and intellectuals have failed to resolve them. Whether you like it or not, this is the infallible truth.

So, the question arises, why are these problems not being resolved despite everyone's relentless efforts? There is only one answer to this: it is because a thorough and profound psychoanalysis of problems has never been undertaken. Indeed, how can problems be resolved without undertaking such an exercise? Therefore, let us straightaway conduct a 'psychoanalysis of problems'. And if you truly wish to triumph over your problems, then pay close attention to what I am about to explain. First, answer this question—who faces problems? Indeed, only human beings face them. The moon, stars or animals are not confronted by major problems. Therefore, the first point you must remember is that any problem, regardless of its nature, is exclusively related to human beings. Except the human being, no entity in this universe encounters any major problem. And here, we have commenced the psychoanalysis of a 'problem'. Using this approach, you must also try to understand how to conduct the psychoanalysis of any entity. Psychoanalysis means starting from the point of origin and progressing step by step towards the final point. And in this context, the starting point of a 'problem' is that it is only humans who are afflicted with problems. Let me tell you at this point that an opportunity to grasp these psychological truths won't be available to you elsewhere. For, even the psychology taught in the most advanced academic courses is not profound enough.

Well, the key point is, any problem is directly connected to humans only, which can be validated from the fact that money too is a problem plaguing the human being, and so is religion and God. In this vast universe, neither money nor religion poses a problem for anyone except the human being. This clearly implies that regardless of the problem at hand, neither can it be comprehended nor resolved without connecting it to human beings. Because it is only human beings who are afflicted with all the major problems. Therefore, whenever there is a discussion on problems, focus only on human beings. Do not shift your focus from this point and do not engage in irrelevant discussions either. The reason I am emphasising this point is, while it is the human being who is facing problems, the solutions are being sought elsewhere. And the term 'elsewhere' includes everything. I am drawing your attention to this point because this has been an age-old practice. Even though it is the human being who is facing the problem, the answer is being sought in religion and God; in other words, God and religion are being experimented with. In short, the problems are being faced by the human being, but the answers are being sought in society. This being the case, how will any problem be resolved? I am certain you are intelligent enough to grasp the compelling hint I have given you.

Well, we have comprehended the starting point of a problem that all problems are directly related to the human being. But this prompts the question: why

> "Before you **engage** in **any** **deal**, ensure what you're gaining is **useful** and **meets** your **needs**

is it that only human beings face so many problems? To answer this, we will have to understand the difference between humans and other entities. And the distinguishing factor is that the mind and life are available in their entirety exclusively to human beings. Such completeness of life is not available to anyone else in this entire universe. And, of course, to have life in all its completeness is not a problem; on the contrary, the availability of mind and life in its entirety is nothing but Nature's blessing bestowed upon human beings. So, why is the human being riddled with a plethora of problems? The reason lies in the fact that human life is bound by countless laws of 'mind, life and Nature'. At this point, you may well exclaim, "So be it! What is the problem with that?" Well, you are correct; there is no problem. If life is bound by laws, what could be the harm in that? Nothing at all!

So then, answer this question—why do humans alone face a multitude of problems? It is because the human being is knowingly or unknowingly violating the laws of 'mind, life and Nature' which is why problems are arising in his life. There is no other reason behind all the problems plaguing human beings. I have given quite a significant hint here. Well, this further prompts the question: why are humans violating these laws? It is because the majority of people are completely ignorant of these laws. When viewed from this perspective, the primary problem of humans is their abject ignorance of the laws governing mind and life that have been created by Nature. Indeed, human beings are violating these laws because of their ignorance, and since they are breaking the laws, they are finding themselves mired in complications. Grasp each and every word that I am stating here. In fact, through these statements, I am elevating your psychological understanding to a level that is beyond your imagination. For, every subject I expound is marked with profundity. As opposed to this, superficial, fanciful and grand proclamations that inspire false hopes are made regularly, but they inevitably fail to solve problems.

Comprehend clearly that regardless of the nature of the problem, it has arisen due to disregarding the laws of mind, life and Nature. In fact, you will realise that in the course of our seemingly casual discussion, we have actually pinpointed the fundamental cause of problems! Henceforth, to seek a solution to any problem, you will have to look for it well within the framework of the laws governing the mind, life and Nature. Although, presently, our focus remains on the subject of money-engendered problems, and in this context, it goes without saying that we shall now progress towards resolving money-engendered problems in keeping with the laws of the mind, life and Nature. Just remember that the method we will use to eliminate money-engendered problems can be applied to resolve other issues as well. All you need to do is grasp the profundity of every word written in this book, because even the seemingly simple points mentioned in this book are quite profound.

Let us now return to our main point, which is addressing money-engendered problems. And in this context, we have already grasped that eradicating money-related problems by eliminating money itself is not a feasible solution, simply because money has attained a status of such magnitude that its removal or eradication is now impossible. Any such attempt would only cripple the human being further. For, money is not akin to a superficial boil on the body that can be snipped off and the problem would be resolved for good. Money has now become an integral part of the human being's life. Therefore, eliminating money is impossible. In that case, we are left with only one option—apply the special theory of problems. In other words, rein in the factors that are fuelling the problem. Essentially, we need to sever the root that lends money its power. For, as soon as its power diminishes, the nuisance it has created will abate automatically. And undoubtedly, the root which gives power to money is 'need'. But the predicament is, in the case of money, eliminating needs is not possible either because it goes against the supreme law of life. And I have already explained through the psychoanalysis of problems that the solution to problems will have to be sought only within the framework of 'the laws of mind, life and Nature'. It is only because the human race has failed to do so that problems have remained unresolved for ages.

Well, clearly, the problem cannot be resolved by ceasing the circulation of money. The second option, therefore, is to 'rein in needs'—the prime factor that lends power to money. However, this is not possible either as it goes against the supreme law of life. And I have made it amply clear that one must respect the laws, come what may. This being the case, it becomes essential to comprehend what the supreme law of life is. Undoubtedly, it is progress, advancement and development! After all, the human being, born with the highest potential for creativity, is meant to reign over the universe. And this principle of development cannot be breached. Moreover, it is only through the continuous surge in needs that such development is possible. So, curbing needs is not feasible at all. On the contrary, needs must multiply, because only then can the human being progress. And development is the supreme law of life. Therefore, curbing needs due to a fear of the nuisance of money would go against the supreme law of life. In fact, the moment this law is violated, a far greater nuisance will emerge. As soon as development ceases, the human race will regress to the era when human beings wandered around aimlessly, clad in leaves. And needless to say, living a primitive life such as this will only lead to countless new frustrations! And each frustration will further trigger a multitude of crimes. All in all, we do not have the option of weakening the power of money by curbing needs.

Evidently, this complication arising out of money is not easy to resolve. Ridding ourselves of the problems engendered by money is not a cakewalk. Otherwise, elimination of the 'cause' of a problem usually eradicates the problem. For instance, if there is a lump in the body which is posing a health problem, the solution would be to remove the lump and resolve the problem. If a place is filthy, it is clearly a problem, but cleaning the filth eliminates the problem. If someone causes distress, banish that person from your life, and the matter is resolved. If a politician is corrupt, vote out the politician, and the problem is taken care of. If a certain tradition or belief system is causing trouble, then stop adhering to it, and the problem is solved. However, this formula cannot be applied in the case of money. For, although the problem stems from money, 'money' itself cannot be eliminated. It is such a perfect system that if disturbed, it would lead us back to the times when the barter system prevailed. In other words, the entire system would collapse like a pack of cards. All in all, comprehend well that money cannot be removed akin to a lump in the body. Here, the gland has to be treated without tampering with it. And that is precisely why liberation from money-engendered problems is not easy, for, money is the most complicated issue in the world; and this is why everyone is troubled by money the most. It is for this reason that we have dived deep into psychology with the very aim of extricating ourselves from the clutches of money-engendered problems.

Although we are making the best possible efforts, the problem is, money is indeed a complicated issue. Unlike a

> “
> Even the **joys** and **sorrows** that a mind experiences is now being **determined** by **money**

corrupt politician whom you can vote out to resolve the problem, money is not something you can simply eliminate. For, in this case, regardless of the nature of the 'politician', there is absolutely no scope of replacing him. In such a scenario, the alternative approach would be to eliminate that which is empowering or fuelling the 'cause'. If you cannot vote out the politician, eliminate the factors that are encouraging the corrupt nature of the politician. In other words, if you cannot eliminate the cause, remove the factor that is triggering the cause. Basically, as per the psychology of problems, these are the only two feasible solutions to tackle a problem. Simply put, if you are experiencing a headache due to an issue in the stomach, you need to fix the issue in your stomach and the headache will naturally vanish. There is no need to directly grapple with the headache every time it occurs. If assassinating Duryodhana is a problem because he is a brother, then Uncle Shakuni should be removed from the path, as it will automatically weaken Duryodhana. This means that if you cannot eliminate money, then curb the needs that fuel its power. However, this is a tricky ground we are treading on, for, if we restrict our needs, progress will stall, and progress is the supreme law of life. Once progress halts, humans will become even more frustrated, and this will lead to the emergence of a nuisance far bigger than money.

Therefore, curtailing needs is not a remedy that can free human beings from the nuisance of money, as this will close all doors to progress. And such an eventuality is totally unacceptable. If one has taken birth as a human being, then carving a splendid life and scaling the dizzying heights of progress is a must. And towards that end, one requires both money as well as needs. Therefore, neither can money be eliminated nor can needs be curbed. In other words, this problem called money cannot be resolved even with the help of the psychology of problems. Indeed, that is why it is hailed as 'The One and Only Money'. The scale of its power is such that it contravenes even the principles of the psychology of problems. Otherwise, as a rule, one simply needs to eliminate the cause or factor that is triggering the problem to rid oneself of it. And indeed, this principle can be applied to resolve all other problems except money. However, money has gained so much importance that despite all the anguish it causes, neither can it be removed, nor can the needs that breathe power into it be eliminated. That is exactly why I had mentioned at the outset that in the present day and age, the power of money has surpassed even that of God. And verily, this has complicated the problem to a level that is beyond one's imagination.

So, does this mean we have to suffer the nuisance of money forever? Will we have to remain mired in money-related stress all our lives? Are we destined to spend our days overwhelmed by the pressure of money? Must we lead our lives in an environment rife with crime and crookedness spawned out of money? Is there no resolution to the problems created by money? For, if it is impossible to eliminate money and curtail needs, then we are surely left with no choice but to endure the havoc wreaked by money. Indeed, the issue of money is like a catch-22 situation. If we eradicate money, we will be compelled to endure frustrations and gradually regress to the era of the barter system. On the other hand, if we do not eliminate money, we would be forced to live in a society fraught with crime and vileness. We will be condemned to suffer ever-new tensions and pressures for the sake of money on a daily basis. In other words, money has created a situation wherein we are caught between the devil and the deep sea.

Well, the question remains—is there a way out of this quandary or not? Is it not possible that money continues to exist but its nuisance disappears? Can't the human race continue to progress, dwell in bliss and yet remain unburdened by the pressure of money? Of course, it is possible and easily achievable too. In fact, there is no problem that cannot be tackled through psychology. It is only due to a lack of psychological understanding that problems become overbearing. And it is because the issue of money is a complex one, finding a solution to resolve it is becoming cumbersome. I have stated repeatedly that money is akin to a beautiful woman—both are equally desirable. Life without either of them becomes dull and boring. However, living with either of them is not a breeze either. When it comes to money, we yearn for it and that too, in abundance, but its nuisance is undesirable. We yearn for a lover or wife and want them to be stunningly beautiful too, but their tantrums are unwelcome. This being the case, both money and women fall under the 'handle with care' category. We desire them, but we also want to shield ourselves from them. That is why a solution to effectively deal with either of them eludes us even after applying the 'psychological principles of problems'. In fact, these two entities are breaching even the principles of a problem!

All said and done, dealing with both, money and women is not a cakewalk. However, we shall address the issue of women while discussing the psychology of women. At present, we shall immediately seek ways to deal with money and its nuisance. One way or the other, we will strive to create a world wherein progress shall surely exist but without the pressures of money, a world wherein our needs can definitely soar high, but we will be far removed from the tension being caused by money. We will certainly achieve these goals; all you need to do is focus on assimilating what is being discussed here and augment your psychological understanding.

In our discussion so far, we have grasped how complex the issue of money is; in fact, it is so tricky that it cannot be resolved even by applying the psychological principles of problems. In other words, it is beyond the scope of the psychology of problems too. However, this certainly does not mean it is impossible to liberate oneself from the problems created by money. For, a problem without a solution simply does not exist. Therefore, money can surely be reined in. Admittedly, money is the lifeline of the modern era, so eliminating it is not an option. In a similar vein, eliminating 'needs' that boost the power of money is not a viable solution either. But this definitely does not mean that one cannot triumph over the nuisance caused by money. As explained earlier, it is the human race alone that faces problems; apart from the human being, not a single entity in this universe faces any major problem. In essence, humans can resolve every problem by increasing their psychological understanding, and to that end, we simply need to learn how to tackle money. We will have to seek a remedy for every form of nuisance it creates. Essentially, we will have to triumph over it by advancing step by step. Indeed, of what consequence is a human being if he succumbs to a mere piece of paper? So, we must definitely not concede defeat. And for that purpose, you must continue to assimilate each and every aspect of the psychological treatment that I will outline here in a step-by-step manner. This meticulous approach will help us triumph over every aspect of the nuisance of money. As a first step, let me clarify that if the human being is afflicted with a problem, then to resolve it, he alone will have to bring the required change within himself. And I will now explain, one by one, the changes that are required. Those who assimilate these learnings will undoubtedly be liberated from every kind of nuisance created by money.

There is no debate about the fact that money is the root of all troubles, and admittedly, the nuisance it creates is limitless. It puts everyone under extreme pressure and causes stress as well. While all of this is true, an even bigger truth is that survival is impossible without money. Although the sun unleashes scorching heat, life is still inconceivable without its presence, is it not? So is the case with money. Despite the tremendous nuisance it creates, it is still absolutely essential for life. 'Fire burns, so shun fire.' 'Women are incomprehensible, so spurn women.' Desist from making such defeatist statements or even thinking on these lines at least where 'money' is concerned. For, just like air and water, money too has assumed paramount importance in our life. In this day and age, one cannot deny the reality that life without money would be a hellish existence! Whereas, our foremost priority is to turn life into a veritable paradise—and that is simply unthinkable without money!

So, we will surely discuss ways to eliminate the nuisance of money, but let us first fathom the importance of acquiring money. To continue with the analogy stated earlier, we will first comprehend how to attract a woman in our life before learning how to tackle her tantrums. For, one cannot build a home without a woman. And in the present times, it is impossible to run a household and look after one's family without money. So, we definitely need both. Of course, dealing with both is a challenging task, but it certainly does not mean that we do not need them. Both are formidable but neither of them can be shunned. Therefore, let us first welcome both into our life and then we can even discuss ways to shield ourselves from their detrimental effects. Oh! By the way, my comments on women are spoken in jest, so kindly do not take offence and launch a protest!

'Money' can exist without God, but it is impossible for 'God' to exist without money

Well, regardless of how tormenting the nuisance of money is, we definitely need money. Even fulfilling our basic needs of food, clothing and shelter is inconceivable without money. Therefore, our foremost priority is to earn money, while warding off the nuisance of money is our second priority. Hence, we will first focus on ways to earn money, for, survival itself is impossible without money. Therefore, let us first focus on our own survival and then we can discuss ways to save the world too. And consider 'earning money' as the first step in the process of doing away with the nuisance of money.

All in all, earning money is our foremost priority, so kindly do not harbour any confusion in this regard. Now, when you have no option but to earn money, you must also comprehend that money is not a natural gift like sunlight that will be bestowed upon us inevitably. In other words, money is an absolute necessity of life, but it is not something that will fall into our lap of its own accord. In fact, if I were to state a deep insight, it is that human needs can be segregated into two categories. The first category is of needs that are fulfilled automatically by Nature such as the need for air, water, light, minerals and so on. The human being does not have to strive much to attain any of these. The second category comprises the rest of the needs, ranging from basic necessities such as food, clothing and shelter to everything that is essential to live a splendid life, the fulfilment of which demands hard work and intelligence on your part. And you are already aware that living without these essential commodities is impossible. Moreover, you are cognisant of the fact that 'money' is required to fulfil all these needs. Therefore, understand well that earning money is the biggest necessity of today's life. So, do not harbour any misconception about this at all.

Surely, by now, you must have grasped what I am hinting at. If you haven't, then let me explicitly state that working diligently and applying intelligence to earn money is the foremost duty of a human being. And one cannot shirk this duty at all. Eliminating the nuisance of money is undoubtedly the goal, but before we do that, it is imperative that everyone fulfils their duty of earning money. And needless to say, the sole path to fulfil this duty is through 'action'. Therefore, your foremost duty is to wholeheartedly and devotedly work towards earning money. Eliminating the nuisance of money is the second priority. Hence, etch it in your mind that in order to earn money, you have no choice but to devote a minimum of eight to ten hours a day to work. And this cannot be avoided at all. If anyone tries to wriggle out of this duty by citing money's nuisance as an excuse, he will only run into bigger trouble, just like the renunciants of the olden times who found themselves trapped on account of forsaking women. So, do not commit the same mistake! Coming back to our analogy, your first task is to build a home with a woman and thereafter learn how to shield yourself from her whims and quirks!

I am explaining all this because there are various categories of people in the world, some who lament over the nuisance of money but shy away from making any effort to overcome the nuisance, while there are many who wish to enjoy life but balk at the idea of working hard to earn money for that purpose. Tell me, who doesn't enjoy travelling, fine dining and indulging in extravagances? However, none of this is possible without expending money. Therefore, one has to earn money, come what may. Indeed, one cannot turn a blind eye to this reality. And money can be earned solely through work. This arrangement cannot be altered, no matter how badly one wants to. But despite this reality, many people try in vain to alter it. Such individuals want to attain everything but shy away from making efforts towards that end. If you happen to be one of them, be cautious, else you will create for yourself a nuisance far bigger than money.

In essence, there is definitely no alternative to earning money for sustaining one's livelihood. And if one has to earn money, one will surely have to engage in work. So, neither should you shirk work nor look for excuses to while away your time. Remember, everyone has to fulfil their own needs, as this is verily Nature's design for human beings. And because the fulfilment of needs is impossible without money, it becomes imperative for everyone to earn money. This system is so well established that no one can alter it. Therefore, I am emphasising the point that whoever shirks action should not harbour great expectations from life. In conclusion, one has no option but to engage in action. So, do not ever allow laziness, idleness or excuses to come in the way of it. Otherwise, life will be ruined completely. Be wise and heed my warning!

In short, money is a necessity of life and you have to earn it yourself through diligence, hard work and intelligence. And to that end, you must necessarily work for eight to ten hours a day. For, money will certainly not drop into your lap on its own. I hope you have grasped all these points well and I am presuming that after fathoming the importance of money, you will surely dedicate yourself to working for eight to ten hours a day. It was essential for me to emphasise this point because there are certain people who keep lamenting about the lack of money without engaging in any work. And verily, such people do not have the right to complain about the nuisance of money. That is why I have first expounded upon the importance of 'money' and also made it clear that everyone must necessarily work for eight to ten hours a day to earn money.

Now that the importance of money and the necessity to work towards earning it has been established, let us explore another aspect of this matter, which is—if we engage in work, it should definitely lead to the best possible outcome. In other words, if we are working towards earning money, then we should also be able to earn the maximum amount of money possible. And to ensure you achieve this goal, I will first explain in depth the "Psychology of Karma (Action or Deeds)" so that it becomes easy for you to earn the maximum amount of money possible. In this context, firstly, you should never assume that deeds are performed by the physical body. The body is merely a machine that follows the commands of the mind and brain. All tasks are performed solely by the 'mind'. And I'm sure you are well aware that tasks are executed seamlessly only when they are performed wholeheartedly. In the eventuality that a task is performed half-heartedly, the body is merely pretending to execute the task. You are also aware that any task executed in a wholehearted manner can well be completed within an hour, whereas the same task can often take a week if performed half-heartedly. In other words, tasks are carried out swiftly only when the mind is fully involved in executing them. And that being the case, it is needless to point out that the better the quality of work, the better will be the outcome. Furthermore, I need not explain to you that the only thing one receives from the external world in exchange of work is 'money'. For, it is only money that can be exchanged. Therefore, whether it is in the field of employment, business, art or science, everyone receives money as compensation for their efforts. And verily, it is 'money' that we require to carve a splendid life. And our purpose behind working too is solely to earn money. For, one can acquire things only in proportion to the money one possesses. This is verily how the system works in the present times. And indeed, we should strive to maximise our income so that it allows us to enjoy life by way of acquiring a greater number of things. Therefore, do not harbour any misconception about why one should maximise one's income. And to earn the maximum amount of money, I have already explained that "no matter what you do, do it wholeheartedly".

Undeniably, money is the supreme necessity of life and acquiring it is impossible without putting in the required work. We are also aware that in order to work, we have at our disposal eight to ten hours a day. It is, therefore, imperative to ensure that those eight to ten hours of work yield excellent results. And to that end, it is essential to perform tasks wholeheartedly. I am placing great emphasis on this point because it is my earnest desire to see you attract the maximum amount of 'money', which is verily the supreme necessity of life. All I am trying to explain is that those who genuinely devote their mind and heart to their work are able to perform better. And better performers are invariably rewarded with increased compensation in addition to receiving better opportunities. This logic applies to all fields of work, be it art, science or business. Regardless of the field or nature of work, progress is attained only by those who work wholeheartedly, for, only such people achieve superior results in their endeavours. Moreover, comprehend clearly that in today's times, progress is determined solely by how much money one earns, for, progress has become synonymous with money. Money denotes 'progress' and progress is unattainable without 'money'. And whether it is money or progress, both will be attained only by performing wholeheartedly and producing outstanding work.

In other words, not only do you have to earn money, but earn it in abundance. This is your religion as well as your duty. Consider this entire discussion as the first step towards curbing the nuisance of money. For, in this day and age, the 'nuisance generated from the shortage of money' is far greater than the nuisance of money itself. Therefore, do not be confused about why one has to earn abundant money. To summarise, our primary objective is to triumph over the nuisance of money, but the issue of money is so complex that to achieve even this goal, earning money becomes imperative. This is the sole reason I had to first explain why it is important to earn money.

It has now been established that no matter how grave the nuisance of money is, one cannot do away with 'money' fearing its nuisance. Nor can one shirk one's duty to earn money. Because, in today's times, the absence of money would create an even bigger nuisance. Indubitably, money is the foremost necessity in the present day and age, as survival is impossible without it. Therefore, for survival's sake, everyone has to earn money, for, life without money is bound to turn into a living hell. The point I am trying to convey is that if you intend to rein in the nuisance of money, then even to that effect, you must first have money in your pocket. The one who does not possess sufficient money will not be able to triumph over the nuisance of money easily. Simply put, money is that poison whose antidote is 'money' itself.

Therefore, comprehend clearly that you have no option but to earn money. And money can be acquired only through intelligence and hard work—there is simply no alternative to it. Those who find hard work a challenge or find it difficult to employ their intelligence should not even nurse the hope that they would be shielded from the assault of money. For, nothing can save one from the assault of money except 'money' itself. This is similar to the case of Gabbar Singh, the notorious villain of the famous Hindi movie, Sholay. In the movie, Gabbar Singh claims that "Only 'Gabbar' can save people from his own fury," similarly, it is 'money' alone that can save one from the devastating impact of money. To state another analogy, this is not a case where the lion is separate from the hunter, because here, the lion itself is the hunter. Hence, if you expect the hunter to save you, you are mistaken. In essence, to earn money, it is everyone's duty to work for eight to ten hours a day. To put it bluntly, neither this book nor this precious human life is meant for those who shirk work.

So, be prepared to work for eight to ten hours daily, and that too with complete dedication. For, only then do you have the right to speak about curbing the nuisance of money. Harbouring grand dreams in life and not putting in the required effort will not work anymore. Therefore, dedicate eight to ten hours unfailingly towards working diligently. Merely building castles in the air without engaging in work is the same as shirking work. Here, let me warn you that once you lose the habit of working, resuming work will become difficult; qualities such as laziness and the tendency to shirk work will become second nature to you. It is certainly ideal if you are able to engage in work of your choice, but even otherwise, you must ensure that you remain engaged in some or the other work. Comprehend clearly that 'you' are not the sun, earth or air that functions like a wound-up toy whose mechanism powers it continuously. You, on the contrary, are the kind of toy that needs to power itself by working for eight to ten hours a day. If the key isn't properly wound to power these eight to ten hours, the functioning of the toy is bound to go awry. That is why I reiterate—make it your religion to dedicatedly work for eight to ten hours on a daily basis. And this is verily your foremost duty too. If you harbour any confusion about this, you will be subjected to both the nuisance of money as well as the nuisance resulting from the shortage of money.

Essentially, in today's times, the foremost duty or primary religion of a human being is to work dedicatedly for eight to ten hours daily to earn the maximum amount of 'money' possible. In comparison, every other so-called religion is spurious. It is with great emphasis that I am stressing on these points so that you can rid yourself of the nuisance of money. For, in the absence of money, you will not be able to evade the 'nuisance of money'. And verily, the nuisance resulting from the paucity of money is no less than death! This is precisely the complication of money that is tormenting everyone. And it is my ardent wish to deflect all money-related troubles away from you. However, the challenge is, I can only explain this to you; if you truly wish to eliminate your troubles, you will have to take the required action yourself. And that is why I am preparing all of you to engage in your work with sheer tenacity.

I am sure none of you would ever wish to struggle, dying a little every day just to survive in this world. I am hopeful that you must have accepted working wholeheartedly for eight to ten hours daily and earning optimally in those eight to ten hours as your primary religion. You can be certain that in today's scientific age, your religious identity as a Hindu, Muslim or Christian will not hold as much relevance as the aforementioned religion. For, working diligently for eight to ten hours daily and earning as much as possible is your '*swadharma*' (duty towards self). Even Krishna has categorically stated in the Bhagavad Gita that the human being's *swadharma* surpasses all other religions. Therefore, I am confident that having embraced your swadharma as your foremost duty, you are now determined to take the first step towards reining in the nuisance of money.

On this determined note, let us now discuss the remedies for liberating ourselves from the nuisance of money. And in this context, you must first comprehend that when you work earnestly, you will earn the best possible amount of 'money' in exchange of it. Let me caution you once again that this book is certainly not meant for those who work disinterestedly or consider their work a burden. For, such people will never attract a significant amount of money, and consequently, they will have to endure the nuisance resulting from the shortage of money all their life. Indeed, when even Nature cannot help shirkers, what can this book possibly do? So, know well that I am specifically referring to those who are dedicatedly working for eight to ten hours daily, as they alone are entitled to find liberation from the nuisance of money.

In short, you must have surely grasped that earning money is your foremost duty and henceforth, you will definitely work for eight to ten hours daily, sincerely and dedicatedly, as part of your *swadharma*. This means that you have already become eligible to rid yourself of the nuisance of money, and surely, you must free yourself from this nuisance at any cost. For, how can it be acceptable that you toil hard and yet endure the nuisance of money? Neither is it acceptable, nor should it ever be. Therefore, to rid yourself of the nuisance of money, first comprehend that when you work dedicatedly for eight to ten hours, you will certainly attract money as a result of your hard work. And since you are engaging in work wholeheartedly, the money you attract will also be the 'best possible amount'. This simply means that presently, your efforts will yield only a specific amount, and not a penny beyond that amount. Nevertheless, it is certain that whatever amount you do earn is your own 'money'—and you have

> "**Money** can only be controlled by those who **perform** their **work** **earnestly**. Those who **shirk** **work** are **punished** by **money** day in and day out

absolute right over it! In fact, you are the sole owner of that money. However, you must also keep in mind the principle of psychology which states that no ownership ever comes without 'responsibility'. So, whilst you are undoubtedly the owner of the money you have earned, it is also your responsibility to use it wisely. Comprehend this point thoroughly, as it is a significant hint that I am giving you—your responsibility does not end merely with earning the money, as proper utilisation of that money is also essential. And consider this responsibility of spending wisely as the second lesson to triumph over the nuisance of money. I'm sure the first lesson is quite clear: it is your primary duty to earn the maximum amount of money possible.

The main point you must grasp is that money, by its very nature, is complicated. That is why even the most accomplished people fail to deal with it in an effective manner. In short, money is a nuisance in itself and the painful reality is that despite this, earning it is a prime necessity. This being the case, shirkers and idlers are bound to perish without a trace. But, amusingly, money does not spare even those who work tirelessly. For, earning money does not resolve all money-engendered issues either. The majority of those who are earning are also distressed by money, and this is because to be able to utilise the earned money prudently is crucial as well; else, it makes no difference whether one earns or not. This is the very reason I reiterate that 'money' by its very nature is complicated.

Therefore, comprehend well that if you want to eliminate the nuisance of money, you must act responsibly in both earning as well as spending. Those who fail to fulfil the responsibility of 'properly utilising money' will also lose its ownership—and this is an immutable principle of psychology. In fact, the inability to fulfil responsibility has unsettled even the greatest kingdoms of the world, so of what consequence are you? Therefore, comprehend clearly that you are the master of your own money, but if you fail to utilise it efficaciously, consider yourself doomed. Pay heed to my warning of devoting as much attention to the utilisation of money as you devote to earning it. Do not make the slightest mistake in this matter and consider this the most significant lesson of this chapter.

Well, the question that now arises is: in what way can money be utilised best? To that end, first answer this: what is the utility of money? Undoubtedly, the utility of money lies in its 'exchange power'. In exchange of money, one can acquire just about everything. Therefore, it goes without saying that we must exchange our money in the best possible manner. For, the sole utility of money lies in its exchangeability. This leads to the question: what should we exchange money for, if we are to rid ourselves of every nuisance that it creates? In other words, where should money be used? Well, in this regard, comprehend clearly that money should only be invested in the 'purpose of life'. Spending money elsewhere will only land you in grave trouble. And kindly do not harbour any confusion regarding the purpose of life. In fact, before you begin to cudgel your brain over this, let me state clearly that the primary purpose of life is 'determined by Nature'. Therefore, do not commit the mistake of considering the goals originating from your mind, ego or brain as the purpose of your life, else you will go astray and disrupt the balance of life. This is, indeed, a profound secret of your life that I am revealing to you. I have already stated earlier that I only speak of profound and ultimate truths, for, all other teachings are psychologically incorrect and therefore, they can never provide solutions. Frankly speaking, it is such teachings alone that have created a terrible mess. But kindly do not commit this error yourself. Just immerse

"Don't just **earn money,** earn it in **abundance!** This is your **religion** as well as **your duty**

yourself in profound psychological insights and never go against Nature's design. Rest assured, following even this little bit of advice will improve your life to a large extent.

Agreed, we must refrain from going against Nature's design, and admittedly, our purpose in life is determined by Nature. But what is that purpose? Well, towards that end, first comprehend this: what is Nature's design for us—in other words—who are we? Of course, we are human beings. And when we all belong to the same species, how can the purpose of our lives be different? And verily, our purpose is not different at all. We all share the same purpose and that purpose is determined by Nature. For instance, every rose plant cannot have a different purpose. Every cow cannot have its own individual purpose. Similarly, every human being cannot have his own individual purpose either. One need not even apply too much intelligence to comprehend this simple truth! But humans are victims of false knowledge, due to which the vast majority of people are clinging on to their own individual purposes. Therefore, grasp clearly that if someone has predetermined his purpose in life, separate from what Nature has determined for him, then he is surely deluded about life. Otherwise, the truth remains that we are all human beings and we all share a single common purpose, which is determined by Nature.

Alright, we have grasped that every human being cannot have his own individual purpose. We have also understood that we are all humans and our purpose is determined by Nature. But kindly tell us what that purpose is. Well, we will come to that eventually; what's the rush? The matter is as profound as it is important, so it is better to comprehend it step by step. At present, answer this question: why is the human being distinct and precious compared to all other entities? It is because he is endowed with a 'complete and all-encompassing life'. Therefore, nothing can be more valuable for a human being than his complete and all-encompassing life. If you consider anything else to be more valuable than such a life, then you have failed to fathom the marvellous play of Nature. This completeness of human life is due to those beautiful experiences that only humans can feel. Otherwise, just being able to inhale and exhale cannot be called life, for, even animals live in this manner. Therefore, if you perceive life to be limited to just the act of breathing, then you are completely mistaken.

Comprehend clearly that in the entire realm of Nature, it is only humans who are endowed with a complete life; and the absoluteness of their life is defined by their sublime feelings and experiences. Therefore, it is needless to state that the only important thing in this entire universe is solely these beautiful emotions which the human being dwells in. These are verily the lovely emotions that no other entity can experience. And truth be told, the entire universe exists solely for the sake of these precious human emotions. If there were no beings capable of experiencing these sublime emotions, then the very existence of the universe would have been pointless. And needless to mention, happiness, fun, joy, peace, contentment, bliss, love, creativity and so on are the very emotions that I am discussing here. Surely, nothing in this universe or beyond is as precious as these emotions. Even your so-called gods and religions are no more significant than the happiness, peace and joy of humans. Therefore, grasp clearly that the happiness and peace of humans cannot be snatched away for the sake of anything in this world. Hence, if you truly wish to curb the nuisance of money, do not consider anything else to be more important than these beautiful feelings and experiences of life. The bitter truth is, those who consider religion and God to be more important than these emotions are actually the ones who are stripping human beings of their happiness and peace in the name of religion and God. While, in reality, nothing surpasses 'humanity' and that is Nature's irrefutable truth. Besides, it is impossible to go against Nature. Therefore, it is only those who embrace this truth that can actually rid themselves of the nuisance of money. Why can't you comprehend the simple notion that the purpose of all rose buds is to become a 'rose'! Similarly, the purpose of every person in this world is to become 'human'. So, how can one consider anything else to be above humanity? The question simply does not arise. When humanity itself reigns supreme in this universe, how can your life have any other purpose apart from being human? And who is a human being—a creature who lives his life dwelling in sublime emotions. These are simple truths that should not give rise to any confusion at all.

Well, I hope that all your confusions regarding the purpose of human life have now been cleared. By now, you must have thoroughly comprehended that amassing sweet emotions and experiences is the sole purpose of human existence. Moreover, understand well that your closest companions in life are your own emotions; and to dwell in these sweet emotions and experiences is the sole purpose of your life, as ordained by Nature. Consider all other purposes as mere fanciful ideas that will lead you astray, whether they are related to religion, God or career. Comprehend clearly that all other purposes are merely a means to fulfil the 'main purpose of life'. And 'means' can never become the 'purpose' itself. The path can never be the destination; it will always remain the means to reach the destination. So, henceforth, kindly do not be confused between path and destination either.

Grasp clearly that dwelling in emotions such as happiness, peace, tranquillity and joy is the sole purpose of human life, as ordained by Nature. One should harbour no confusion in this regard. Apart from this, if you make anything else the purpose of your life, then you will inevitably be compelled to suffer the nuisance of money. I am repeatedly cautioning you that it is totally futile to go against Nature. So, comprehend well that if earning the maximum amount of money is your *swadharma*, then investing the money you have earned in the 'purpose of life' is also your duty. If rich and famous people have fallen victim to the nuisance of money despite possessing ample money, it is only because they have strayed away from the primary purpose of life. They have erroneously assumed that becoming a doctor, engineer, businessperson or religious proponent like a pundit, maulvi or priest, or something else altogether is the purpose of their life. However, these are simply the means, not the purpose. One may definitely aspire to become a doctor or a businessperson, but the ultimate aim is only to experience sweet emotions. Therefore, becoming a doctor cannot be the purpose; after all, it is just a means to experience beautiful emotions. The true purpose of life can only be defined as dwelling in pleasant and sublime emotions. Comprehend this difference between path and destination and you will have grasped a profound psychological truth.

Basically, the sole purpose of life is to live joyfully. And if you wish to rid yourself of the nuisance of money, you will have to consider this the sole purpose of life. And with this being the sole purpose of life, comprehend another fact as well—to fulfil your needs in life by working towards it is the very system that Nature has designed for humans. However, this does not mean that the human being should consider fulfilling his needs a burden. It is an irrefutable fact that everyone has to perform their tasks, but here I wish to convey that these tasks can also be performed happily. And honestly speaking, one should discharge the responsibility of earning in a cheerful state of mind. For, the purpose of your life is to enjoy. So, working devotedly for eight to ten hours daily is a must, but you should not perceive it as a burden. In other words, the money earned from working should not only be spent for the purpose of enjoyment, but the work itself should be performed joyfully, with a merry song on your lips. To state it differently, you should not lose sight of and deviate from the primary purpose of life even while working.

Hopefully, this explanation should suffice, so let us now return to the main point of our discussion. And the key point is, 'money' acquired through work should only be invested in the purpose of life. And if I were to explain the purpose of life in simple terms, it is nothing but 'using one's earnings to procure happiness for oneself and one's loved ones'. And needless to say, money's biggest power lies in its 'exchangeability'. So, the money earned through your hard work should only be converted into joy, bliss, fun, peace, contentment, love and creativity. In other words, spending money should invariably result in the attainment of at least one of the afore-mentioned things. Of course, in case of an adversity, money can also be converted to minimise one's sorrow and troubles. This implies that when one is ill, it is definitely wise to spend money on healthcare. To put it simply, when everything is progressing smoothly, one should spend money to procure happiness, but when adversity knocks at your door, money should be utilised to alleviate hardships. Comprehend clearly that the conversion of money for anything apart from this will only lead your life astray. And honestly, it is this incorrect conversion of money that has ensnared the larger majority. Therefore, if you wish to eliminate the nuisance of money, convert your hard-earned money into beautiful emotions and experiences only. Procure happiness, joy, peace and love for yourself and your loved ones with every penny you earn.

I am sure you will argue, "This is exactly what we are doing," and my response to that would be, the lives of those who do so can never be besieged by such immense sorrow, stress and anxiety. Those who convert their money smartly can never be tormented by the nuisance of money. Had you taken this approach, I would not have emphasised this point so strongly. Therefore, from now on, observe whether you convert your money into happiness, joy and peace, or conversely into cars, furniture and other material possessions. Surely, you are converting your money into material possessions. Of course, at the time of conversion, you presume that this exchange of money into material goods will bring you happiness. In other words, you do not seek happiness directly; you seek it indirectly, through material possessions. And psychologically speaking, there is a significant difference between procuring happiness directly vis-à-vis buying a car to secure happiness. That is why the outcomes of these two approaches differ as well. Those who procure happiness directly are always content and unaffected by the nuisance of money, while those who procure happiness indirectly have to suffer the nuisance of money day in and day out. The problem is, there is a very fine but crucial line of distinction between these two approaches. And to comprehend this, one needs to have a profound knowledge of psychology. But unfortunately, even a basic knowledge of psychology is not readily available in the world.

In short, you may be trying to garner happiness, but more often than not, you do so in an indirect manner. Considering the significance of this matter, let me elaborate it in some more detail. A home, car, furniture, television and similar possessions are indeed the necessities of life, and if you have the funds and resources, you should definitely fulfil these necessities. However, the key question is, what is your state of mind during the process of acquiring these? Are you procuring happiness or a car? This very mindset alters the entire scenario. There is a big psychological difference between focussing on the car while purchasing it, and focussing on the happiness you derive at the time of purchasing the car. Focussing on 'happiness' means that you are purchasing the car solely for your own happiness and that of your loved ones. But focussing on the 'car' may indicate a variety of reasons for buying the car. You could be purchasing the car to elevate your status. And if that is the case, then your focus is not on your own happiness, but rather on flaunting your car as a status symbol to boost your image in the eyes of others. Similarly, you may acquire a car to arouse envy in someone or to belittle them. It is also possible that you are purchasing the car because your competitor has already bought one. All these possibilities indicate that you are not buying the car for your own happiness. What I am trying to explain is, if you buy a car for any reason other than your own happiness, it will ultimately bring sorrow in its wake. And honestly speaking, most people are converting their money into such sorrows only. In fact, they are

> ”
> **‘Money trap’ is far more dangerous than ‘honey trap’**

converting money less for themselves and more with their focus on others.

Basically, you must convert money only for the direct attainment of joy, merriment and peace of mind—this is the only correct way to utilise money. And it is only then that you will feel you are living life as it ought to be lived. If you convert money erroneously, it will attract ever-new problems in your life and create every possible nuisance. The aforementioned statement holds great significance and I shall eventually explain it in detail too. But, for now, comprehend clearly that you must convert your money solely to experience positive emotions. While converting money, do not focus on anything other than garnering positive experiences. This is Nature’s design for human life and you must respect it fully.

In fact, you must respect not just this but every creation of Nature. Since Nature has bestowed this precious life for the purpose of living, you will find yourself hopelessly trapped if you try to come up with any purpose other than what Nature has determined for you. Admittedly, life cannot be sustained without money, and to that end, one needs to devote eight to ten hours of diligent work and apply intelligence as well. However, one has a choice whether one wants to engage in that endeavour feeling utterly miserable or with a smile on one's face. And only those who work diligently and cheerfully for eight to ten hours are entitled to live a splendid life. As opposed to this, those who work with a gloomy disposition are as good as dead! This is the reason why I have explained that becoming a doctor, engineer, businessperson or artist can never be the 'purpose of life'. These are all paths, not the destination. If you aspire to become a doctor, then by all means do so, but ensure that you do it without losing sight of the purpose of life. Become a doctor only if you find joy in it. However, if you try to become a doctor grudgingly, you will surely stray away from the purpose of life. And if that is the case, then steer clear of becoming one. It is better to pursue a line of work that brings happiness to you and puts a smile on your face. But regardless, you have to choose a career and you definitely need to work eight to ten hours a day. This implies, if you cannot do anything cheerfully, then you surely have no right to live! Those who feel compelled to perform every task glumly are mere idlers. And idlers can never shake off the nuisance of money.

To summarise, the sole purpose of life is to live joyously, for which money is essential; and earning money requires working for eight to ten hours daily. Learning and studying are also tasks in themselves; in other words, a person has to engage in work right from the age of six or seven. This is how life has been designed for human beings. Wise are those who respect this arrangement with a smile on their face and perform their tasks cheerfully.

However, never forget that your responsibility does not end with merely working for eight to ten hours in a joyous state of mind. For, it is also your responsibility to garner every possible joy for yourself and your loved ones from the money you have earned. And it is only when you fulfil both these responsibilities diligently that you can safeguard yourself from the nuisance of money.

In essence, the only true and balanced approach is to work cheerfully. Acquire everything the world has to offer, but only for your own happiness. This approach is not only spiritually correct but psychologically perfect as well. On my part, I have elucidated a simple truth of life and I am confident that you will assimilate this truth and steer your life in the right direction. In other words, you will earn the maximum amount of money possible in a cheerful and joyous state of mind and utilise it to acquire happiness directly, that is, you will invest your hard-earned money to fulfil the purpose of life.

Now that we have covered a great many aspects of money, answer this question: is there anyone in today's world who is not hounded by the problems created by money? Perhaps very few! Indeed, it is the issues related to money that are causing the greatest distress in everyone's lives. In fact, this is the very reason you are unable to achieve the primary purpose of your life, which is to live life joyously. Viewed from this perspective, it can be said that it is the nuisance of money that is largely responsible for the negativities in the mind and ailments in the body. Therefore, it goes without saying that he who can liberate himself from the nuisance of money has more or less attained harmony and well-being in his life. And I am re-emphasising that if you truly wish to free yourself from the nuisance of money, then first and foremost, immerse yourself in your work cheerfully and dedicatedly for eight to ten hours a day. It is imperative to do so and bear in mind—unless you do this, you will fail to accomplish anything substantial! Thereafter, utilise every penny of your earnings from those eight to ten hours of work to procure direct happiness for yourself and your loved ones. In other words, invest each and every penny of yours in fulfilling the purpose of your life. First, resolve firmly that you will accomplish these two goals and only then contemplate making further progress. I am emphasising these two goals repeatedly so that I can set your mind to accomplish them under any circumstance. And it is essential to set your mind because the present-day world is suffering from an acute shortage of money. Earning money is surely no child's play. Therefore, set your mind firmly on accomplishing these two goals so that it eases further discussions for both you and me. For now, peruse the following charts for a better understanding of the context of the present discussion.

List of Top 10 Countries with Highest Per Capita Income:

NO.	Country	Annual Per Capita Income (USD)
1.	Luxembourg	1,18,001
2.	Singapore	97,057
3.	Ireland	94,392
4.	Qatar	93,508
5.	Switzerland	72,874
6.	Norway	65,800
7.	United States of America	63,416
8.	Brunei	62,371
9.	Hong Kong	59,520
10.	Denmark	58,932

List of Top 10 Countries with Lowest Per Capita Income:

NO.	Country	Annual Per Capita Income (USD)
1.	Somalia	130
2.	Mozambique	490
3.	Central African Republic	520
4.	Madagascar	520
5.	Afghanistan	530
6.	Democratic Republic of Congo	530
7.	Sierra Leone	540
8.	Liberia	580

9.	Sudan	590
10.	Eritrea	600

(Source – International Monetary Fund, April – 2021)

You must have surely perused the charts given above listing the per capita income of some countries, in other words, the income per person in each of those countries. On scanning the list of countries with the highest income, you would have noticed that their average per person income is approximately INR 60 lakhs (six million) annually. Conversely, if you take a closer look at the countries with the lowest per capita income, you will notice that their average per person income is a mere INR 40,000 annually. The charts given above hold immense significance as they shed light on various aspects. First, they highlight the substantial disparity in the per capita income of various countries of the world. The per capita income of the top ten wealthiest countries is approximately 150 times higher than that of the ten poorest countries of the world! This is undoubtedly a vast disparity between them. Now, in the countries where the annual per capita income is INR 60 lakhs, there is obviously no dearth of money. However, in the nations where the per capita income is a mere INR 40,000 per year, there exists a significant scarcity of money. This fact is particularly noteworthy because even to secure freedom from the nuisance of money, one needs money... but the reality is, money is scarce!

In other words, the state of affairs is so dismal that there is a paucity of money in the world, but unfortunately, survival is impossible without money. Empty pockets mean that one cannot afford even a piece of bread, and that being the case, how can one even hope to fulfil the rest of the necessities of life? Another point worth considering is the innumerable contributions made by science in providing comfort and convenience to humans; evidently, scientific inventions such as electricity, car, television, refrigerator and mobile phone have now become necessities that are as indispensable as food, clothing and shelter. However, the acquisition and maintenance of these commodities is far from easy, especially for people in countries with a low per capita income. In fact, in today's scientific age, it is undoubtedly agonising that although such amenities are abundantly available, a meagre income does not permit one to acquire them. From luxurious cars to magnificent houses, from private jets to private yachts, is there anything that is not available in this scientific age? Moreover, science has made space travel possible too. And to top it all, the ever-restless human mind, prone to weaving grand dreams, is proving to be even more torturous. For, who would not want to enjoy these marvels of science? However, on scrutinising the existing per capita incomes, it becomes clear that only a few can truly savour the joy of these scientific inventions. For, indulgence demands money... and money, as we all know, is scarce.

The scenario is such that whichever way he turns, the modern-day man finds himself hopelessly trapped, because on one hand, there is the utterly restless and wishful mind, and on the other are abundant material possessions offering comfort and convenience. And to make matters worse, the paucity of money torments him no end. For, despite his relentless efforts, earning sufficient money remains an uncertainty. So, under such circumstances, how can he ever purchase happiness with his hard-earned money? On the face of it, it is evident that people can buy happiness with their earnings, but the harsh reality is, with such an acute scarcity of money, how can they generate enough income to fulfil their desires? The question is perfectly valid. A person should certainly be wise and procure happiness in exchange for money, but to that end too, he needs adequate money, doesn't he? With not a single penny in the pocket, what is the point in discussing the purpose of life and so on? In fact, the scarcity of money has become the primary cause of distress, worry, frustration and conflict today. This being the case, what can a person do, helpless as he is? For, the issue of money has become extremely complicated. First of all, one is not interested in working hard, but this does not change the fact that hard toil is necessary to earn money. An even more distressing fact is that one is not guaranteed sufficient income even after toiling hard. And even if one manages to earn a reasonable amount of money, it is imperative to exercise prudence in spending it. And it is only natural to commit mistakes and make miscalculations in this whole process.

All things considered, the fact remains, in today's world, money is indispensable when it comes to fulfilling needs and ensuring a happy life, but at the same time, the shortage of money for one reason or the other is the stark reality of this world. In other words, the world at large is distressed by the all-pervading scarcity of money. And, know well, the problem merely begins from this point onwards! For, an even bigger monster looming before us is that many people are resorting to crime to rid themselves of the paucity of money. Viewed from this perspective, it is this very scarcity of money that is solely responsible for everything, right from the distressed state of human beings to the prevalence of crime in society. And I have already indicated that in the present times, 'the shortage of money' is a bigger nuisance than money itself. That was the reason why I had referred to earning the maximum amount of money possible as one's foremost duty. For, the situation created by the shortage of money is so deplorable that even those who work dedicatedly to earn well have failed to remain unscathed by it. In such a scenario, one shudders to even imagine the plight of those who do not earn at all!

> "To be **deceitful** is **money's nature.** It shows **loyalty** to whoever **owns** it at any given point

Nevertheless, the fact remains that the scarcity of money is the harsh reality of this world, and this very shortage is the biggest cause of distress today. India's annual per capita income is merely INR 130,000. But, of course, the ever-restless mind does not comprehend this ground reality! And this being the case, how can a person ever satisfy his insatiable mind with his hard-earned money, no matter how desperately he wishes to? How can one achieve the primary purpose of life, which is to live joyously? Simply put, eliminating distress from human life and crime from society is not an easy task at all, especially considering the fact that money cannot be generated overnight. A significant improvement in global per capita income is bound to take centuries, and it can happen only when everyone works perseveringly towards that end. Therefore, it is only justifiable to question whether the distress from human life and crime from society can ever be eradicated. Truly, in light of all this, the task appears to be impossible. No one knows at what point everyone will earn sufficient money and when their most cherished desires will be fulfilled. But unless these two issues are addressed, any decline in the nuisance of money will remain just a pipe dream. However, let me clarify here that although the issue is challenging, its resolution is by no means impossible. So, do not be disheartened. Distress from life and crime from the society can indeed be eradicated completely—and it must be done at all costs! And that is precisely why we are conducting an in-depth psychoanalysis of money. For, how can it be tolerated that the human being strays away from the primary purpose of life, ensnared in the illusory web of money? We should not have to wait for centuries to see human life liberated from pain and distress and a society free of crimes. At the same time, one must comprehend how challenging a task this is, considering the fact that there is a tremendous shortage of money. And that is precisely what I am trying to convey, that if the nuisance of money is the world's greatest problem, how can the process of liberating oneself from it be easy?

Surely, money must be invested in fulfilling the purpose of life, and it must be employed solely to acquire happiness for ourselves and our loved ones. However, the question remains: does one have adequate money for that purpose either? Even if we work hard and exercise prudence, we would still need money to acquire happiness, won't we? The argument is absolutely valid. For, the fact remains, in the absence of money, it is impossible to free ourselves from the nuisance of money. And considering the per capita income of most countries, no one can hazard a guess as to when the shortage of money will finally be eliminated. Well, another question worth considering is, even if the per capita income increases, what could possibly change? The increasing per capita income will trigger a simultaneous increase in needs, won't it? After all, nothing can ever satiate the mind. As a matter of fact, per capita income has risen exponentially over the past century, and yet the nuisance of money remains unabated. On the contrary, the nuisance has become even more pronounced. In short, the scarcity of money alone is not responsible for the escalating nuisance. This implies, we should not wait for a spike in our income to liberate ourselves from the nuisance of money. For, although there has been a steep rise in the overall income earned in the past century, the nuisance of money has certainly not declined as a result of it. Therefore, we have to act now, and that too, in the given circumstances! In short, we do not have to wait for the ideal situation, in other words, a spike in our income, to take action. We need to set everything right today itself! In any case, no problem is ever resolved by procrastinating. So, if you wish to resolve the problem, it has to be done right here, right now! Indeed, those who procrastinate their problems are never truly free of them. Here, I have revealed the supreme principle of resolving problems, and wise would be the one who takes advantage of every psychological principle that is being hinted at.

In essence, you must realise that those who wait for a change of circumstances to resolve a problem have completely failed to comprehend the psychology of problems. Although this book does not focus on the psychology of problems, we are certainly discussing the problems engendered by money. And verily, we need concrete solutions to the problems spawned by money today itself! We must not wait for tomorrow, that is, for circumstances to change in order to rein in the nuisance of money. In our discussion so far, we have at least realised that there can only be a single purpose of life, which is to lead a life brimming with fun, joy and peace while simultaneously making great strides. We have also grasped that sorrow, distress, tension, frustration, the pressure of money, crime and so on are the biggest obstacles in the achievement of this purpose of life.

So, how can we overcome these obstacles? For, the paucity of money is a stark reality of this world, and this scarcity will surely bring its own share of pain and distress. At the same time, one cannot deny the possibility that many people will also resort to crime in order to acquire money. So, what is the solution to this? Well, you must have definitely heard of the term 'spirituality'. In fact, I have used this word several times in this book as well. And now, you must also grasp that true and profound spiritual principles are nothing short of magic for humans. They hold the solutions to all the problems of human beings. But, of course, how many people actually discuss profound spiritual principles and how many truly comprehend them? Nevertheless, for now, understand well that spirituality does not wait for the next moment to find solutions to problems. For, the next moment does not even exist for spirituality! Therefore, do not ever mistake anything that postpones action until the next moment to be spiritual. This is a major hint I have given you. So, pay heed to it and henceforth, bear in mind this key difference between spiritual and non-spiritual matters.

Well, another principle of spirituality states that everything is governed by the laws of Nature. And everything truly means everything, therefore, 'money' is no exception to it either. So, when everything exists in accordance with the laws of Nature, nothing is inherently bad. Here, once again, let me clarify that spirituality makes no differentiation whatsoever. In other words, differentiation which labels things as good or bad is non-existent in the dictionary of spirituality. This is yet another significant hint, so ensure that you grasp it in all its profundity.

Comprehend this; as per the principles of spirituality, anything that is bad, wrong, evil or negative exists solely within human beings, as they misuse things due to their own imprudence. For instance, what is inherently wrong about a gun? It is a valuable tool when used against terrorists. The same principle applies to 'money'. It is only the manner in which it is tackled that is wrong. In other words, the flaw lies in the human being himself, not in money. This is precisely why in the Bhagavad Gita, Krishna says that he is Kubera, the lord of wealth, which means that the one who is wealthy is verily a form of Krishna. This implies, there is nothing inherently bad about money. On the contrary, the more you have it, the better it is. As for the nuisance of money, humans are themselves responsible for creating it. The fault does not lie with money, because a spiritually enlightened person does not consider anything to be evil or negative in this entire realm of Nature. Therefore, grasp clearly that if humans wish to liberate themselves from the nuisance of money, they will have to transform themselves. For, when there is nothing inherently wrong in money, the question of bringing a change in it does not arise at all. The problem lies in the human being, so it is he who will have to change. And only he who brings about the required changes within himself will become immune to the nuisance of money. To that end, all he needs to do is learn to tackle money prudently.

In essence, comprehend clearly that there is nothing inherently evil or wrong in money. Therefore, it doesn't make much of a difference whether money is scarce or abundant. For, when there is absolutely nothing wrong with money, how can it be blamed for the troubles arising on account of it? The fault, if at all, lies with us, as we are not spiritual. So, neither those who lament the shortage of money, nor those who label money as evil are spiritual. For, true spirituality states that the fault doesn't lie in external objects, rather it lies within oneself. Instead of blaming things, spirituality teaches us to utilise them correctly. That is why, in the Bhagavad Gita, Krishna even goes so far as to proclaim that he is desire, anger and ego as well. Now, why did Krishna state this? It is because one can use even desire, anger and ego in an appropriate manner and transform them into nectar. Therefore, instead of cursing money or lamenting its scarcity, we must learn the correct way to tackle it. All I am trying to convey is, the paucity of money is an undeniable reality, but we must not relinquish our life's purpose on account of it. Once you master the art of tackling money, you can definitely fulfil the purpose of life despite the scarcity of money.

So, etch firmly in your mind that there is no inherent flaw in money, for, it is also a part of Nature. Therefore, if you are distressed due to money, seek the flaw within yourself. And if you genuinely wish to shield yourself from the assault of money, then assimilate this principle of spirituality for good—do not label anything as flawed or evil. You must realise that you haven't yet mastered the art of utilising it suitably. Know well that at present, you are unable to handle things properly. This is a profound spiritual hint that I have provided, and wise are those who can grasp even the subtlest hints.

In short, those who label certain acts as sinful and raise strong objections against them are simply admitting that they haven't yet mastered the art of tackling things. Krishna never felt the need to label anything as bad because he was adept at the art of tackling everything. Therefore, comprehend another point clearly—spirituality concerns only the individual; it never addresses family, society or nation. Even in the case of the nuisance of money, spirituality can definitely guide you—as an individual—on how to ward it off; however, spirituality does not prescribe non-psychological measures such as saving an entire family or nation. Of course, if every individual is reformed one by one, then not just the family but the entire world can also be saved from the nuisance of money. In essence, it is 'you' who must take the initiative to try to save yourself from the nuisance of money, and verily, this is the only possible solution. For, others are free to act as per their own understanding and will. I am sharing these profound truths so that I can protect you from the nuisance of money; therefore, focus on yourself first. Spirituality states that when each and every person is reformed, a day will dawn when this world too will be transformed into a better place. Spirituality is not a religion wherein the preachers, despite being totally ignorant about their own selves, have embarked on a mission to transform the world at large!

Well, now that I have spoken at length on spirituality, let us return to our main topic of discussion—'money' and our aim to seek liberation from the troubles caused by money. As for spirituality, we have our entire lives to delve into profound spiritual principles. In the present context, it is evident that in today's times, money is synonymous with life itself. Moreover, one cannot deny the fact that there is an acute scarcity of money in the world. Therefore, to liberate ourselves from its nuisance, we must learn to tackle money efficiently. The straightforward solution is that everyone must work diligently for eight to ten hours a day to earn the maximum amount of money possible. It is also clear that a person can earn a substantial amount of money only by devoting himself wholeheartedly to his work. Now, what I seek to explain with the help of spirituality is that if you wish to liberate yourself from the nuisance of money, pause right here, right now. Those who will take a pause at this point will never encounter money-related distress. I have already stated that spirituality does not wait for some point in the future to provide solutions. So, whoever pauses here itself will be saved. However,

> "
> **Money plays** with your **psychology** with **great style**

nobody pauses here, and that is the primary reason why they are compelled to suffer the nuisance of money. The core problem lies with the human being, because he does not pause at this point. And once again, I have made quite a significant observation. In case you have failed to comprehend, read it once again. If you wish to rid yourself of the nuisance of money right here, right now, then consider this a foolproof solution.

However, if you are still struggling to grasp it, then let me explain it using a different approach. In fact, allow me to elaborate on the matter in greater detail. For, it is likely that you may not have had much exposure to profound 'psycho-spiritual discussions'. So, answer this question: all things considered, what is actually in your control? The only aspect that you can control is performing high-quality work dedicatedly for eight to ten hours daily to earn money. Beyond that, you do not have much control, at least for the time being. If you do have, then let me know. And truly, there is nothing. However, so-called intelligent people can surely present a list of things which they believe are under their control. In the Mahabharata war, Arjuna had just one option—to fight the war wholeheartedly. And that is exactly what Krishna advised him to do unquestionably and wholeheartedly. But Arjuna was intelligent, so he continued to offer numerous bizarre options to Krishna. In other words, he kept giving strange reasons for not engaging in battle. That is why I mentioned that intelligent people can very well list a number of reasons. However, you must not become extra intelligent like them, because such people are actually foolish. So, apart from dedicatedly working for eight to ten hours, nothing else is in your control. This is the ultimate reality of life. And whoever genuinely accepts this reality, or this very limitation of humans at large, will definitely be able to ward off the nuisance of money.

To summarise, amassing happiness is the main purpose of life, but even to fulfil this purpose, one requires money. However, considering the scarcity of money in the world, it is evident that money is insufficient. And when there is a lack of sufficient money, earning it is certainly cumbersome. This is obvious, but what I wish to explain is that whether the path to earn money is easy or ridden with difficulties, efforts must be made to earn the maximum amount of money possible. And the first and foremost step in this direction is to dedicate eight to ten hours of diligent work daily to accomplish this objective. Do this and stop right there, for, you have done your best. And once you have worked devotedly for eight to ten hours, you will surely earn the money that you rightfully deserve. So, first of all, set yourself within the limits of the money available at your disposal. This simply means utilising the money at your disposal to procure whatever joy, happiness, fun, bliss, peace and serenity that you can. Of course, when procuring happiness, I hope you demonstrate enough spiritual wisdom to know that happiness is not confined to travelling in a luxurious chartered flight. One can find far greater joy even in a leisurely bicycle ride, provided one is not hankering after chartered flights! This is the very reality of everyday life which you are well aware of. Indeed, it is not that happiness can be acquired only by spending money. Even something as simple as one's favourite meal can surely send one soaring to the seventh heaven of gastronomical delights!

Therefore, evaluate yourself honestly and answer this question: which of the two really matters to you—flying in a private jet or being happy? Undoubtedly, what truly matters is happiness. And when being happy is all that matters, there is hardly any obstacle in your path to obtaining it. All you have to do is focus your attention on seeking happiness with the money available at your disposal. And speaking of happiness, it abounds everywhere; you simply have to become a smart buyer of happiness. A great number of affordable things can bring you so much joy that there is absolutely no need to lament the 'paucity of money'. For the purpose of entertainment, you have the entire YouTube channel at your fingertips at the nominal price of an internet connection. Countless TV channels are accessible for a mere hundred rupees. Delicious meals are not expensive at all. You can chat with your loved ones free of cost. Does one really need money to enjoy sports? Is there any tax imposed on giving and receiving love?

Agreed, there is an acute shortage of money in the world, and putting in an honest day's work for eight to ten hours does not necessarily guarantee sufficient earnings. This aspect is undoubtedly true, but what can you do? This, however, does not mean that you are condemned to suffer the nuisance of money lifelong. This also does not mean that the primary purpose of life, which is to live a life filled with cheer and enjoyment, is unattainable just because you have limited financial resources. You must ensure that you never stray away from the purpose of life, and towards that end, all you need to grasp is that once you have worked honestly for eight to ten hours a day, you have fulfilled your duty. After working dedicatedly for eight to ten hours, you fully deserve to sit back, relax and enjoy your life to the fullest. And this you must do! However, to live such a life, you will have to become spiritually wise. In spirituality, the solution to a problem lies in the present, in the here and now. In spirituality, it is just not acceptable to blame others, or in this case, the paucity of money for your troubles. In spirituality, neither do you have to wait for another day for the resolution of a problem, nor do you have to offer justification for the inability to resolve the problem. The spiritual mind provides prompt solutions for absolutely everything. And the immediate solution in this case is that you have earned all the money that you could have possibly earned. Thereafter, all you need to do is satiate the mind with the money available at your disposal thus overcoming the nuisance of money. For, even after toiling for eight to ten hours daily, if you are still compelled to endure the nuisance of money, then it is sheer foolishness. And you must steer clear of such foolishness! Towards that end, all you need to do is focus on amassing a variety of happiness that is affordable rather than focussing on things that are unaffordable. Frankly speaking, the amount of money in one's possession does not determine how wealthy or prosperous one is. It is the lack of spiritual knowledge that has made 'money' the deciding factor in ascertaining who is wealthy or prosperous. Otherwise, the fact of the matter is, money is merely a piece of paper and its value lies solely in its conversion. And in spiritual terms, truly wealthy are those who convert the money at their disposal in the best possible manner. Otherwise, even those who possess hordes of money amass nothing but sorrow by converting their money incorrectly. As opposed to them, those who convert their money smartly are able to procure all kinds of happiness with significantly less amount of money. So, tell me, who amongst the two is truly wealthy? Certainly, it is those who garner all kinds of happiness with a mere thousand rupees in their pocket.

Therefore, first and foremost, dispel the misconception from your mind that having money in abundance is a proof of being wealthy. Secondly, rid yourself of the notion that overcoming the nuisance of money requires a substantial amount of money. Do not cry over the fact that with such an abject scarcity of money in the world, how can one even hope to fulfil the purpose of living a joyful life! For, what is money, after all? It is just a piece of paper whose true value is hidden in its conversion power. Hence, by smartly converting even a small amount of money, you can certainly overcome its scarcity. Despite possessing a modest amount of money, you can surely teach the wealthiest people a thing or two about money conversion! Therefore, become psychologically and spiritually wise and effortlessly triumph over both, the nuisance as well as the paucity of money. In our earlier discussion, we have already gauged how widespread the scarcity of money is after glancing at the per capita income of various countries, so there is no denying the fact that the paucity of money is a harsh reality of the present-day world. In such a scenario, if you too are facing a shortage of money, it does not necessarily mean that the primary goal of living a joyful life will remain unfulfilled. This is what I have been trying to impress upon you all this while.

In short, instead of moping about insufficient funds, learn to smartly convert whatever money you already possess. This single act will liberate you from the nuisance of money, that is, its side effects such as stress, frustration, helplessness and despondency. In any case, if 'negative emotions' continue to plague your life, then no matter how much money you possess, it is of no consequence. These are simple truths that need not be explained repeatedly to intelligent people like you. So, whatever be the amount of money you possess, that becomes your limitation. However, bear in mind, this is the limitation of money, not the limitation of your spirituality. Therefore, no matter what, become spiritually wise and smartly convert the money at your disposal to attain peace, joy and contentment. Bear in mind, your inability to do so will lead you astray from the primary purpose of life, which is to 'live' life to the fullest. Having said that, I request you not to perceive the scarcity of money as its cause; instead, recognise it as a lack of spirituality within yourself.

Since we are discussing this point, here's another aspect you must comprehend: there is one more clear-cut benefit of living in peace, joy and contentment. A mind that is peaceful and brimming with joy will reflect in superior performance in work and also aid you in arriving at the right decisions. This, in turn, will naturally increase your chances of augmenting your income. Then, all you have to do is smartly convert even that increased amount of money. In other words, utilise the augmented income to garner more happiness. This will set into motion a cycle of increased income and ever-increasing happiness. Thereafter, be content with whatever extent of progress you make in this manner while enjoying life to the fullest. For, everything you accomplish thus will not be at the expense of the purpose of life. You have not traded your happiness, joy and peace for it. Money can never trouble those who lead their lives in this manner, which also proves that money possesses no nuisance power of its own. It is human weaknesses that are fuelling the nuisance of money. This also validates the spiritual principle that psychological wisdom can definitely enable one to find prompt solutions to every problem. And you must become such a person of wisdom and triumph over the nuisance of money at the initial stage itself. Going forward, we will discuss the precautions you need to take in order to notch up this victory, but in the meantime, just adopt the principle: 'You work for money and make sure money works for you'.

Frankly speaking, in the present age, there can be no achievement greater than being liberated from the nuisance of money, so firmly etch in mind the solution provided here. And to help you with this, I will once again conduct a brief psychoanalysis of the entire topic. This is not a reiteration, but rather a 'psychological tablet' that will ensure complete assimilation of the solution given here. Indeed, if you can recite tomes penned in Sanskrit and Persian languages a thousand times over without truly comprehending them, I'm sure you can revisit these valuable learnings explained from a fresh perspective.

The essence of our discussion is, money is the biggest necessity of life in the present times. Without money, survival is impossible in today's fast-paced world. Therefore, the primary duty of an individual is to earn the maximum amount of money possible, and to that end, he must work devotedly for eight to ten hours every day. At the same time, it is evident from the data on the per capita income of various countries that there is a tremendous scarcity of money worldwide, which implies that a satisfactory income is not guaranteed even after putting in an honest day's work. To make matters worse, the mind is so tricky and treacherous that no amount of money can satiate it. Therefore, the fault lies more with the mind rather than with the paucity of money. So, essentially, the issue is more about a lack of spiritual knowledge than money itself. And the true and simple spiritual lesson is that one cannot do much except work honestly for eight to ten hours a day to earn money. After having worked diligently, everyone should realise that for the time being, this is all that they can do. Hence, it is essential for everyone to work honestly and dedicatedly for eight to ten hours a day and consider the resultant income as the boundary set for their present life. In fact, the very essence of the Bhagavad Gita is encompassed in these words "O Arjuna! You have a right only over the performance of your karma (deeds), not over their fruits." In a similar vein, you too have a right only over performing your work honestly for eight to ten hours. Thereafter, you must consider the money you earn as Nature's blessing. However, this does not imply that you should stop focussing on earning more money; neither does it mean that you should stop making progress. Continue to perform your work consistently, but remember that all these efforts and the earnings accruing from them belong to the future. So, continue making efforts for the future, but do not rely on the probable money that will be earned in the future. At present, consider the money you earn by working honestly for eight to ten hours as the 'limit of your income'. The quantum of money you earn in this manner does not matter, for, the reality is, only a specific amount of money is available today. And as they say, those who shut their eyes to reality are nothing but fools! Therefore, as soon as possible, confine your needs and those of your loved ones within the limits of the money presently available at your disposal. The only thing you must decidedly do is smartly convert every unit of that money to procure happiness, joy and peace. Your efforts are already underway, so when you earn more money in the future, reset this increased income as your new boundary.

In essence, the only firm decision you should make is to always set the current amount of money at your disposal as your limit and continue to convert it smartly. That is all you can do. Once you have done that, your job is complete. And thereafter, you must firmly resolve that you will never nurse the feeling that 'money is scarce'. Once you take this step in a spiritual sense, you will instantly triumph over most of the nuisance arising on account of money. There may be a great many things available in the world, so be it! Learn the art of living joyfully within your set boundaries. After all, the sun has its limitations too. Is it illuminating the entire universe? No! Isn't it radiating its light cheerfully, considering the solar system as its prescribed limit? Then what is stopping you from living joyfully within your limits? I hope you have comprehended this straightforward spiritual solution to ward off the nuisance of money. I also hope that by adopting this spiritual approach, you will wholeheartedly immerse yourself in fulfilling the primary purpose of life—to 'live magnificently'. And towards that end, you will no longer lament the scarcity of money. Of course, for those who are adamant and naïve, even Krishna himself cannot help them! However, I am confident that you certainly do not belong to that category.

We have grasped by now that working honestly and dedicatedly for eight to ten hours daily and defining the resultant income as your limit can certainly evade the nuisance of money to a large extent. Thereafter, you only need to smartly convert that money, that is, utilise your limited money to procure happiness for yourselves and your loved ones. However, converting money smartly is not as straightforward as it seems. Money wields such tremendous power that avoiding its nuisance is not easy at all. This is because, firstly, earning money is essential, after which it is imperative to set one's lifestyle within the confines of one's income. Moreover, one must be careful enough to utilise the income only to procure happiness. And even after you have navigated all these steps perfectly, 'converting money smartly' is still challenging. Honestly speaking, if the nuisance of money has to be tackled, then one needs to demonstrate a strong sense of 'spiritual smartness' at every step. Otherwise, the nuisance of money will grip you in its clutches at some point or the other. If nothing else, it will create hurdles in your endeavour to smartly convert your money. Just think about it—had you been able to convert money smartly, the nuisance of money would have never tormented you in the first place. But as I have mentioned, converting money smartly is not as easy as it seems. Therefore, do not take the task of smart conversion of money lightly. For, even if you work hard, set your mind accordingly, and decide to procure only happiness, you may still not succeed in amassing joys with the money available at your disposal. Indeed, even those who are adept at financial matters are stumped when it comes to converting money.

At this point, you may wonder whether you are really so clueless about how to smartly spend your money and what is so difficult about it anyway? Well, the difficulty is that money is smarter than all of us put together! Its psychology is extremely volatile and that is precisely why I am emphasising that converting money smartly is not as easy as it seems. To give you an analogy, the celestial damsel Menaka simply had to employ one technique to distract the sage Vishwamitra, but money can divert your attention in countless ingenious ways. Money is a mischief maker and an impostor too. In fact, one could easily lose count of the various methods and weapons money possesses to divert a person's attention. Indeed, money has cast countless elaborate traps. And bear in mind that 'money trap' is far more dangerous than 'honey trap'! And this is the very reason why humans are unable to tackle 'money'.

This implies that if we consider our total income as the limit within which we must confine ourselves and utilise that money solely to buy happiness, we can ward off the nuisance of money to a large extent. However, as simple as it may sound, it is equally challenging to implement this. For, just as you have your own free will, money too has a will of its own. And that is what I am trying to indicate. Even if a person wishes to procure happiness, money does not permit it. One way or the other, it manages to ensnare everyone in its innumerable 'money traps'. And for this purpose, not only does money possess its own hands and feet but also a brain of its own! Its cunning and fickle nature is truly beyond description. Indeed, it is not without reason that it holds sway over the entire world. Therefore, never underestimate money, the nuisance it creates and its conversion power. Verily, if money is causing distress for one and all, it must definitely possess some extraordinary power.

It is true that money possesses astonishing qualities, but its most prominent quality is its 'character'. The character of money is so paradoxical that if on one hand, the lack of it causes

'Money' is the very reason why stress and scramble, strife and crime have become an inseparable part of life

distress, on the other, owning money is also a huge problem. Tackling the scarcity of money is a challenging task and so is managing the money in one's possession. In other words, money is such a peculiar affliction that the lack of it causes distress, but its presence too is not easy to deal with. Indeed, no other entity in this entire universe is as mischievous and troublesome as money. It is so crafty in nature that although you earn it through hard toil, it refuses to obey you. Ideally, it should be your slave but because of its craftiness, it ends up becoming your master. That is precisely why I keep reiterating that it possesses all the qualities of a wife or a girlfriend! Money deludes you into thinking that it is your slave, lulling you into the belief that you can spend it as per your desire. However, the reality is totally different. By setting up ingenious traps, money finds a way to impose its will. It possesses traits that are so dangerous that they are truly beyond one's imagination! For this reason, I am explaining the entire psychology of money in depth to help you recognise all its nuances and clear up your misconception that you are converting money smartly as per your own will. I am explaining all this to forewarn you about the innumerable traps money lays out for you and to help you understand that converting money smartly is not an easy task. Indeed, you need to sharpen your wits and become so smart that you are able to outsmart money. Otherwise, you will always find yourself at its mercy.

In conclusion, money is so shrewd and treacherous that it truly defies description. It lays out traps that are incredibly mind-boggling. Therefore, it is crucial for you to be on your guard and fully vigilant when it comes to money matters. Comprehend well that merely earning money does not relieve you of all your responsibilities related to money. To draw an analogy, money is like a daughter, and as you are aware, simply giving birth to a daughter does not relieve you of your responsibilities. Right from her education to getting her suitably married, you have to look after your daughter's well-being. And even after fulfilling these responsibilities, you need to ensure that her marital life is happy and thriving. The same is the case with money. Although earning money is the first step, converting it in the best possible manner is crucial as well. And to convert it well, it is important to exercise both prudence and control. For, the moment you lose your prudence or control, money pulls you into its 'trap'. Therefore, as important as it is to earn money, it is equally important to assert your authority over it. Anyone who loses control over his money can consider his life ruined.

Now, you obviously don't wish to squander away your precious life mired in the nuisance of money. Earning money is already an uphill task and is certainly not a breeze. Just think about the hard work you put in to earn money. But I want you to answer this question: why do you toil hard? Surely, it is to ensure that the money you earn brings you happiness. Indeed, if you work laboriously but are still unable to buy happiness with the money earned, then you will be counted amongst fools. So, let me re-emphasise that your responsibility regarding money is not limited to earning alone. The onus of managing it well also falls upon you; in other words, you need to ensure that everything—right from earning money to its best possible conversion—is executed with perfection. The problem, however, is that you are unable to exercise control over your money. Even if you act with prudence, you are unable to effectively convert money as per your will. For, you don't even realise at what point this seemingly innocent money, which appears to be your slave, suddenly turns into the master! Subsequently, ignoring your will, it begins to sneak in and out of your life according to its own will. And eventually, it makes no difference whether you earn money or not, for, nothing seems to be in your control. And this is precisely the experience of a vast majority of people.

The key point here is that even spending money requires as much intelligence as earning does. Very often, people manage to earn the required money but fail to spend it prudently, thus falling prey to the money trap. That is why I am reiterating that it is important to steer clear of all kinds of 'money traps', else money will slip away from you and happiness too will elude you. And this is exactly the predicament everyone is facing. Therefore, note carefully that even spending money is an art—and one that must be learnt well. However, the problem is, only the one who is able to exercise complete control over his earnings can truly learn this art. So, you must have complete control over your earned money under all circumstances. For, there is simply no other way to avert the nuisance of money.

The reason I am emphasising this is because people really invest their heart and soul into earning money and even manage to earn a substantial amount. However, they falter when it comes to converting this hard-earned money and end up committing grave errors. And this is truly disheartening, because how can one suffer hardships despite applying intelligence and working laboriously? Therefore, do not underestimate the art of 'smart conversion of money'. Unfortunately though, some people nurse the false belief that they actually spend their money as per their will and that they exercise complete control over it. They even assert that they are adept at converting money smartly. Well, if that is true, then it is indeed commendable. However, if this is a misconception, it can spell utter doom. Therefore, let me warn you that breeding such misconceptions in your mind is also a 'trap' laid out by money. As I had mentioned earlier, money is similar to a wife. It is actually the wife who controls you, but you believe that it is you who holds the reins! So, instead of harbouring such misconceptions, focus on comprehending the matter at hand. For, the one who is able to convert money smartly must surely be free from enduring its nuisance. Therefore, if you are currently suffering the nuisance of money in any form, know that you haven't yet learnt to convert your money smartly.

Comprehend well that the smartness of money far surpasses your intelligence, so to steer clear of money traps, you too will need to become smarter. You will have to show determination and also gain clarity in your understanding of money. Hence, grasp clearly that if money possesses any power, it is nothing but its 'power of conversion'. And it is not money per se, but its inherent power that holds value for you. The day it loses this power, its value will also diminish. And obviously, you too earn money not for the sake of money itself, but because of its 'power of conversion'. Therefore, as a first step, decide firmly that you will convert the money at your disposal in the best possible manner for yourself and your loved ones. And what could be the best possible conversion of money? Ponder upon this question carefully. Surely, you engage yourself in converting money day and night, so you must be aware of the most advantageous way of doing it, right? The above question should, therefore, not be difficult for you to answer.

Nevertheless, let me explain the concept of 'best conversion' of money. To begin with, answer this simple question: why do you earn money by toiling hard and applying your intelligence for eight to ten hours on a daily basis? The reason is obvious—to ensure that you can spend the remaining sixteen hours as per your heart's desire. If you are able to make this conversion meticulously, then you can rest assured that you have converted your money in the best possible manner. However, if you fail to do so, you must realise that you have fallen prey to the 'money trap'. I don't think this point can be explained in a language simpler than this. Therefore, evaluate yourself carefully and check whether you are really converting money smartly or if you have somehow misunderstood the concept. For, if you are converting your money smartly, then you must be spending the remaining sixteen hours in peace and enjoyment.

Therefore, the first thing you must do with your earnings is purchase eight hours of comfort, bliss and entertainment for yourself and your loved ones. Thereafter, you should buy everyone around you a calm and peaceful night's sleep for the next eight hours. This is verily the finest form of money conversion, and if you stick to this formula, money will not be able to 'trap' you easily. However, no sooner you deviate from this path even slightly than money will ensnare you. So, focus on the money available with you and simultaneously keep your purpose in sight, avoiding all other distractions. And the purpose is only one—utilise the money earned from eight to ten hours of hard toil to acquire sixteen hours of peace and happiness. Bear in mind, the moment your focus wavers from this purpose, money will spring into action and trap you instantly. Then, in spite of possessing money, you will remain distressed. And despite making relentless efforts, you will remain mired in troubles. Therefore, be clear in your mind that your earnings must be utilised to procure 'peace and a good night's sleep' as well as 'comfort and enjoyment' for yourself and your loved ones. Moreover, till the time these conversions are executed properly, refrain from focussing your attention on any other conversion of money. Only if you firmly adhere to this course of action will you be able to evade the money trap. Otherwise, money will easily trap you in its snare.

Etch firmly in your mind that you are putting in eight to ten hours of honest work so that you can enjoy the remaining sixteen hours of your day. Hence, till the time you don't possess sufficient amount of money, refrain from focussing on any other type of conversion. Once you ensure this, money will no longer be able to trap you easily.

For now, let us learn about the money traps that do not allow one to amass joy and happiness even after earning well and spending money wisely. In this context, we will explore in detail the most prominent money traps one by one. We will also simultaneously discuss strategies to evade these traps. All you need to do is thoroughly comprehend every money trap and try to relate it to your own life experiences. At the same time, resolve that you will not fall into any money trap ever again. For, it is only then that you will be able to evade the vicious snare of money and buy happiness for yourself.

Comprehend How Money Plays Tricks on You

Most people have a persistent feeling that money is scarce and that more of it is required. The paucity of money continues to niggle at the back of their mind. Let me ask you this—is this feeling real or imaginary? Are you really in dire need of more money or is the amount you possess sufficient? These questions are worth pondering upon as everyone is distressed because of the shortage of money. Everyone is desperate to earn more money. In such a scenario, it is essential to comprehend whether the money in their possession is genuinely scarce or not? Do they really have to suffer the pain caused by the paucity of money? And if one is compelled to live with such distress, then what is the point of living such a life? Life is meant to be enjoyed in its many-splendoured hues, but if we are unable to achieve even this fundamental purpose due to the constraints posed by money, then can such a life really be called a 'life'? It, therefore, becomes crucial for everyone to ask themselves whether the 'pain and distress they are experiencing due to the paucity of money' is real or not. The question is significant because there is no pain greater than the one caused by the insufficiency of money. Hence, it becomes necessary to find out whether one is enduring this distress for no reason at all.

The fact is, a vast majority of people are living under the illusion that the money they possess is grossly inadequate. But let me reveal a secret to you—it is 'money' itself that has created this illusion! That is the reason why I am constantly cautioning you that the smartness of money is unparalleled. And that is precisely why we are conducting an in-depth psychoanalysis of money. Moreover, on closer observation, you will realise that the thought that 'money is insufficient' is less of your own and more of a notion planted by money. Money is a remarkable con artist that hollers into your mind that 'more and more money' is required. This is an extremely dangerous aspect of the psychology of money, which manages to trap everyone easily. Hence, you will notice that the more money one possesses, the more one craves it, which proves that money itself fosters in you a sense of scarcity of money! And this is the very 'trick' of money that traps everyone. However, you must steer clear of this bewitching trap of money under all circumstances.

So, before you find yourself falling into the trap that deludes you into thinking "I need more money," carefully assess whether you are truly short of money. Observe closely whether the money you have is actually insufficient or is it just a false notion? For, honestly speaking, living your entire life in pain and distress due to the scarcity of money is worse than death itself. Therefore, do not harbour this pain for no rhyme or reason. Remember, your existence as a human being is to fulfil the 'sole purpose of living life magnificently'. Therefore, ensure that you do not commit the foolishness of straying away from life's main purpose by getting caught in the money trap. Don't set out on a path whereby you are compelled to needlessly spend your life lamenting the paucity of money, dying little by little every day. Of course, those living below the poverty line are no doubt enduring the acute scarcity of money. The middle class, however, does not face such an abject shortage of money that prevents them from leading a decent life. If they are distressed, it is only because they have themselves contributed to their plight. Due to their ignorance of the psychology of money, they are being ensnared in various kinds of 'money traps'—especially the trap of 'shortage of money'. And the trap of 'shortage of money' is so treacherous that its pressure leads to numerous wrong conversions of money. Hence, comprehend clearly that more often than not, people actually do not face a shortage of money; it is, in fact, their misguided conversions on account of undue pressures that have weakened them financially. And this is quite a significant hint I have provided. Therefore, ensure that you check yourself vis-à-vis the fact highlighted in the statement above.

So, the middle class, at the very least, does not face such an acute shortage of money. It is only because they are trapped in the mind games played by money that they end up bemoaning the scarcity of money. And the moment you begin to agonise over the paucity of money, it ensnares you in various other traps. The feeling that 'I have less money' and 'I need more money at any cost' are the very traps through which money ensnares a person. And the moment one is caught in this trap, one is bound to spiral down a pit of countless other traps. So, this is the point where you must become cautious. And if you truly wish to evade this treacherous trap of money, the simplest approach is to accept the reality that the money in your possession is all that you have, and you have to lead your life within those means. Therefore, avoid falling prey to the notion that 'I need more money'. One does not have to spend one's life in this pain and

"**Embark** on **adventures**, but only in your **field** of **expertise**. If you are **not** an **expert** yet, first become one. Otherwise, **money** will **turn** its **back** on you

anguish needlessly. For, harbouring this agony is not going to help you attract more money. However, this certainly does not mean that you should cease all efforts to earn more money. Make consistent efforts to earn more money, but settle yourself with the money you possess at present, and that too determinedly so that thoughts of scarcity of money do not make way into your mind. This is the only approach to safeguard yourself from the 'trickster' that money is and establish your absolute control over 'money'. I, therefore, urge you not to torment yourself by bemoaning the 'insufficiency of money'. Instead, focus on exactly where you are converting your money erroneously. I promise that if you stop engaging in wrong conversions of money, your 'concerns about the scarcity of money' will be eliminated on their own. Pay heed to this advice, else life will turn into a living hell. For, the anguish resulting from the shortage of money is far worse than the suffering caused by countless ailments put together! This particular distress often ensnares people in several mental illnesses such as tension, depression and frustration, and these very mental ailments, in turn, spawn numerous physical ailments. With this explanation, I'm sure you can gauge how dangerous it is to nurture the notion that 'I have less money'. Therefore, the feeling of scarcity of money must be snipped off, come what may. Otherwise, this apprehension in itself is more than enough to ruin one's life.

Hence, I urge you once again to shift your focus from crying over the scarcity of money to rectifying the wrong conversions of money you are making at present. Roughly speaking, fifty percent of money is being converted wrongly. So, if this trend is put to an end and money is converted appropriately, the shortage of money will naturally dissipate. And the simplest solution for correct conversion is to convert every single penny earned through eight to ten hours of work into procuring sixteen hours of peace and joy. Decide for yourself that not a single penny shall be spent anywhere else apart from this. Only by firmly resolving thus, will you be able to safeguard yourself from the tricks of money; otherwise, the feeling of scarcity of money will keep gnawing at you, suffocating you and destroying you bit by bit every day. Therefore, never fall into the trap of thinking that there is a scarcity of money. I am re-emphasising and stressing upon this point only because there is no greater anguish than the feeling of scarcity of money. Moreover, I do not wish for anyone to nurse this anguish without any reason and endure this pain needlessly. I urge you to also make every possible effort to safeguard yourself from this agony. Shield yourself from this anguish and I assure you, you will have won a significant battle in life. I hope you will safeguard yourself from this pain and stop yourself from falling into the trap of believing that 'money is scarce'—a trap set by money itself. I have already stated that to evade the nuisance of money, you will have to become smarter than money, and I hope you will outsmart it.

Reject All Pressures Exerted By Others On Your Money

There is an old adage which states, "True wealth is that which positively impacts your being." In other words, money is valuable only if it brings pleasure to the mind and imbues the heart with contentment. If money fails to accomplish this purpose, then it is of no consequence. However, the psychology of money is so deceptive that it traps you in ingenious ways, befuddling you completely. Comprehend this: why do you apply your intelligence and work so hard to earn money? You do it only to savour the pleasures of life, don't you? But somehow, things do not work out as intended. You fail to realise how money ends up deluding you into spending your earnings on a myriad of unnecessary things. And everyone must learn to steer clear of this deceptive web of money. Indeed, how can it be tolerated that our hard-earned money goes to waste without us deriving enjoyment from it?

In short, the focus of your money should solely be on your happiness. Therefore, no matter what, do not ever allow money to take its eyes off your happiness. How is it even acceptable that your money casts its gaze in every other direction and gets easily distracted? This cannot be allowed at any cost! Therefore, under all circumstances, keep your money under your absolute control, with the firm instruction that it should refrain from casting its gaze on anything else other than your direct happiness. And since we are on this subject, comprehend one more point: you must determine for yourself what makes you and your loved ones happy. Let your entire family collectively decide this, and while making this decision, focus only on yourselves. Do not allow anyone from outside your family or any external system, pressure or influence to interfere in this process. Comprehend clearly that others' wishes do not translate into your happiness. Never forget that you have earned this money only to garner happiness for yourself and your loved ones. Besides, how on earth can anyone know better than you where your happiness lies? Therefore, you must determine the criteria of your happiness yourself! If you allow others to decide the criteria of your happiness, you will be stripped of your money and you will never be able to acquire happiness. Unfortunately, this is precisely what is happening all around. While the money belongs to someone, it is someone else's will that is at play. But this cannot be allowed to continue!

In essence, if it is your money, it is your will alone that should prevail. And towards that end, you must learn to keep your money entirely under your control. Here, let me also make it clear that controlling money is a mind game. And in the external world, there is a battalion of people employing mind games to claim authority over your money. Some are eager to stake a claim over your money in the name of society and social customs, while others try to siphon off your money in the name of religion. Some seek control over your money by citing traditions and beliefs, while others want to fleece you through emotional exploitation. And there are still others who employ pressure tactics to compel you to spend your money in the name of caste and community. And while this nefarious game is being played out, it is your mind that is suffering all these pressures. That is exactly why I have stated that the entire game of money conversion is a 'mind game'. The moment your mind weakens, others make off with your money.

Therefore, on waking up every morning, strengthen your mind by affirming that, “I have earned money to acquire happiness for myself and my loved ones. To that end, I have even worked hard and applied intelligence. So, I will not allow anyone to rob me of my money.” You will have to strengthen your mind by saying that, “Religion, society, traditions and emotions change with the passing of time and eras. So, why should I succumb to the pressures of these ever-changing factors?” Of course, those who have unlimited money are unaffected by such matters. For them, all of this is merely a pastime. However, for those with limited financial resources, it is imperative to learn to shield themselves from external influences and undue pressures. Verily, people with limited means need to ensure that their money is not wasted due to external pressures and influences. For, succumbing to pressures or influences can never grant you true happiness. On the contrary, the ones who influence or pressurise you, derive pleasure in this. Therefore, you must ensure that you are never outwitted in the 'mind game' played by those who seek to influence or pressurise you.

Grasp clearly that just as you have to compulsorily shell out a 'tax' (aka bribe) for gangsters, corrupt individuals and blackmailers, even those who pressurise and influence you impose a tax on you. The only difference is, the latter are white-collared conmen. However, whether a thief is white-collared or grey-collared, he should never be allowed to rob you. Never be duped into shelling out a thousand rupees for a charmed ring, sacred thread, amulet or cross that is worth only ten rupees. You are all aware that earning money is an arduous task, so it is crucial to protect your hard-earned money from conmen. And towards that end, you must strengthen your mind to beat everyone in this ongoing mind game of pressure and influence. Once you triumph over them, they will not dare to dupe you again. And you must do this because broadly speaking, these crafty people are siphoning off ten to fifteen percent of everyone's money. And it is only due to a lack of psychological understanding that this issue is skipping your attention. But henceforth, focus on this a little and you will realise how a significant percentage of your money is vanishing due to undue pressures and influences. In essence, I implore you to safeguard your money from being robbed through this 'mind game' and convert that saved money into buying direct happiness for yourself and your loved ones. Instead of crying over the paucity of money, do this and you will see that you are far happier in life. For, herein lies wisdom and you are indeed wise and sensible. So, I hope, going forward, you will take this hint and learn to protect your money from undue pressures and influences.

Never Convert Your Money for the Purpose of Show-Off

Money is such a mischievous entity that it demands intelligence both in earning as well as spending it. And honestly speaking, spending money demands considerably more intelligence than earning it. To put it simply, money can be converted in two ways: one, for buying happiness for oneself, and two, for making a show of being happy. Ideally, money should be converted only for one's own happiness. If happiness, peace and contentment cannot be obtained directly, then one must avoid converting money altogether. In fact, till the time a suitable conversion of money is not found, money should be saved. One must refrain from spending it till the time one chances upon a treasure trove of (direct) happiness. However, the problem with the majority of people is that they find more pleasure in trumpeting that they are happy instead of actually acquiring happiness. And this is where they get hopelessly trapped. If you are miserable but others assume that you are happy, does their assumption change the truth that you are actually miserable? Just because the world perceives you as wealthy, it will not alter the fact that you are indeed grappling with the scarcity of money. Therefore, shift your attention from others and focus it on yourself. Why should it be anyone's concern whether the money you have is less or more? You are not seeking monetary assistance from others, so why should you bother about their validation? In short, avoid all forms of show-off and learn to live with your reality, for, this alone will usher true happiness in your life.

When it comes to earning money, what is it that lies within your power? It is simply working devotedly for eight to ten hours a day. Beyond that, you do not have control over anything, neither in the present nor in the future. So, you have already done that, which means you have put in every effort within your capacity to earn money. Therefore, naturally, the money you are earning presently is your limit at this particular point of time. And confining yourself within this very boundary, you have to amass a world full of happiness for yourself. Certainly, those who garner such happiness within the confines of their financial resources are wise, while the rest are just over smart. And needless to say, it is precisely because the world is replete with extra smart people that there is so much distress regarding money. However, you must become a simple, wise person, for, that is all you need to live a joyful life.

Essentially, you should steer clear of the mad race to put up a pretence of happiness and instead focus on being genuinely happy. If your financial position allows you to host a function for fifty people at your daughter's wedding, then host the function for fifty people only. Refrain from organising a function for five hundred people just to impress others. Really, tell me, how does it matter to them? They will arrive at your event, eat and drink, shower praises and leave. But you must understand that extending yourself beyond your financial capacity may put you in trouble for several years to come. Therefore, never indulge in such foolishness. Besides, why don't you comprehend that when you choose to engage in pretentious display, your happiness remains contingent upon the opinion of others! The very basis of your happiness is then dependent on what others think. And surely, you are well acquainted with the behaviour of others. No matter how splendid the bride's attire is, how delectable the food is, or how magnificent the decorations and arrangements are, others will invariably find faults in them. Someone will question the quality of the food, while another will express reservations about the arrangements. Their comments and criticisms will instantly dampen your spirits, turning your joy into despondency. In other words, this whole exercise will ensure that you are not just incurring huge expenses but also accumulating grief. So, tell me, where is the wisdom in that?

It is understandable if those who possess abundant money or whose business depends on networking organise such grand functions; however, those who have limited financial resources must necessarily value money. They should abstain from all such pretentious displays where their happiness is contingent upon the opinions of others. They should spend money solely for their own (direct) happiness. Instead of splurging on extravagant events, they can choose to gift that money to the newlywed couple. Subsequently, the couple can use those funds to either plan their future or even take off on a few honeymoon trips every year, if they so desire. This will at least ensure that the money is spent directly on the couple's happiness. Similarly, whether you buy a house or car, acquire it for your own happiness. If your actions are aimed only at flaunting your wealth or making others envious, you are the only one who will suffer. Comprehend well that even if you purchase a car to impress others, it does not necessarily guarantee that they will get impressed! And even if they are impressed, what will you gain out of it? It is merely a matter of a day or two that the impression will last. Thereafter, it is you who has to foot the bill towards the maintenance of the car, and that maintenance will compel you to sacrifice several small joys of life. So, before you indulge in such acts, ask yourself, “Am I being wise or foolish?”

The biggest problem is, these days, there is no limit to showing off, and this is particularly evident in the case of children’s education—securing admission in prestigious schools seems to have become the norm, even if it means that one has to suffer untold hardships to pay exorbitant fees. In fact, one doesn’t bat an eyelid even if the entire family finds itself grappling with the shortage of money for the whole month! But such people firmly believe that children must be educated in reputed schools at

> "Instead of grumbling about **insufficient funds**, learn to **make 'smart conversions'** of the **money** you have

any cost. The question is, why is this so essential? History bears testimony to the fact that even uneducated people have succeeded in life, let alone those with limited education. I am definitely not advocating that you should not educate your children. Good education is indeed important in the present age. However, putting the entire family's joy and life at stake for the sake of children's education is certainly not wise. When even uneducated people can attain greatness, how is your child's future being jeopardised just by attending a regular school? Moreover, does the suffering of the entire family for fifteen years guarantee a bright future for the child? Despite having attended top-notch schools, millions of people around the world are suffering hardships, running from pillar to post. Therefore, if you are facing a paucity of money, you should refrain from staking fifteen years of your family's life and joy solely for your child's prestigious education, especially considering the fact that even after making this sacrifice, it will still not guarantee a bright future for the child. Moreover, the troubles resulting from such a toxic culture of show-off do not end here. It is very likely that upon securing admission into prestigious schools, your child will find himself amongst classmates hailing from affluent families. And this disparity would become evident when the latter would arrive at the school in luxurious cars while your child would pedal to school on a bicycle. Children from affluent families would enjoy yearly vacations abroad, whereas your child will not be able to travel to exotic locations.

This may still sound alright to you, but the problems do not cease here. You cannot even gauge how severe the impact on your child's psyche will be when he hears the boastful talks of his classmates. To be honest, by securing your child's admission to a school that is beyond your means, you are actually buying an 'inferiority complex' for him. Consequently, most children are unable to overcome this complex for the rest of their lives. To sum it up, first, you turn your family's present life into a living hell in order to pay the exorbitant school fees; thereafter, you put your child's future at stake by making him susceptible to developing an inferiority complex. Therefore, exercise prudence at this point itself. The world is replete with all kinds of pressures, but if you truly wish to lead a good life, you will have to learn to navigate those pressures. You must comprehend that it is talent that builds one's life, not one's educational institution. Therefore, focus on honing your child's skills rather than needlessly sacrificing your family's happiness and that of your own.

The truth is, life is a psychology—a mind game if you will. But no one understands this, and blinded by their ignorance, they are digging their own grave. Let me explain this with an example. You are well aware that enrolling your child in a prestigious school is a good decision, but you fail to comprehend the potential negative consequences of overextending your financial resources. You are totally ignorant of the adverse psychological impact on your child when he is admitted to a school far beyond your financial means. The extravagant lifestyle of other children may lead your child to harbour numerous complaints and grudges about your weak financial position. Besides, as he grows older, you too may harbour several complaints about him. This is because you have curtailed your desires and sacrificed your joys to enrol him into a prestigious and expensive school; therefore, it is quite natural for you to hold certain expectations from your child. In other words, due to a single wrong decision, you are actually laying down the foundation for a rift between you and your child! Tell me, isn't a person engaging in such actions digging his own grave? And you must comprehend that this entire game of digging your own grave is psychological in nature. That is the reason why I assert that a 'supreme knowledge of psychology' is the foremost requirement for a human being. For, the psychological consequences of every decision you make continue to impact you for years. You may not remember the decision, but its domino effect hounds you for life. That is precisely why the present-day world desperately needs the knowledge of psychology.

At present, all you need to comprehend is that you should never extend yourself beyond your financial means. You don't have to spend even a single unit of your hard-earned money in a place where others' opinions become the benchmark for measuring your happiness. So, avoid engaging in any kind of show-off. On an average, ten to twenty percent of everyone's income is inevitably spent on such pretentious displays. And amusingly, most people don't even realise this fact. But you must use your intelligence and prudently save the money that would otherwise be spent on showing off. I am repeatedly emphasising that spending money requires more sagacity than earning it—and you must apply that intelligence! Instead of crying over insufficient funds, focus on curbing the erroneous conversions of money. For, whether you acknowledge it or not, you are erroneously converting around fifty percent of your income under some or the other influence. This implies, if you are earning one lakh rupees, then approximately fifty thousand rupees are either getting siphoned off by someone or are being spent on show-off. To make matters worse, your income is also being frittered away in some or the other money trap that you are ensnared in. And these are the very reasons that the scarcity of money is tormenting you ceaselessly. Therefore, realise once and for all that the money you have is not insufficient. So, stop harbouring the anguish of scarcity of money and start converting it in the best possible manner. Once you learn this art, you will witness a remarkable improvement in all aspects of your life, right from your mind to your physical health.

Money Wants to Wriggle Out of Your Pocket – Escape That Trap

It is no secret that one has to jump through innumerable hoops in order to earn money. The question is, why is everyone striving so hard to earn money? Certainly, it is to ease one's life. But if money complicates life, then it is surely a folly on one's part. If life's hardships escalate because of money, then it is nothing but foolishness. And everyone should definitely avoid committing such follies. Remind yourself every day that money must create a life of ease and bliss, not make it cumbersome and complicated.

At this point, I'm sure you will exclaim, "But why would we ourselves make our lives complicated?" So, in this regard, understand clearly that most people are actually making their own lives difficult. And how are they doing that? Let me give you a few hints. Grasp these hints thoroughly and wherever you deem necessary, inculcate them to bring about the necessary changes within yourself. For, it is important that money eases your life and makes living worthwhile.

Comprehend well that money aims its strongest attack on your psyche. It plays with your psychology with great style, by first attacking your psychology and then luring you into a trap.

And the trap set by money is so treacherous that escaping it is not easy at all. This is because money is psychologically so powerful that it has taken control of a person's mind, brain and intellect, and to such an extent that it effortlessly plays with anyone and in any way it wants to. So, if you want to weaken this trap laid out by money, you will need to bring about a number of psychological transformations within yourself. Since money has enslaved your psychology, it goes without saying that it can be outwitted only psychologically.

For a better understanding of this matter, familiarise yourself with a few key traps laid out by money. One of the few dangerous traps of money is its tendency to fuel your 'needs'. And this money trap is absolutely unerring! To prevent yourself from getting ensnared in this trap, you will have to exercise a reasonable amount of prudence. You will have to refrain from fuelling your needs unnecessarily. In other words, you will have to block all avenues that fuel your needs. Understand well that money does not want your attention to waver from it even for a moment. As I have mentioned earlier, money possesses all the qualities of a wife; and at the very least, men do not need to be explained what the two most significant qualities of a wife are. The first is, a wife yearns for her husband's constant attention, and this quality is deeply ingrained in the psychology of money. During the day, you work for eight to ten hours to earn money, so your focus invariably remains on money in that span of time. However, money craves your attention even during the rest of the time. That is why it keeps fuelling your needs continuously so that you remain preoccupied with thoughts related to your needs and desires. It compels you to immerse yourself in thoughts such as, "I don't possess this", "I need to acquire that", "Why don't I own this?" and "I need that at all costs!" Now, it goes without saying that money is indispensable to acquire whatever you may desire, therefore no matter how hard you try to divert your attention, it is constantly drawn back towards money; and this is precisely what money desires.

In essence, your attention is focussed on money for eight to ten hours of the day, as you work hard to earn it. And for the next sixteen hours, money grabs your attention by fuelling your needs. In other words, similar to a wife, money too tries every possible trick to grab your attention. And frankly speaking, to remain absorbed in thoughts of money day in and day out is not how 'life' ought to be lived. If money dominates your heart and mind, how would you be able to truly enjoy anything in life? Therefore, do not take my words lightly, for, it is these very quirks of money that have created havoc in your life. And as mentioned earlier, the issue of money is extremely complicated because every assault of money is psychological in nature. Therefore, if you wish to ward off the nuisance of money, you will need to bring about various psychological changes within yourself. And verily, we are discussing each one of them step by step.

Well, another psychological trait of money is that it is always eager to jump out of your hands! And I'm sure you have experienced this behaviour of money, but it has probably skipped your attention. To cite an example, you step out of the house for a stroll but end up returning with a few purchases. Why? It is because the money in your pocket wants to sneak out. It urges you to splurge with the reasoning that "This is good" or "The kids will love it" and the list is endless. You visit a hill station only to spend some leisure time but return with suitcases full of purchases. Why? It is because the extra money you had taken along is frisky, ever eager to jump out of your pocket! And it is not just the money kept in your pocket that is eager to hop out.

Even the money kept at home or in a bank account wishes to escape, urging you to spend on a myriad of things and compelling you to invest in questionable ventures. In other words, no matter where the money is kept, it is always looking for ways to wriggle out and escape. And it ultimately manages to coax you into purchasing useless items and making pointless investments. The outcome of all this is, money ultimately vanishes leaving behind needs that remain unfulfilled. Thereafter, the shortage of money begins to pinch you once again and consequently, you are forced to shift your entire focus back on money. In other words, you remain trapped in this vicious cycle created by money. And this is precisely what 'money' desires.

To beat money at its game and to evade this money trap, you will have to exercise prudence. You will have to make your psychology more powerful and realise that while there are countless things available in the world, it is not possible for everyone to acquire everything. After all, to procure anything at all, money will have to be paid in exchange. And the money you possess is limited. You have earned it through your hard work in order to buy happiness. You have definitely not earned it to fall into a money trap and cry over it. Therefore, let the world offer whatever it has to; you can only acquire as many things as the money in your pocket permits. And if this is the ground reality, why get ensnared in the trap of money in the first place? Money will try to slip out of your pocket, but you don't have to slip with it. Shift your focus away from what is available in the world and instead focus on how much money you possess. For, you will be able to acquire things from the world only to the extent the money in your possession allows. However, if you try to procure more than what the available money permits, you will inevitably stray onto a path of darkness, one that you may never be able to return from. Your home will be cluttered with all the wrong things and in the process, you will deprive yourself of all the essential items. And this is precisely the state of affairs all around us. Money sneaks out of the pocket and everyone ends up bringing home useless things! And since your precious money is getting spent on such things, you end up feeling that money is scarce. So, be wise and comprehend that in reality, you do not face such an abject shortage of money. Problems are arising only due to the psychological assault of money, and the most dangerous psychological attack is money's tendency to jump out of your pocket by constantly creating needs. And whoever falls victim to this psychological attack even once, can well be considered a victim for life. For, this is a mental illness that is totally incurable, because a person who falls victim to this psychology will always feel the need to acquire things that require ten times the money he currently possesses. Moreover, in the future, even if he accumulates ten times the money he possesses today, he will invariably need things that require ten times the amount he possesses at that time! In other words, no matter how much money he earns, he will forever find himself mired in the deficit of money. For, the fault lies not with money or the needs, but with his own psychology. Hence, such an individual will always experience a shortage of money, regardless of how much money he acquires or how many needs are fulfilled. And as a result, he will always be steeped in misery.

Therefore, learn to restrict your needs within the confines of the 'available money'. Do not nurture the psychology which makes you think that your needs are too many, while the money available is very less. Tell the money in your pocket to stay calm and curb its restlessness. State emphatically to the money you possess that you are aware of where your happiness lies and what your needs are, and that you will continue to convert the money in hand to procure joys. At the same time, warn the money that it should cease all attempts to trap you, as you will not fall prey to its psychological assault anymore. Repeat this mantra daily until you gain complete control over your money. For, in the real world, one's needs can be fulfilled only to the extent that one's financial resources permit. This is an infallible principle which no one can alter. So, why harbour a psychology that yields negative results? Why even deviate from the main purpose of life, which is to 'live joyously' and instead create for yourself a mountain of self-inflicted sorrows?

To sum it up, surplus money always attempts to sneak out of your pocket. By creating needs, it invariably casts a spell and compels you to spend on non-essentials. If there is surplus money lying in a bank account, it generates some or the other scheme and manipulates you into making ill-advised investments. All these actions on its part are simply aimed at wriggling out of your grasp. At the same time, it continues to fuel your needs. In other words, money makes every effort to create its own shortage while simultaneously multiplying your needs. And once you are ensnared in this psychological trap of money, you are doomed. For, this is a deadly psychological labyrinth which is extremely difficult to escape. Therefore, ensure that you are never trapped in this dangerous web woven by money.

In short, you should never fall prey to this treacherous trap set by money. Instead, focus on utilising the available money to amass happiness for yourself. And believe me, most people possess enough money to acquire joys for themselves and their family. Who says that luxurious houses and fancy cars are the only sources of happiness? If the psychology of such people falls prey to needs, they too may have to endure the anguish of yearning for bigger houses and fancier cars than they already possess. Therefore, always remember that a joyful life is not contingent upon fulfilling extravagant needs. This is an illusion that money creates with its deceptive nature so that your entire attention remains focussed on it. Therefore, first and foremost, do not be under the false impression that only expensive cars and luxurious mansions can provide joy. Just focus your undivided attention on amassing happiness with the money available at your disposal. Besides, the world offers countless little joys that do not require you to splurge on them. Have a delectable meal and derive joy from it. Listen to melodious music and experience a sense of calm and tranquillity. Take pleasure in watching entertaining shows and movies. How much money do you really need to experience these joys? Comprehend well that if all you can afford is a trip to Shimla, then enjoy that trip wholeheartedly. Who says that enjoyment can be found only when one vacations in Switzerland?

This implies, you must strike a balance between the money available at your disposal and the joys it can usher in, for, this balance alone will make your life joyful. And let me also make it clear that if the entire family establishes this balance, then it would truly be the icing on the cake. Thereafter, not even a single family member would experience the scarcity of money, nor would the breadwinner ever have to bear the brunt of taunts for not earning enough. All of them must collectively garner the greatest possible happiness for themselves with the available financial resources. The choice is clear—you can either enjoy life with the available money or spend a lifetime of misery crying over the shortage of money. Here, let me clarify another point: the one who uses the money at his disposal to acquire happiness, perpetually lives in a contented and cheerful state of mind. And needless to say, a cheerful mind performs better and utilises opportunities more efficaciously. Consequently, such a person also progresses rapidly. However, those who constantly lament the paucity of money always find themselves in a disturbed state of mind. A disturbed mind can neither perform well nor can it leverage opportunities. Such people only engage in empty talk; neither are they able to live in peace nor make any progress. The crux of the matter is, focus on amassing happiness with the available money, and your joys in turn will ensure that everything else falls into place too. Rest assured, 'the joys amassed with the available money' will not only attract more money but also facilitate progress.

Since we are on this topic, let me suggest an effective solution. It is true that the world has a plethora of offerings; and every medium, right from television to newspapers and even conversations with others revolves around various commodities and services available for purchase. Admittedly, curbing desires in such a scenario is definitely not easy, and that being the case, it is truly challenging to rein in money which anyway refuses to stay in your control. For, such is the crafty nature of money that it first entices the human mind and fuels needs, and if the desires remain unfulfilled, money creates the feeling of scarcity. Consequently, the hapless human being begins to perceive himself as poor and weak, and once this feeling sets in, he falls prey to an inferiority complex of such magnitude that he just cannot break free of it. Granted, this trap of money is dangerous, but one has to evade it under all circumstances.

Hence, to break this dangerous psychological sequence, I am presenting an exceedingly simple solution. For, irrespective of what happens, one must never succumb to the inferiority complex created by the scarcity of money. Hand in glove with the external world, 'money' will try to sow the seed of inferiority in you, but you must ensure that you do not get ensnared in its trap. Know well that this overpowering sense of inferiority, which makes you think that you are weak, will turn your life into a living hell. Therefore, let me elaborate upon the most effective psychological remedy to obviate such a situation—and that is a sense of 'superiority', which is the only antidote to inferiority. Here, I have once again stated a profound principle of psychology. Assimilate it and apply it wherever required, as it will help you achieve long-lasting freedom from all forms of inferiority.

The crux of the above explanation is, you must live with a sense of superiority that 'money is abundant' rather than harbouring the feeling that 'money is scarce'. This is a straightforward and simple solution to evade the dangerous trap of money. And to that end, all you have to do is consistently engage in charitable acts, donating one to five percent of whatever amount of money you possess. Pay someone's fees or provide clothing to an orphan. Whatever you do, ensure that you engage in some or the other charity on a monthly basis in keeping with your financial position. If nothing else, donate a small amount of

> "**Remind yourself** every day that **'money' must create** a **life** of **ease** and **bliss**, not make it **cumbersome** and **complicated**

hundred or five hundred rupees, but do it unfailingly. This small gesture on your part will instantly suffuse you with a sense of abundance. The logic behind this exercise is, you are practising charity because there is an abundance of money. Believe me, this feeling of abundance will not only protect you from all kinds of inferiority created by money but will also make you responsible. More importantly, it will rein in your needs. And even more significantly, this small step will instil humaneness in you to the core. Verily, everyone in this world lives just for themselves; it is only those who reach out to others and lend a helping hand that can be called human beings in the truest sense.

Trust me, this small step taken by you will always safeguard you from all forms of nuisance created by money. Additionally, it will elevate the joy of living to a whole new level. In fact, I would suggest that those who possess surplus money should definitely donate at least ten percent of their income to charity. The more you spend on others, the more you will develop a sense of being a 'king'. And true joy lies solely in being the 'king in one's own mind'. Needless to say, money never creates any trouble for 'kings'. And the psychological definition of this is—those who are not troubled by money are verily 'kings'. If you wish, by regularly donating a certain percentage of your earnings, you too can become a 'king' instantly. So, I hope you will surely take this step for the sake of your own happiness and that of your loved ones and transform your entire family into a family of 'kings'. Believe me, no family in the world can be happier than the one whose lives are spent experiencing a sense of being 'kings'. So, seize this opportunity with both hands! Show the world that you are, indeed, a king.

Comprehend well that becoming a king doesn't require much; you just need to realise that it is money's habit to hop around in your pocket, so let it jump around. You don't need to do the same, for, you are a 'human being', and you must behave like one. Why do you need to emulate money, frisking around like a monkey? First, to hop around, then to create needs and finally to disappear...this is verily a money trap. So, why get ensnared in it? What is the need to be so restless? I have already mentioned that true wealth is that which positively impacts your entire being. Hence, firstly, spend money only on delicious food, exquisite attire, living comfortably and travelling to your favourite destinations. Spending money on these things alone creates a positive impact on your being. Therefore, your primary focus should be only on these four things. Apart from these, don't ever give money the opportunity to jump around. But yes, once the needs pertaining to these four areas are fulfilled, feel free to jump around with your money, that is, feel free to indulge to your heart's content. But, at present, most people do the opposite—they display stinginess with food, clothing and travelling, while boldly engage in every other foolishness. This is verily the money trap that you are getting ensnared in. But you do not have to fall into this trap. So, spend liberally on good food, fine attire, living comfortably and travelling to your favourite places, and engage in charity every month, even if it is a mere hundred rupees. Do this and you will become a 'king'! Always remember, money does not create any nuisance for kings.

In today's highly competitive age, earning money is an arduous task. Only the individual himself knows the kind of trials and tribulations he goes through to earn money. These facts need no elaboration; however, it is essential to point out that it is your responsibility to ensure that you are not robbed of the money you have earned by dint of hard work. It is your duty to ensure that every penny you own is spent to gain happiness. Now, you may retort that you are well aware of this and that you pay close attention to this matter, but had you really done so, I would not have felt the need to emphasise this point.

So, comprehend clearly that the reason behind all these observations of mine is that everyone keeps lamenting over the 'scarcity of money' but very few pay attention to how and where the money they possess is slipping away. First and foremost, grasp clearly that money is the basic requirement for not just you but everyone else too. And that is how it ought to be, because this is the truth of the modern-day world. However, the problem is, those who are engaged in robbing people of their money far outnumber those who are working honestly towards earning it. Now, money is just 'money', so whether you earn it through honest means or dishonest methods, it facilitates your purchases either way. This observation may be harsh, but it is the bitter truth. Presently, no such machine has been invented to alert vendors that the money they are receiving is stolen; no such method exists to discourage them from selling their goods to a thief. This being the case, how can thieves and robbers be reined in? An additional problem is that not all thieves project themselves as 'bandits'. Most of them roam around freely in the guise of decent, noble and honest people. So, before you can even recognise them and glean their intentions, they scoot off with your money. Jog your memory and you will recall several such experiences when you were robbed of your money. Therefore, do not be under the false impression that your money is not being stolen.

Alright, let us leave that aside. Instead of dwelling on the past, it would serve us well to focus our attention on the actions to be taken henceforth. And the only action required of you is to resolve that you will never allow your precious money to be plundered. Instead of crying over the 'paucity of money', you need to prioritise safeguarding the money that is being looted. And I am offering a straightforward solution to help you protect your money from such thieves. As I have mentioned repeatedly, a permanent solution for every problem is possible only through a profound psychoanalysis. And verily, we need to protect ourselves from these thieves permanently. So, to do this, we will have to conduct an in-depth psychoanalysis of the act of stealing as well as the process of being robbed. And in this context, grasp clearly that both stealing and being robbed are actions, and there invariably exists some or the other psychological force behind every action. No action is possible without a psychological force at play. Here, I have delineated one of the most profound principles of psychology. You will not get the opportunity to read or listen to such profound psychological principles anywhere else. So, just grasp these principles being conveyed by me and with their aid, transform yourself into a master of psychology. For, each principle will help you fathom a thousand other truths.

At present, however, let us return to the subject of stealing and being robbed. The point worth comprehending is, all actions of stealing and being robbed are guided by a single psychological force—'the force of fear and greed'. The thief steals by instilling fear and greed, while the one who is being robbed succumbs to this fear and greed, thus falling victim to the robbery. Grasp the profound truth that no other psychological force operates behind the acts of stealing and being robbed except that of fear and greed.

Alright, I am moving forward with the assumption that you have no inclination whatsoever to 'steal'. However, if you have any such tendency, then beware! For, thieves may be able to get their hands on the desired money, but it is only a short-term gain as they end up paying a hefty price for this later. Comprehending the mindset of a thief is not at all difficult—they are fearful during the act of stealing, and even after the theft, they live in constant dread of getting apprehended. Moreover, once caught, they also have to endure the consequences of their actions. So, in light of all this, even if they manage to steal some amount of money, it is rather futile, for, they end up suffering far graver consequences in turn. Hence, if you too are inclined towards stealing, discard all such thoughts immediately! For, no matter who the thief is, sooner or later, a day comes when he can no longer enjoy even a good night's sleep; then, it matters little whether he is a politician or a corrupt official. Granted, the fear of arrest does not really bother these two categories of people, because they know how to circumvent the law on the strength of their power and money. However, the stress of hoarding and managing all that money surely gnaws at them day in and day out. And God forbid, if they are caught, then the game is over! That's not all! Such individuals find it difficult to even spend the money they have accumulated through dishonest means. In their day-to-day life, they are compelled to use the officially allotted government car and the same allotted government quarters. What baffles the mind is, why do they carry such a heavy burden on their conscience when they are not even able to enjoy the money they steal? Besides, the stress and tension they endure to manage their 'black money' far outweighs the trouble of

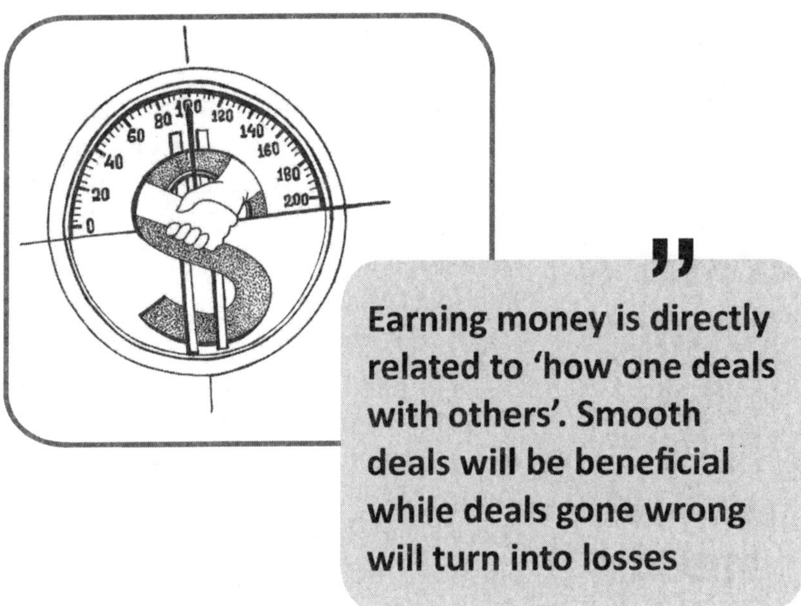

accumulating this kind of money. And what is all this stress really for? They harbour untold stress and tension for money they can't even utilise to buy happiness for themselves! Hence, I consider such thieving politicians and officers to be mentally deranged.

For that matter, the condition of fraudulent businesspeople is even worse than that of the corrupt politicians and officers. They invariably have the sword of Damocles hanging over their heads, for, their frauds do get exposed sooner or later. And I'm sure you're well aware of the hardships they have to suffer once they are caught. Usually, they try to engage in plundering in connivance with the corrupt politicians and officers. But do politicians and officers ever show allegiance towards anyone? Moreover, the government in power and the officers themselves do not stay in term forever. Most importantly, everyone has to face the repercussions of their misdeeds, no matter who it is.

> One of the few **dangerous traps** of **money** is its tendency to **fuel 'needs'**

In fact, in the end, someone invariably exposes their fraud, be it to settle scores or to blackmail them. So, sooner or later, corrupt businesspersons do find themselves trapped. And, even otherwise, deceiving or fleecing people is not a good idea, for, it inevitably burdens the soul. The spiritual principle behind this is: no matter what you obtain after compromising your soul, it will always remain an unprofitable bargain.

Therefore, let us leave all these things aside. We do not want to rob or fleece. Our aim is simple—to safeguard ourselves from such malpractices and ensure that no one robs us. And protecting yourself from being robbed is well within your control. Admittedly, there are various types of 'money thieves' in this world, but you must realise that they cannot rob you forcefully. They can do that only at gunpoint or knifepoint, and such thievery is indeed an exception. More often than not, a person is cheated mostly by sophisticated thieves, and our present discussion is focussed on such white-collared crooks. Here, grasp clearly that it is impossible for white-collared thieves to rob you without exploiting your weaknesses. Moreover, I have already explained that 'fear and greed' are the only two psychological weaknesses that enable others to rob you. If you are not fearful or greedy, no swindler in the world can ever rob you, no matter how cunning he is. If you are being robbed, it is only because of taking shortcuts to feed your greed for money. And the thieves are aware of this weakness of yours. Hence, they stride in confidently with their get-rich-quick schemes and trap you effortlessly. In fact, luring investors with high-interest rates, rich returns and attractive incentives have become a norm in many schemes these days, so much so that large corporates sell their products to you at four times the actual price by enticing you with grand claims. They rob you with promises of every kind, right from a fairer complexion to staying young forever. In fact, the onset of the COVID-19 pandemic saw the market being flooded by flour and oil brands promising products with immunity-boosting powers. As for charmed rings and amulets promising to attract immense wealth, they are being peddled around as easily as street food. That's not all! Methods to earn virtue and a ticket to heaven are also being marketed heavily! No one stops to consider that a ticket for a space journey costs millions of rupees, so what should be the price for a ticket to heaven? Can a charmed ring that is supposed to shower wealth ever be bought for a measly 200 rupees? And the real question is, why is a person who has in his possession thousands of such rings still living in a shanty? The truth of the matter is, greed blinds reason. Once someone gets ensnared by greed, his intellect ceases to function. Then, it makes no difference whether it is greed for wealth, fair complexion or eternal youthfulness. The moment you are gripped by greed, you are robbed, and this is an irrevocable psychological principle. By now, I'm sure you have realised how often you too have been robbed through such scams. Just imagine, had you not squandered away your wealth in this manner, you could have accomplished so much with that money!

Therefore, exercise prudence and rein in your greed. Etch it in your mind that any form of greed is always detrimental. According to Krishna, even nursing a desire for the fruits of your actions is wrong, so do I really need to discuss the repercussions of greed? Greed, be it under the garb of religion or social customs and traditions, ensures that the person lured by it gets robbed. No one can alter this psychological principle. It is only because of the ignorance of psychology that people are failing to comprehend how dangerous greed is. Indeed, the sole misfortune of the human being lies in his poor knowledge of psychology. He fails to comprehend the intricacies of the law of cause and effect. But whoever grasps this principle will never succumb to any form of greed. So, become wise and decide once and for all that you will not allow con men who fan your greed to steal even a penny of your precious, hard-earned money. Although it sounds simple on the face of it, to be able to implement this in your life completely is not a breeze. For, greed manifests in multiple forms and to make matters worse, 'greed' is one of the biggest psychological weaknesses of human beings. Hence, not everyone is capable of liberating themselves from it.

Well, no matter how challenging it may be to rid oneself of greed, it is imperative to do so. For, it is a fact that as long as the mind remains gripped by greed, you will continue to get robbed. If you genuinely want to safeguard your precious money from being robbed, comprehend clearly that both the act of stealing and being robbed fall under the purview of spiritual psychology. Here, I am once again explaining a profound spiritual truth. Therefore, try to assimilate it in as much depth as possible. Grasp clearly that spiritual psychology always has a two-pronged impact. The ultimate truth of spiritual psychology is that no one is enduring anything in this world without reason. Whatever one is compelled to endure in this world is merely the result of his own weaknesses. You can certainly justify your plight by saying, "The conmen and thieves are smart and cunning; what can we do about it?" Well, they certainly do not possess an official permit for looting others, do they? Also, it is not that they are able to rob every single person. Moreover, not every person is getting robbed. This being the case, don't you think you need to give a serious thought as to what sort of people they are able to rob? You will also need to ask yourself why you are letting others rob you. In addition to this, reflect upon the kind of people whom no one is able to rob. You will need to understand the difference between the robbers and the ones who are getting robbed. To put it bluntly, those who are being robbed are also thieves in some respect! Those who are not thieves themselves can never be robbed by anyone. This statement may have shocked you and I can almost hear you retort, "Do you think we are thieves?!" Well, grasp clearly that if you are being robbed, then you are definitely a thief too. For, in this world, it is only the thieves who are being robbed. Admittedly, spiritual truths are exceedingly harsh—to hear, comprehend and embrace them is difficult indeed. This is precisely why people adopt religious beliefs quite easily, but embracing spirituality in its truest sense is immensely challenging. So, grasp well that any white-collared thief in the world can only steal from those who are 'thieves' themselves. Hence, those who are being robbed are also robbers themselves. Do not be mistaken or surprised about this, for, I have already explained that spirituality always produces a two-pronged impact. Therefore, comprehend clearly, he who is being robbed is also, in some way or the other, a thief himself.

I'm sure your head must be reeling after reading the explanation given above. Your mind must be riddled with doubts and you are perhaps feeling annoyed too. And it is natural for you to feel so. After all, I have declared that every one of those who are robbed are robbers themselves! But why do you react so hastily? I haven't concluded my point yet. Let me ask you this: how much money do you think you have authority over? Surely, you have authority only over the amount you have earned after working diligently for eight to ten hours a day. This fact is spiritually perfect. But what about those who wish to earn extra money without lifting a finger, nurturing the hope that by simply wearing a sacred thread priced at 100 rupees, they will attract more wealth? Seen through the lens of spiritual psychology, they too would be viewed as thieves, wouldn't they? Spirituality poses a simple question: why should you ever desire anything without applying your intelligence and working for it? Why should you desire anything for free from others, be it from God himself? You must acquire whatever you desire through your own actions. This is verily the system that Nature has designed for you. Therefore, those who desire something without working for it possess the mindset of a thief, don't they? Spirituality is a profound matter related to a higher level of consciousness, with absolutely no scope for hypocrisy. And this is precisely why being spiritual is challenging.

Well, the key point is, if you want something for free, beyond what your income permits, then you are definitely a thief as seen from the perspective of spirituality. And the world of thieves is governed by a single spiritual principle—the big fish will devour the small fish. In other words, the powerful thieves will wipe out the weaker ones. Grasp well that if the world is in a state of balance, it is solely due to the spiritual system established by Nature. Although spirituality is not the focus of this book, it was necessary for me to touch upon the subject. All in all, those who are being looted are also surely a victim of the mindset of acquiring something for free. But since they are ordinary thieves, the seasoned thieves are able to rob them effortlessly. Here, I have stated a perfect and straightforward truth in an extremely simple language.

So, if you genuinely want to avoid being robbed, be clear in your head that under no circumstances do you require a penny more than what you already earn. And when you do not have the need for it, falling prey to greed will be out of the question. This will make it easy for you to ignore all tricks and schemes and prevent yourself from purchasing useless products. Indeed, you will not even spare a glance at the peddlers of false promises and assurances who are out to rob people. And it is only when you are able to do all this that you can safeguard your hard-earned money. The takeaway is, you are not being troubled so much by the paucity of money as much as you are distressed by losing money due to the whims of your greedy mind. Statistically speaking, on an average, an individual is losing ten to twenty percent of his 'money' because of his greed. And it is not as if he is falling prey to fraudulent schemes or is buying useless products; he is squandering away his money in many other ways as well. To cite an example, many people often spend extravagantly on influential personalities, hoping to gain something from them in the future. While spending and fawning over them, they invariably forget that these influential people actually never help anyone. Amusingly, people are so blinded by greed that they try to bribe God too! They don't even apply their intelligence to consider whether God will ever accept bribes? Nor do they pause to ask themselves, does the Almighty even need anything from them?

Know for certain, it is due to your insatiable greed that your money is being squandered in not one but several places. If you manage to save at least the amount of money being wasted, it would fulfil quite a few of your essential needs. So, henceforth, learn to completely rein in your greed, no matter which form it manifests itself in. If you manage to do even this single thing, you will be free from lamenting the paucity of money to a large extent. And I sincerely hope that going forward you will not allow anyone to rob you.

Well, it is not as if you squander away your money driven by greed alone, for, there is yet another psychological weakness that is robbing you of your wealth to a considerable extent. And that weakness is called 'fear'. Perhaps, you have never paid close attention to the amount of money you squander away due to fear. By instilling the fear that one will burn in hellfire to creating the fear of countless other things, people have been robbed since ages; and if that did not suffice, in this modern age of bureaucracy, swindlers have devised numerous other ways to instil fear in people and rob them. Just like those who employ the weapon of greed, the present era has also seen a rise in the number of thieves who instil fear so that they can rob people. To give you an example, in order to evade harassment by government officials, many people are compelled to part with large sums of money. And why just the officials; even politicians and thugs are not far behind when it comes to instilling fear in the masses. However, one cannot allow one's precious money to be robbed on account of fear. It, therefore, becomes imperative to learn how to fend off these intimidators by vanquishing all forms of fear. These fear-mongers focus their attention especially on the wealth of those who are making great strides in life. In fact, the latter find themselves chased by not just the media but various other blackmailers too. And what could be worse than someone making away with your money through intimidation or fraud? Indeed, this should not happen at all. Therefore, rouse yourself and marshall all your strength. You would do well to remember that just like greed, fear too has destroyed the mightiest of individuals.

After this in-depth discussion, I do not think there is any need to delve further into how one is robbed of money through fear; fear is not as chameleon-like and complex as greed. Therefore, whenever people are robbed on account of fear, the realisation eventually dawns upon them that it is their fear that has made them fall prey to theft. Well, let me now share a few famous anecdotes that illustrate how 'greed' has robbed people of their money. This will surely help you comprehend how dangerous greed is. You will also realise how dangerous those 'little thoughts revolving around fear and greed' can be. In addition, these anecdotes will also aid you in comprehending the various types of money traps a person falls into. Moreover, drawing insights from these anecdotes, you will also learn how to safeguard your hard-earned money from such traps. Most importantly, taking lessons from these narratives, you will fathom the various precautionary measures to be taken in future.

1. Ulysses S. Grant

After having served as the 18th President of the United States (1869-1877), a desire kindled within Ulysses S. Grant to join the ranks of the country's wealthiest people. In other words, greed spread its tentacles within him for no apparent reason. Now, the nature of greed is such that it invariably finds its way, and Grant too found a way to satiate his greed. He partnered with Ferdinand Ward, a prominent figure on Wall Street in those days, to establish the Grant and Ward Company, a financial firm. But little did Grant know that Ward was running a fraudulent scheme. And the outcome of this alliance was as expected. Ward pocketed the investors' and Grant's money and vanished without a trace, leaving Grant with a debt of nearly 150,000 USD. To repay this debt, Grant not only pledged his residence's papers but also handed over the medals earned during his military service to the creditors. And that's not all! Grant, who was battling throat cancer, asked the renowned American author, Mark Twain, to write his memoir, hoping to earn some money from its sale which in turn would help him repay the debt. However, despite all this, Grant departed from this world with the stigma of bankruptcy attached to his name. This leads to the question: how did such a disaster befall him? It befell him because Grant succumbed to greed that made him venture into a field that was completely beyond his capability and comprehension. After all, to what extent can the president of a country fathom the intricacies of finance?

Well, the aforementioned example highlights another scientific aspect of the psychology of money which must be grasped by all. And that is, one obtains money only in proportion to the effort and intelligence one puts in. And both, laborious work and intelligence can be applied only according to one's skills or capabilities. So, if one employs hard work and intelligence in an area where one lacks the inherent skills, all such efforts will be rendered futile. On the contrary, it will often prove to be detrimental. And that is precisely what occurred in the above-mentioned incident involving Ulysses S. Grant. You are no doubt intelligent and I have provided you a hint as well. So, I hope you will never go against the basic tenets of money by committing such a grave error in judgement and will always try your hand only in areas that you are knowledgeable about.

2. Mark Twain

The great, internationally renowned American author, Mark Twain was struck by an idea that led him to invest his entire savings of 300,000 USD into developing the 'Compositor', a typesetting machine. Actually, in those days, the machines used in the printing industry were rather sluggish, while the Compositor had an exceptional printing speed compared to its counterparts. Naturally, Twain had invested his entire savings to develop the Compositor only after a proper evaluation of its printing capacity, but unfortunately, perfecting the machine took an unduly long time. And time never waits for anyone, does it? So, before the Compositor could even be introduced in the market, the Linotype machine was launched and very soon, it strengthened its hold in the market. As a result, the company manufacturing the Compositor as well as Twain both became bankrupt. This begs the question, why did this happen? Where exactly did a person as intelligent as Twain falter? The explanation is simple: when technology was not his specialty or domain, what was the need for him to venture into it? But what could Twain do? Money tends to fuel both needs as well as the ego.

You would do well to remember that however unwilling a human being may be, 'money' has a way of steering him on misadventures. But you must take a lesson from the aforementioned incident. Embark on adventures, but only in your field of expertise. If you are not a master in a particular field yet, first become one and then venture forth. Otherwise, money will turn its back on you. Being a wise person, how can you go against money's psychology? Well, I am confident that you won't and surely, you will take a lesson from every anecdote shared here.

3. Kim Basinger

In the 1980s, Hollywood's renowned actress and Oscar winner, Kim Basinger purchased the entire town of Braselton spread over approximately 2000 acres in the state of Georgia, USA. She purchased the town at a price of almost 20 million USD. Basinger's vision was to establish a massive movie studio wherein she could organise a film festival. In short, she aimed to transform the small town of Braselton into a thriving tourist destination. The dream was no doubt grand, but unfortunately, it could never materialise. For, the project's completion demanded far more funds than Basinger had initially estimated. This led to such a massive strain on her financial resources that she was ultimately forced to declare bankruptcy. In fact, faced with a mountain of debt, Basinger had to sell Braselton itself at a fraction of its worth to repay the money owed to her creditors.

This anecdote highlights yet another aspect of the psychology of money which is worth grasping. It is clear that Basinger possessed the required skills in the field she decided to venture into, for, movies, studios, fame and fortune were an integral part of her life. In this scenario, she had definitely not embarked on a misadventure. So, where exactly did she go wrong? Well, she failed because she violated the principles of the psychology of money. Now, you might wonder what is this new aspect of money's psychology I am referring to! Well, haven't I said before that money is the most powerful entity in the world, so its psychological idiosyncrasies are no less either! And this particular facet of money's psychology is that it responds positively only when a project is completed. If a project faces roadblocks and remains incomplete for whatever reason, money gets upset and turns its back on you. In Basinger's case, her scheme was perfect and she also possessed the requisite talent to take it forward. The allure of her name was enough to attract people to the city too. Therefore, her ideas were not misplaced at all. However, she lacked the funds required to complete the project, and as a result, she faced failure. Despite her sincere efforts, she could not complete the project. The lesson worth learning is, even if you wish to embark on an adventure in a field of your talent, venture into it only when you can guarantee its successful completion. In fact, refrain from taking even a single step forward without having adequate financial resources; otherwise, the project will turn into a quagmire that will drag you deeper and deeper. Let me point out that these anecdotes offer a priceless opportunity to learn from the psychoanalysis of others' experiences, so do imbibe the lessons. You must never allow money to turn its back on you, and do not ever embark on a misadventure which goes against the psychology of money.

4. Debbie Reynolds

The famed Hollywood actress, Debbie Reynolds had garnered much love and adulation from her audience through her acting abilities. But apparently, this did not suffice, and her discontent led her to embark on an adventure. In 1992, Reynolds purchased a hotel with a casino, situated quite a distance away from Las Vegas, for a hefty sum of 2.2 million USD. Later, she spent an additional amount of more than 10 million USD to transform the hotel into a Hollywood-themed museum. Unfortunately though, her adventure failed to pull in the crowds. Essentially, a substantial amount of money had already been invested, but the desired results were nowhere in sight. Finally, left with no alternative, Reynolds even started performing in her hotel in a last-ditch attempt to draw people in and save her business. But despite all her efforts, the venture could not gain traction. The question now arises: what went wrong despite Reynolds making every effort to establish her business? The problem was, her casino hotel was located quite far from the main casino hub in Las

Vegas. Consequently, avid casino-goers did not prefer to go out of their way to visit her establishment. Indeed, with an eclectic choice of casinos available in a single location, who would want to travel such a great distance to visit just one casino? For, the foremost priority of casino enthusiasts is the casino itself; music and entertainment are of secondary importance to them.

All things considered, the allure of Debbie Reynolds paled in comparison to the craze for casinos. It is worth learning from this example that the psychology of money does not tolerate even a single miscalculation. In the case of Reynolds, she had gone completely off the mark in her choice of location, so money was bound to turn its back on her. And staying true to its psychology, it did! Finally, with no solution in sight, Reynolds had to shut down the casino—her dream project—in 1996. And just a year later, she declared bankruptcy. In the following year, her hotel was auctioned off for 10.65 million USD.

The key lesson here is, money will lose no opportunity to strike you the moment you miscalculate. It is worth noting that if Reynolds had opened this very casino hotel in a different city, her adventure would have reaped in great success. Moreover, the icing on the cake would have been her live performances that would have made it the city's biggest attraction. For, in a city, no one could have rivalled her charm. However, her clash with the allure of the collective casinos of Las Vegas proved extremely costly for her. The lesson you must learn from this entire incident is to calculate and evaluate everything perfectly before embarking on any adventure, especially when it is with your hard-earned money; otherwise, money will abandon you. For, money simply hates miscalculations!

5. Burt Reynolds

The ruling star of Hollywood during the 60s–80s, Burt Reynolds took the advice of his business manager and invested in the franchise of PoFolks, a family restaurant, in the year 1980. He acquired a total of 30 franchise outlets. However, after venturing into the business, he realised that the restaurant's food was not as popular amongst the patrons. To make matters worse, the demands of his busy schedule made it all the more challenging for him to devote enough time and attention to this new venture. Hence, to save the restaurants from further losses, he appointed a consultant. The consultant suggested that Reynolds invest in yet another franchise of restaurants, which the latter approved. Unfortunately, this idea also turned out to be a debacle, landing Reynolds in a financial quagmire. Finally, in 1988, PoFolks declared bankruptcy. Years later, Reynolds regretfully admitted that an issue that could have been resolved by incurring a loss of 5–6 million USD turned into a complete disaster after he heeded the consultant's counsel, which led him to suffer a compounded loss of up to 20–30 million USD over a period of time.

> "It is the **'nuisance of money'** that is majorly responsible for **negatives** in the **mind** and **ailments** in **the body**

Well, the above-mentioned loss, followed by an expensive divorce with his second wife, Loni Anderson, coupled with his extravagant lifestyle ultimately led Reynolds to declare bankruptcy in 1996. All of this leads to the question: why did Reynolds encounter a misfortune of such magnitude after garnering so much success? The answer lies in the peculiar psychology of money that constantly yearns to wriggle out of one's hands and lands one in a trap. The lesson worth assimilating from this story is, one should not jeopardise one's happy and blissful life by embarking on futile adventures. Why invest in a venture that one does not even fully comprehend, simply because someone else is recommending it? Blindly following a consultant's advice and diving headfirst into ventures without truly comprehending them is sheer foolishness. For, the consultant may have his own perspective and self-interest too. Most importantly, no investment should be made in a business that you cannot dedicate your time to. By all means, make progress in life and embark on new adventures, but if you violate the psychology of money with your reckless adventures, you will be trapped. Always remember that if earning money is an art, then evading money traps is no less of an art. My very purpose of citing these case studies and also conducting their psychoanalysis is to ensure that you do not fall into money traps. I do hope that the lessons embedded in these case studies will help you evade money traps.

Bear in mind that the world is ever eager to rob you, but it is you who has to realise that every penny of yours earned through hard work and application of intelligence is invaluable. And no one should be allowed to steal it. Remember, the only two reasons why you squander away your money are fear and greed. Greed implies desiring more than what you earn through your hard work, intelligence and talent. And when you crave extra money, know well that there are many in this world who are just waiting to lure you in their trap with false promises and assurances. What is puzzling is the fact that money never falls into one's lap of its own accord—that is not its psychology—so why do you still succumb to greed? Why do you fall prey to false promises and assurances? The tendency to try one's hand in a field that one has no expertise in also baffles my mind. Why do you even jump into a field you have no talent in? Why don't you comprehend the psychology of money which states that only if you possess the requisite talent in a particular field will you attract money! Why don't you understand that money has its own psychology and will never overstep the boundaries of its psychology! So, march forth and embark on exciting adventures; that is essential indeed. Progress is the law of life and leading a magnificent life defines a human being. However, ensure that you venture forth whilst staying within the confines of money's psychology, that is, respecting its psychology. Be cautious not to fall flat on your face in your eagerness to forge ahead. And to that end, I have tried to explain a few crucial points with the help of these case studies. For, I am well aware of the relentless efforts you put in and the struggle you go through to earn money. Therefore, I wish that you savour the fruits of your labour and enjoy the benefits of the money you have earned. I also want to see you make great strides in life. But I absolutely do not want anyone to steal your money. Nor do I want you to embark on an adventure that goes against the psychology of money and in the process, get trapped. And certainly, I do not want you to get ensnared in any kind of money trap. Life is a wonderful opportunity to live to the fullest and I want to see you lead a beautiful life.

There is no denying the fact that the amount of money one possesses is all that one has. And to live well, everyone has to procure joys only with the money available at their disposal. Indeed, it is important to garner happiness in this manner because we will never be bestowed with a similar life again. And this is a reality that everyone is aware of. The only question is—why are people not able to live contentedly within the limits of the money available at their disposal? More surprisingly, there are many others who are struggling to live their lives well despite possessing abundant money. The question remains, why do people behave thus when it comes to this entity called money? The reason is, money has established its reign over everyone's mind. It lures people in ever-new and ingenious traps, and they fall into these traps hook, line and sinker. Hence, it becomes imperative for everyone to learn how to evade money traps in order to lead their lives well. In this context, we have extensively discussed the most prominent money traps. But bear in mind, the traps laid out by money are infinite; in fact, it has in its arsenal innumerable methods to entrap people. Hence, in the following pages, I shall draw your attention towards these treacherous traps, hoping that with the aid of the cues I provide, you will learn to evade these traps as well. For, it is these very traps laid out by money that are robbing you of your peace.

In light of this, let us begin by discussing one of the most bewitching traps of money wherein it uses its 'charm to entice people'. Interestingly, money evokes such passion and affection for itself in people's hearts that it starts appearing more valuable than even interpersonal relationships. In fact, for many, money has become dearer than life itself. And this is truly a one-of-a-kind trap of money. Very often, money wriggles out of one's grasp and slips away. And in the eventuality that you are able to

History bears testimony to the fact that money has showered its blessings exclusively on creative people

prevent this from happening, it plays the card of fear and greed to rob you. It entices you into purchasing useless items and then vanishes from sight. Many a time, it even lures you into impractical adventures, only to disappear without a trace. And God forbid, if one manages to steer clear of all its traps, then money creates an altogether new trap to ensnare you. It then makes its victims so hopelessly addicted to hoarding money that they cling on to it with all their might, unable to part with it. Such people forget that money is merely a means to garner joy and happiness. They become so obsessed with it that they are no longer capable of acquiring happiness in exchange of money and eventually end up in a 'lose-lose situation'. First, they toil extra hard to earn money, and in the process, harbour extreme stress and tension, and then amusingly enough, they cannot even procure happiness with the money they earn. For, the fact remains that one has to spend

> "**Happiness** abounds **everywhere.** All you have to do is **be** a **smart buyer** of happiness

money in order to amass joys, but such individuals are unable to do so because of their 'obsession with money'. To sum it up, money will ensnare you in its trap and vanish or in the eventuality that you manage to evade its trap, it will bewitch you with its charm and destroy you. This means that either way, it will ensure that you are unable to amass happiness with the money you possess.

Well, let us return to the discussion about those who are ensnared by the charming spell of money. Frankly speaking, the only aim of such people is to live to see their bank balance increase year after year. They fail to realise that irrespective of the amount of money stacked in their bank accounts, it is useless as long as it is not converted into happiness. Unfortunately, this bit of common sense eludes them, and as a result, these miserly people, ensnared by the spell of money, end up ruining their own lives. By slogging all day and enduring stress, they first end up compromising their health. On the other hand, since money holds prime importance for such people, they remain deprived of the joys of relationships too. It is due to this very obsession with money that they end up ruining even the most precious bonds of affection. More often than not, almost every relationship of theirs becomes devoid of love; and to be honest, if interpersonal relationships run out of warmth and affection, then how does it really matter whether one is dead or alive? But unfortunately, these emotionless people, mesmerised by money, become as heartless as a stone. And the truth is, countless lives are being ruined due to this very 'obsession with money'. Ironically, these individuals are not afflicted by the paucity of money at all, but even then, money does not spare them. This in itself should help you gauge how dangerous an entity like money is.

So, kindly ensure that you are never ensnared by the allure of money. Never lend so much importance to increasing your bank balance that you neglect utilising your money to procure happiness. Always remember that money is merely a means to an end—which is to accumulate joys. Therefore, focus on building your bank balance only when the money available with you is helping you amass happiness. If you are not able to procure joys with the money you already possess, then what is the point in stressing over earning additional money? In a life that is illusory and ephemeral, the size of your bank balance is not important at all; what holds significance is whether or not you are able to convert your money into garnering happiness. And as for those who fall prey to the allure of money, such people lose their senses completely! Even with millions of rupees lying in their bank account and despite struggling with health issues at an advanced age, such individuals hesitate to spend even five to ten lakh rupees for their medical treatment. In fact, individuals who are sent to a mental asylum upon being diagnosed as insane are not all necessarily insane; however, those who have fallen under the spell of money and are roaming around freely are all, without exception, unhinged! A word of warning here: ensure that you never allow such insanity to consume you.

In essence, let us recap a few important points regarding money. Human beings are the only entities that require money; and the human being has arrived on Earth on a visa of 80–100 years. As soon as his time runs out, he will have to depart forever.

While departing, he cannot carry his money along. Have you ever heard anyone claiming that an individual has departed from this world with fifty million rupees? We always say that the person has left behind fifty million rupees. In other words, you will have to leave behind the money that you do not utilise. This is a fact that everyone is aware of, and yet, millions of people continue to spend their lives entranced by 'the spell of money'. Tell me, what should such people be called if not insane?

So, if you want to maintain your sanity, ensure that you are never caught in the web of money. Always remember, as important as it is to earn money, it is equally crucial to spend it. For, happiness can be procured only by spending money. Besides, whatever money one possesses is the outcome of one's hard work and intelligence, and it is meant to garner happiness for oneself and one's family. Therefore, money must be utilised for that purpose alone; otherwise, everything will be in vain.

Why don't you comprehend that money is deceitful by its very nature?! You may nurse the belief that you own it, but the reality is far from it. Money belongs to whoever owns it at any given moment. Faithfulness and loyalty are alien to its nature. Money is loyal to you only if you procure joys in exchange for it—etch this truth in your mind forever. Another trait of money is that it is capricious by nature. The more you earn, the more it will multiply. If you refrain from spending it, it will remain undiminished. But that certainly does not mean it will remain loyal to you. The money lying in a bank account definitely tries to escape, doesn't it? If you refrain from utilising it to procure joy and happiness, it will still find a way to escape by luring you into ill-advised investments. And God forbid, if anyone succeeds in evading its psychology of wriggling out of grasp, money will ensnare them with its charm and destroy them. In other words, it will either wriggle out of your hands and escape or it will cast its spell and destroy you. In short, it will do everything in its power to prevent you from amassing happiness. This alone should help you gauge how psychologically powerful money is. In fact, this will also give you a fair idea of how dangerous it can be.

In essence, one must fathom the cunning psychology of money, as it spares not a single person from its harassment. While the lower strata of the society are grappling with the scarcity of money, the middle class is distressed, caught in various kinds of money traps. And even those having abundant wealth should never nurse the false belief that money will spare them. For, money has in its arsenal a number of tricks and weapons to unleash trouble. If money is scarce, its paucity destroys a person. If it exists in abundance, it wriggles out of grasp and escapes. And if you are not swayed by its tendency to slip out of your pocket, it makes you miserly and ruins you anyway. Therefore, in order to evade money traps, you must calmly continue to amass happiness with the money available at your disposal. Otherwise, life will slip through your grasp, and one day, death will come knocking at your door. You will keep fretting over money all your life and also depart this world in the same state of mind. So, rouse yourself, for, the time has come to wake up from this slumber. I am sure you are now well acquainted with the majority of money traps. Hence, keep converting money in the best possible manner, so much so that money itself is overcome by an acute feeling of frustration. Let it scream in annoyance and say, “This smart person has cleverly evaded every single one of my traps!” The day you achieve this, trust me, the joy of living will scale to an altogether different level!

From the discussion we have had so far, I'm sure you have gained an in-depth understanding of money traps, and I hope from now onwards, you will not get ensnared in them. So, moving on, grasp another crucial point about money, and that is to exercise complete control over the money you have earned through your diligence and hard work. Here, the term 'complete control' holds tremendous significance. It basically means that none of the tricks that money usually employs should have any effect on 'your money'. I have oft repeated that the entire play of money is a mind game. And there can be only one winner in every mind game. Needless to mention, only the person who is psychologically strong triumphs in a mind game. Therefore, if you wish to triumph over money, the only solution is to make your psychology more powerful than 'the psychology of money'. For, if money gains control over your 'mind', it will inevitably pull you into its trap. However, if your 'mind' gains control over money, you won't face any problem.

Of course, gaining control over 'money' is no easy task, for, money has enslaved most people's minds. Indeed, the powerful psychology of money has checkmated everyone's mind, and this is precisely why they are not able to spend their money as per their wishes. In fact, no one is able to exercise their will even on their own 'money'. The situation has worsened to such an extent that money not only streams in and out of one's life on its own terms, but also compels one to spend as per its whims. A person comes to his senses only when money does the vanishing act after having played its trick. This is the reason why one can witness everyone in this world 'constantly lamenting over money'. However, since it is your money, it ought to be spent in accordance with your wishes alone.

Well, coming back to the main point, money should only be controlled by the person who earns it. Of course, the entire family and everyone else connected with you are entitled to the happiness bought with that money. In fact, family has the first claim over the happiness thus acquired. However, when it comes to 'control', it is best if the one who earns the money is in complete charge of it. And this is an important psychological fact about money that I am highlighting, so treat it with utmost seriousness. For, I am firmly asserting that the control over money should rest with the person who earns it. The primary reason is, the person who earns is arguably the one who fully appreciates the value of his hard-earned money. As opposed to this, the one who does not earn can never truly appreciate the value of money. Let me also make it clear that money is never able to easily trap those who earn as compared to those who do not earn. Countless examples abound where money has ensnared and ruined families after families because those who earned the money had no control over it. Therefore, I am re-emphasising that regardless of the person who earns the money—be it the husband, wife, children or grandparents, they alone should have control over the money they earn. Of course, every member of the family has a right over the

> "**Everyone cries** over the **scarcity** of **money** but very few **pay attention** to where their **money** is **slipping away**

happiness acquired through that money, and for this purpose, the entire family should be considered a single unit, enjoying the happiness collectively. However, the control over money should rest solely with those who earn it. Unfortunately, in most cases, this principle is breached, and as a result, money is able to entrap people with ease.

It is a pretty straightforward fact that only the one who earns money appreciates its value and significance. So, ideally, control should also rest with the person who understands the value of money. However, people fail to adhere to even this simple practice. If the wife's income is higher than the husband's, the latter tends to exert his control over her money. Similarly, a father will exercise control over his son's earnings and vice versa. Although this is an internal family matter, it is quite dangerous when perceived from a psychological viewpoint. For, when the wife's money is under the husband's control, he often tends to splurge it. When children begin to assert undue control over their parents' money, they often stray towards the wrong path. This may seem a trivial matter, but it is quite significant, so treat it with all seriousness. A family is like a team and there is no debate on this matter, but the team's captain should be the one who purchases the required sports equipment for his team, in other words, the person who earns and provides for the entire family. If you break this rule, money will trap you easily and the entire family will have to suffer the consequences. And since this is the case with almost every family, deliberate upon this matter with all due seriousness. I have provided you a compelling hint to safeguard your family's interests; it is now up to you to fathom its significance and implement it. You must realise that family after family is heading towards ruination because the control of money has fallen into the wrong hands.

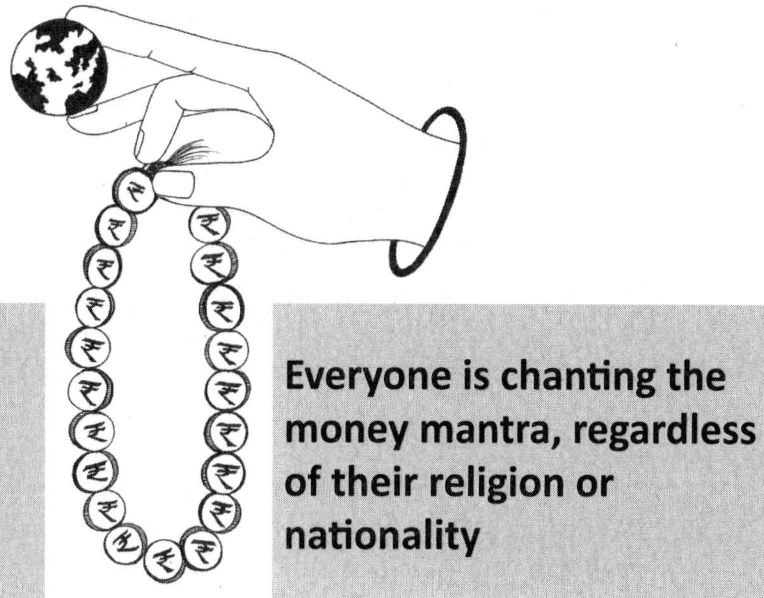

Everyone is chanting the money mantra, regardless of their religion or nationality

In essence, all you need to grasp is that the absolute control over money should rest solely with the person earning it. This principle applies equally to everyone across all strata of society. For, while ensnaring you, money does not make any distinction about which strata of society you belong to. Therefore, individuals belonging to the upper strata of society should not presume that they can evade the money trap. Even amongst them, the absolute control over money must rest with those who earn it. It is not that this rule should be followed only by those who experience the paucity of money. Truth be told, this practice must be followed more so by those who possess a substantial amount of wealth. Consider this: if one amasses so much money that spending it becomes a challenge, what should one do? Should one spend it frivolously? Certainly not! In the present age, money has assumed great significance, becoming as important as God. Through its conversion, you can bring smiles to countless faces. Hence, to engage in any kind of profligacy is nothing short of a crime. To spend money when there is no need for it, when it is not bringing you happiness—but only to impress others or just because you have a surplus of it—is akin to insulting its godlike quality. If money has assumed such immense value in today's times, then an adequate control must be exercised over every surplus unit of it so that profligacy is prevented under all circumstances. Therefore, those who possess substantial wealth carry on their shoulders an even greater responsibility. In their case too, it is crucial that the one who earns the money maintains absolute control over it.

In short, never harbour any misconception about money. Your primary duty is to amass happiness for yourself and your loved ones by spending your money wisely. With an increase in your income, you may splurge on indulgences. But when your income soars even further, become all the more responsible with your money. When it comes to children, everyone wishes to bequeath money to them, so go ahead and do so. But the question remains, how much should you leave behind for them? Once again, it is contingent upon the amount of money in your possession. You must surely bequeath immovable property to your children, and if you wish to venture beyond that, then set aside enough money for them to be able to live their lives comfortably. However, those who possess wealth that far exceeds their requirements, should under all circumstances, maintain complete control over their earnings. Leave aside as much as you wish for your children, but before you depart, manage the rest of the surplus money in your presence as per your desire. For, amassing happiness with money is the very first stage of converting money. But if money becomes abundant, then the one who has earned it is entitled to 'purchase contentment' with the surplus money. No one should strip him of this right! Grasp clearly that 'contentment' is the most supreme emotion of a human being, and the one who has earned the money has an absolute right to experience and dwell in that emotion. Family members should refrain from depriving anyone of this right on account of their own greed and selfish motives.

This raises the question, what exactly is 'contentment' and how does one attain it? In this respect, comprehend clearly that contentment can be attained only by doing something meaningful for others. Of course, finding 'contentment' is effortless for individuals such as scientists and artists, because through science and art, they bring joy to everyone and thereby attain contentment. However, for the rest, true contentment comes only from spending their surplus money on others. Remember that spending on oneself or loved ones brings happiness, while spending on others begets contentment. And verily, the one who attains contentment in one's lifetime has achieved everything! For, in this world, there exists no greater feeling than contentment. Ask yourself, what could be greater than the contentment our soul experiences on having fulfilled its purpose on earth? And attaining this state of contentment by utilising the money a person has earned is their right as well as their duty. Therefore, if such an opportunity presents itself, never let it go. But yes, as long as there is a shortage of money, utilise the money to garner happiness exclusively for yourself and your loved ones. In the eventuality that you are able to earn abundant money, by all means use it to derive contentment. And in case you are unaware, let me tell you, people donate money in billions only to experience the feeling of contentment. If this surprises you, just take a glance at the below-mentioned list of the most charitable people in the world.

Following are the 20 greatest philanthropists of the world and their charitable contributions in the 20th and 21st centuries:

Sr. No.	Name	Amount Donated
1.	Jamshedji Tata	102.4 bn USD
2.	Bill Gates & Melinda Gates	74.6 bn USD
3.	Henry Wellcome	56.7 bn USD
4.	Howard Hughes	38.6 bn USD
5.	Warren Buffett	37.4 bn USD
6.	George Soros	34.8 bn USD
7.	Hans Wilsdorf	31.5 bn USD
8.	Josiah K. Lilly Senior	27.5 bn USD
9.	John D. Rockefeller	26.8 bn USD
10.	Edsel Ford	26.7 bn USD
11.	Robert Wood Johnson	23.7 bn USD
12.	Azim Premji	22 bn USD
13.	William Hewlett & Flora Hewlett	21.4 bn USD
14.	David Packard	16.4 bn USD
15.	J. Paul Getty	14.6 bn USD
16.	John MacArthur	14.5 bn USD
17.	Will Keith Kellogg	14.5 bn USD

18.	Andrew Carnegie	13.4 bn USD
19.	Ailsa Mellon Bruce & Paul Mellon	12.9 bn USD
20.	Sam Walton & Helen Walton	12.8 bn USD

(Source: 2021 Edel Give Hurun Philanthropists of the Century)

I'm sure it is now clear to you from the list given above that people have made charities of generous proportions to attain 'contentment'. This should help you gauge how exalted the feeling of 'contentment' is. And that is precisely why I am emphasising the importance of maintaining complete control over your surplus money, because only then will you be able to convert it to gain contentment. Otherwise, you will not even realise how sneakily money will entrap you and make you squander every surplus unit of it. Pay heed to these words of caution, for, you are completely ignorant of the fickle nature of money. I am stressing upon this point repeatedly because if you do not use your surplus money to gain contentment for yourself, you will lose out majorly. First and foremost, you will be deprived of experiencing the sublime feeling of contentment. You will fritter away this wonderful opportunity earned through your hard work and intelligence. And even otherwise, what could be more worthwhile than spending your money on others and spreading 'smiles'? At this point, you may ask, "But what if we are unable to do this?" Well, money is deceptive and fickle, after all. If you don't spend your surplus money on others, it will be snatched away from you sooner or later. Perhaps, your own friends and family will coax you into squandering it. And even if none of this transpires, your money will certainly not follow you after you depart from this world. Inevitably, it will betray

"

The **simple** and **straight-forward** method to **earn money** is to deal with **integrity** and **fairness** and **engage** in deals only with **professionals**

you and acquire a new owner. Thereafter, all that excess money will fall into the hands of your children. Besides, do not misunderstand money, considering it to be nectar sent from the heavens. Only those who know how to earn it are aware of how to keep it under control. But your children have not earned this money, have they? They have simply inherited it. So, keeping control over the money will not be an easy task for them. More often than not, children who unexpectedly inherit substantial wealth fall into bad company and are drawn towards drugs, alcohol and gambling. Enticed by their money, swindlers suddenly become their 'friends', and consequently, such children end up committing misdeeds. Therefore, leave behind only the essential amount of money for your children that enables them to lead a decent life. If you leave them with more than the essential amount of money, then know well that you are ruining their lives. And since you harbour great love and affection for your children, I am certain you will not commit such mistakes henceforth.

The crux of the matter is, money is a means to live life well, therefore continue to convert the money you have earned into happiness. When there is a spike in your income, purchase greater joys, but ensure that your earnings are spent solely for your happiness and that of your loved ones. However, if you manage to acquire surplus money beyond what you require to fulfil your needs, then use that amount solely for deriving contentment. Resolve firmly that you will depart from this world only after carefully managing all your surplus money. Bequeath as much as you wish to and generously donate as much as you desire, but fulfil all these obligations in your presence. For, bidding a peaceful farewell to this world is as important as living peacefully in it.

Since we are on this topic, let me convey another point. And what I am about to explain is a matter of spiritual psychology. This is a profoundly significant point, so grasp it well. And in order to comprehend it, just answer this question: Is this life truly yours? Is this body really yours? If your answer is in the affirmative, then answer this—have you acquired this life and this body through your own planning and hard work? If the answer is in the negative, then neither is this life yours nor is this body. Then, to whom do these two belong? Undoubtedly, they belong to the entity that has bestowed them upon you; in other words, they belong to Nature. Well, now that it has been proven beyond a doubt that your life and body belong to Nature, the key point is, you are the one who controls them. That being the case, what is your responsibility? It is to live your life as Nature's trustee; to consider yourself a trustee of your body and your talents, while acknowledging the fact that Nature is the actual owner. This is the only true and simple spiritual way to live your life.

Now, answer this: who is a genuine trustee? Of course, the one who fulfils his owner's wishes. And since Nature is the owner of our life and body, it becomes essential to understand Nature's wish for us. Nature's sole desire is the happiness and progress of human beings. Therefore, true spirituality states that you must fulfil this very desire of Nature. First and foremost, utilise your body and talent for the purpose of acquiring happiness and making progress for yourself. Then, work towards ensuring the happiness of your family and others around you. Thereafter, on the strength of your abilities, appoint yourself the trustee of whatever you acquire over and above this and utilise that surplus money to secure the happiness and progress of all the other children of Nature.

In this way, become a genuine 'trustee' in every sense of the word, considering Nature to be the sole owner of everything that you attain over and above your needs. Just take this step and I promise, you will depart this world with so much contentment that you will experience sublimity on an altogether different level. And for that purpose, it is crucial to exercise complete control over your money. But if your mind is ruled by money, it would become impossible for you to implement any of the measures mentioned above. You will neither be able to amass happiness nor attain contentment. In fact, in the eventuality that your family claims a stake over your money, you will still not be able to achieve any of the above. This is the sole reason I am strongly emphasising on taking 'complete control' over your money. Basically, whether you seek happiness or contentment, being the owner of your money is imperative. Simply put, those who are enslaved by money find neither happiness nor contentment. So, here's hoping that you will definitely become the 'master of money', not its slave.

In our discussion so far, we have grasped that money is, indubitably, the foremost priority in today's times. Nevertheless, how can one tolerate being harassed by money? Indeed, one cannot allow that at any cost! This raises the question: why does one need money in the first place? Obviously, to live a grand life. And what stops one from living a good life? It is, undoubtedly, the troubles that stream in one after the other. In other words, the situation is truly complicated. For, one cannot live without money, and money always arrives with troubles in tow. This is still alright, but the problem is, even after money steps into your life, it does not stop troubling you. So, what is the remedy to rid oneself of these troubles? Honestly, the root cause of troubles is not money, but the obsession with money. Admittedly, it is impossible to live without money in the present age, but one cannot live one's life obsessing over money either. Therefore, the only solution is to possess money but without obsessing over it.

If one manages to achieve even this single goal, the majority of money-related troubles will be alleviated. And in this day and age, a person who is not burdened by money-related problems can well be considered to have scored victory in eighty percent of life's battles. You too can triumph in this battle effortlessly—in fact, you must. For, what is the point of living when despite possessing money, you are still mired in troubles? Life is meaningful only when one possesses money, but is not troubled by it.

Indubitably, you must be harbouring the desire to liberate yourself from money-related troubles. And to that end, tell me, who falls prey to money? Who are the ones money is ensnaring in its ever-new traps? In answer to this, comprehend clearly that your 'mind' is the sole prey of money. It is the mind that experiences the delirium caused by the shortage of money, and it is the mind alone that is gripped by the madness resulting from excess money. If you observe closely, these are both psychological issues, and the majority of people are grappling with either of these psychological problems. They are either victims of the delirium caused by the 'paucity of money' or are consumed by the madness resulting from possessing 'excessive money'.

In essence, those facing a scarcity of money have their own set of problems, while those having excess money also face their own share of challenges. This clearly means, there is no correlation between problems and the amount of money one possesses. For, both situations, be it lack or excess of money, create their own set of troubles. So, does it mean that money is always the root cause of trouble? No, that's not true either. The truth is, money by itself holds no power to be the cause of your distress. It is your own psychological weakness that is allowing money to trouble you. Hence, by simply tweaking your psychology, you can forever liberate yourself from all money-related problems. For, the source of distress is not money; it is the psychological attack of money on your mind that is causing problems. In such a scenario, gaining a psychological victory over 'money' is the sole solution to liberate yourself from all money-related problems.

Well, it is clear that the presence or absence of money is not the problem, for, those who possess it as well as those who face a scarcity of it, are both distressed by it. Indeed, they are helpless, for, the psychology of money is so mischievous that it is capable of troubling people on both sides of the spectrum. And today, the majority of people are, indeed, enduring money-related problems due to some or the other reason. Viewed from this perspective, let me state clearly that a psychological victory

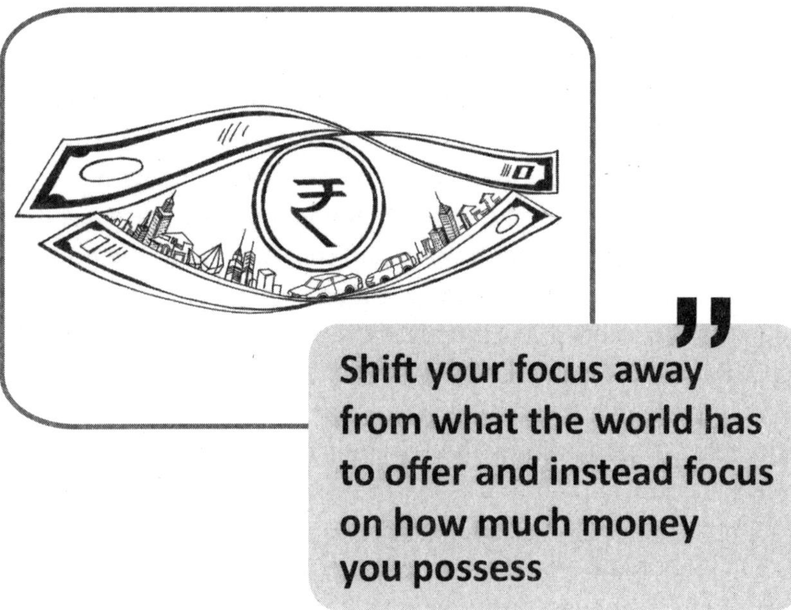

over money is the most crucial need of human beings in the present times. Let people say that anchoring yourself in the soul is the purpose of life. They may even urge you to align yourself with God. However, I am responsibly stating that all such goals are far-fetched; you must first establish harmony with money. Begin with gaining a psychological victory over money and focus on everything else later.

Alright, let us leave that aside. For now, grasp well that although emerging victorious in the 'psychological war' against money is essential, this is not a battle wherein you eliminate the enemy altogether. Do not forget that money is the supreme necessity of life, not an adversary that needs to be annihilated. In fact, it is impossible to win this war if you eliminate money. Look around you; any spiritual leader who doles out such advice has already been vanquished by money. For, whether it is their ashrams or churches, both have been built with the help of money. As a matter of fact, their very survival hinges on 'monetary donations'. So, know for certain that triumphing in this battle by eliminating, despising or cursing money is impossible. The only way to emerge victorious in this war is to reconcile with money, and reconciliation simply means that you must establish a setting between your mind and money. And this is, indeed, the greatest necessity of life in today's times. Grasp clearly, a mind that is not aligned with 'money' will find it impossible to align with the soul or God. And this is the spiritual truth of the present era, no matter how unpalatable it may seem. I speak only about the ultimate principles of psychology and spirituality, therefore comprehend well that only a mind that is in sync with 'money' will eventually find alignment with the soul and God.

This truth could seem a bitter pill to swallow for some and many may even disagree with it, but that does not change the reality. Besides, this truth is evident to all. So, you might as well answer this question: despite ninety percent of the people being vested in religion and its ways, why are they unable to align themselves with the 'soul or God'? It is because their minds are not yet aligned even with 'money'. And how can a mind that is not able to align even with money, possibly align itself with the soul or God? Even millions of so-called religious gurus are unable to align themselves with the soul or God simply because they have not yet been able to sync their minds with money. Even at this stage in their journey, they need grand ashrams, magnificent churches and splendid mosques. And how can any mind that harbours the tiniest complaint, desire or obsession related to money, possibly align itself with the 'soul or God'?

Essentially, establishing a rapport between your mind and 'money' is a fundamental requirement of both life as well as spirituality. And a thorough comprehension of the psychology of mind as well as money is imperative to establish this rapport. It is for this reason that I am going to delve straight into the psychological core of both the mind and money. Therefore, do not miss out on this opportunity to align your mind with money. Read every word attentively. But before you do so, take a moment to contemplate upon the relationship between the two. I will, of course, explain as we move forward, but the more you reflect upon it yourself, the more it will enhance your psychological understanding.

Well, to put it simply, money is an entity that can help you buy happiness, while the mind is that which can experience happiness. This is the direct connection between the mind and money. So, where exactly does the problem stem from? The problem arises because money is not being able to procure happiness, and the mind is not being able to remain happy. And what could be the reason behind this? The reason is the absence of a tuning between the mind and money; and till the time such a tuning is established, it will be impossible to achieve either objective. Until then, neither will money be able to procure happiness nor will the mind be able to experience joy. And as long as both these objectives are unfulfilled, life will be nothing but a hellish existence. This in itself should help you gauge the importance of establishing a 'setting between the mind and money'.

At this point, you may well ask, what should we do so that money brings in happiness and the mind too remains anchored in a state of bliss? Oh, have you not grasped yet? The simple and only solution is, the mind must learn to always remain happy with whatever joys money brings. There is no other way to forge an alignment between the mind and money. And when I am stating

> “ **Man** is being **cheated** mostly by **white-collared thieves**

that there is no other option, it verily means that no such option exists. For, my statements are always rooted in spiritual psychology, and spiritual psychology is a set of principles that leave absolutely no room for ambiguity.

Therefore, etch it in your mind that money is the biggest problem in the present times, and this is because living without money in this day and age is impossible. Nevertheless, grasp clearly that it is not money per se that is causing the problem. The real problem arises due to the psychological assault that money wreaks on the mind. And if you wish to shield yourself from the psychological onslaughts of money, you will have to establish a permanent alignment between your mind and money. Indeed, there is no other way to evade the psychological attack of money. In case you fail to establish this alignment, be certain that money will continue to torment you. And both, those with less money as well as those with substantial wealth will have to suffer these money-related problems. Viewed from a spiritual perspective, the lack or excess of money is not the cause of problems; the issue is the absence of a tuning between the mind and money. In other words, only a person who succeeds in establishing an alignment between his mind and money will be able to eliminate monetary troubles.

The question now arises: how does one establish an alignment between the mind and money? So, towards that end, you must first grasp a few points. Everyone needs money, and admittedly, money is the foremost necessity of human life. That being the case, grasp clearly that no one will want to part with their money easily. In other words, earning money will never be a cakewalk. And you too are well aware that everyone is trying their best to hold on to their money. In fact, the world at large lives by the principle, 'Life may perish, but money must not vanish.' In other words, money has taken precedence even over life. Everyone is engaged in the pursuit of acquiring as much money as possible in an attempt to surpass others. Employers are reluctant to give a salary raise to employees, whereas employees have their eyes trained on salary increments. Indeed, intense negotiations abound everywhere regarding money. In such a scenario, earning money is certainly an uphill task. And it is better to acknowledge this reality of life that there is nothing more arduous than earning money.

Now, let us come face to face with another truth of life, and that is, no matter how challenging earning money may be, one has to earn it to sustain one's life. There is no alternative to this either. So, answer this question: ultimately, what is the most that you can do towards that end? You can work for eight to ten hours with all your heart and soul, but beyond this, nothing lies in your control. Therefore, just continue to work devotedly for eight to ten hours a day. Fulfil this duty with utmost honesty, because this alone will pave the way to a proper tuning between the mind and money. Those who do not work devotedly for eight to ten hours must simply discard the idea of establishing a tuning between their mind and money. Grasp clearly that all remedies or solutions provided by spirituality are meant only for karmaveers (people of action). Those who shirk karma (action) are anyway not entitled to live a magnificent life. And I'm sure you would recall that the great scripture of 'Bhagavad Gita' commenced on the basis of the same spiritual principle.

Well, the amount of money one receives after working for eight to ten hours a day depends on various factors. But we will not delve into those factors here; instead, we will focus directly on our main point and take the discussion forward. And the key point is, whatever money a person earns after putting in those dedicated eight to ten hours of work becomes his wealth—to put it bluntly, that becomes his financial limit. And whether one accepts it or not, this reality remains unaltered. Now, it is possible that for some, their earnings may indeed be insufficient, but even so, one cannot do much about it. For, the only aspect that is in your control is the honest effort you put into those eight to ten hours. Of course, in these eight to ten hours, some people earn large sums of money while others earn exceedingly large amounts, and there are even those who may not be able to earn as per their heart's desire. The key point to comprehend here is, whatever amount a person earns after eight to ten hours of hard work has nothing to do with the alignment between their mind and money. Tuning the mind with money is not at all contingent upon one's income. In fact, the tuning of the mind and money is a matter of spirituality; in other words, it is an art. And what does that mean? It means that it is not necessary that those who earn money in abundance will be able to tune their mind with money. At the same time, it does not necessarily mean that those who earn less cannot establish a tuning between the two. In essence, comprehend well that tuning one's mind with money is an 'art' which is certainly not dependent on the amount of money one possesses.

This begs the question—how should one align one's mind with money? So, towards that end, just reflect—which entity between the mind and money has a limit? Undoubtedly, it is money that has a definite limit, for, the amount of money in one's pocket is all that one has. On the other hand, the mind is boundless, as it can soar to dizzying heights as per its desires. There are neither taxes nor restrictions on its flights of fancy. And verily, it soars unbridled, which is precisely what hinders the tuning of the mind with money. It is also true that it is the mind that soars first, after which the person begins to chase after money. The fact that everyone fails to realise is, no matter how much they chase after money, they cannot ever match the pace of the mind. For, the mind will always remain unsatiated, as the desires of the mind are unlimited while money is limited. Therefore, if one wishes to tune one's mind with money, it is imperative to rein in the soaring mind. To achieve a long-lasting harmony between a constant and a variable, one would have to experiment with the variable entity only. This is an irrevocable principle of psychology, and no matter where you apply this principle, it will always yield a perfect outcome. And this is verily the beauty of psychological principles that they always yield accurate results. Of course, it's a completely different matter that the knowledge of genuine psychological principles is almost non-existent in today's world. At present, however, grasp another aspect regarding the mind and money. Granted that the mind is a variable entity, so one has to work with that alone, but the problem is, curbing the mind excessively renders life meaningless. To live a penurious life is nonsensical, as life ought to be lived as magnificently as possible. Therefore, kindly avoid being swayed by talks that glorify the notion of living an austere life. Of course, when it comes to the mind, one cannot deny that the matter is a bit complicated.

In essence, comprehend well that living magnificently is the purpose of life. And while it is true that one has to experiment with the mind, it certainly does not imply that one should throw one's hands up in the air. Learn from Krishna's life and not from

Strive for a palace by all means, but if all you get is a shed, live 'joyfully' nonetheless

those who flee in fear. Try to make life as grand as possible, and towards that end, ensure that you work devotedly for eight to ten hours a day. Having said that, know well that if stress and sorrows persist in life, then living the good life is impossible. Thus, one must seek the path that will lead one on a many-splendoured journey, devoid of stress and tension. Simply stated, money is welcome but stress is not. There is no point in earning money while harbouring stress. It is also foolish to harbour stress despite possessing money. And sacrificing your health to earn money will obviously jeopardise everything. So, what should you do? Well, the goal remains the same—attune your mind to money and that is precisely what we are trying to do. In fact, I am endeavouring to eliminate, one by one, the very obstacles that stand in the way of this attunement. And in this context, understand well that you need to adopt a balanced attitude. Of course, you must earn money, but not at the cost of compromising your health or peace of mind. And this is possible only if you avoid putting undue restraints on the mind, while also ensuring that you do not give it unnecessary leeway to soar high. This simply means, you must adopt a 'completely balanced attitude' in dealing with the mind.

So, how can one achieve this balance? Well, to that end, first put your entire focus on working diligently for eight to ten hours every day, and that too consistently. As you continue to work, money will definitely stream in. And when it does, you will obviously not spend it all recklessly. Surely, you will put some in savings and investments. So, keep up with this practice. Utilise money to amass as much happiness as you can while staying within your limits. But even while doing all this, keep a keen eye on finding a way to permanently attune your mind to money. Try to set your soaring mind in and around the limits of the earned money. For, the money you possess is all that you have. Hence, keep striving to confine the flights of your mind within the boundaries of the available money. Of course, this will not happen in a day, but with consistent and mindful efforts, it will surely be accomplished. At the outset, just continue to assess your practical needs and those of your loved ones, while keeping a vigilant eye on the amount of money you possess. Then, evaluate the distance between the aspirations of your soaring mind and the money at your disposal. For example, you may adjudge that the aspirations of the mind have reached the figure of eighty, while the money in hand is forty. Never mind! Do not lose heart. For, you are at least aware that the distance between the mind and money is that of 'forty'. The next step is to think about how to bridge this gap. And there are only two ways to do this—either the requisite money comes in as per the aspirations of the soaring mind or the mind aligns itself with the available money. Keep in mind that this attunement will not happen overnight. But you have nonetheless adjudged the distance between the two. Rest assured, this single step will initiate the 'setting of the mind and money' because by judging the distance between the mind and money, you have taken the first step. The next step would then be to focus on reducing that distance. Curb some of the fanciful flights of the mind and simultaneously make efforts to increase your income. The day your savings and fixed income along with your current earnings align with the needs of your mind, you can pat yourself on the back for having scored a major victory in life.

In case you have not fully grasped the essence of the point stated above, let me explain it from a different perspective and in greater detail. Fathoming this point is essential, because the matter pertains to the permanent setting of your life. So, to begin with, answer this question: what is the problem at present? The problem is, the mind harbours needs numbering in thousands, while the money in hand is a mere two hundred. Whereas, setting the mind with money means that if the mind has a hundred needs, then the money to satisfy those needs should be equal or more. It implies reaching a state where money fulfils all the requirements of the 'mind'. And once this is accomplished, stress and tension will be eliminated from life, replaced with joy, merriment, happiness, celebration and bliss. For, in this day and age, a person who has vanquished the troubles spawned by money has triumphed over life itself! Therefore, you will have to fight tooth and nail to establish this unparalleled setting. And this is only possible if you continuously try to reduce the distance between the mind and money. Rein in the mind to some extent while also striving to enhance your income, and persist with this endeavour until the two are aligned permanently. In fact, I would urge you to never cease in your efforts till the time such a setting is established. Hence, every day, reason a little with the mind and whenever an opportunity to earn extra money presents itself, seize it with both hands. But do whatever it takes to establish a setting between the mind and money as quickly as possible. Remember, the sooner you establish this setting, the better it is for you, because you will experience the true pleasure of living only after this setting has been established; until then, life will seem utterly dismal.

> " **Money** deludes you into thinking that it is your **slave**, but in **reality**, it has become **everyone's master**

Well, the day you succeed in establishing a setting between the mind and money, you must take a pause. And this opportunity definitely presents itself at some point or the other in the lives of those who work with honesty and integrity. For some, it may arrive after ten years, while for others, it might take twenty years. But you must comprehend clearly that this opportunity presents itself only to those who work honestly for eight to ten hours a day. Those who work reluctantly or shirk work never come across such an opportunity. Having said this, you must also realise that working honestly for eight to ten hours a day is just the first step. For, even then, this opportunity arrives in the lives of only those who continue to focus on 'aligning their mind with money'. Otherwise, in spite of possessing abundant wealth, a great majority of people still fail to reach this stage. Despite possessing limitless money, the harmony between the mind and money eludes them all their life. There are still many others who surely possess enough money that if they so desire, they can immediately begin living in a state where their mind and money are aligned. However, as I mentioned earlier, aligning the mind with money is an 'art' which has nothing to do with 'the amount of money you possess'. So, I urge you, if you or your family possess enough wealth that allows you to align your mind with money today itself, then go ahead and do it without wasting a moment. You already possess sufficient money, so all you need to do is align your mind with it. Otherwise, despite possessing a vast amount of wealth, your life will be spent in vain.

Well, it is now clear that the alignment of the mind and money is an art. It is also evident that till the time such an alignment is achieved, life will not be enjoyable. So, please keep an eye out for opportunities to establish this setting. The day you feel that having acquired sufficient wealth and aligning it with your mind, you are able to live a magnificent life, take a pause. Mind you, I am urging you to take a 'pause', not to stop working. Taking a pause means that you no longer have to toil under pressure to earn money; in fact, you must now liberate yourself from the pressures and complications associated with earning money. Of course, you must continue working and ensure that work never stops. Life is actually nothing but a continuous stream of actions, flowing rhythmically. To sit idle and twiddle your thumbs cannot be called life. Therefore, as long as a person is physically capable, he must put in eight to ten hours of work every day. Aligning the mind with money does not imply that one should cease working. Setting the mind with money only means that you will now work, not for money, but for the joy it begets.

Comprehend another point that whether you work for money or for the joy it provides, your work will surely bring in the 'money'. So, allow the money to flow in. Of course, you no longer require that money because your money and mind are aligned, so all you have to do is utilise that surplus money towards charity to derive contentment. And verily, the one who has amassed contentment has fulfilled the purpose of life.

I'm sure by now, you must have grasped what I mean by the 'alignment of the mind and money' and how exactly to establish this tuning. You must have also realised how crucial this alignment is. But the main question is: how can one ascertain whether one has actually achieved this alignment or not? So, assess this with the help of the following points. This exercise is crucial because until your mind and money are in sync, money will continue to create problems for you. Therefore, do not harbour any misconception in this matter. It is better to check whether the alignment has been established or not. So, carefully read the points stated below and examine if you have truly aligned your mind with money or you are somehow mistaken about this.

1) Firstly, aligning your mind with money does not mean that you will now quit working. You may still engage in work, but you will now be working solely for the joy you derive out of it, not for the money it begets. The day you reach this state, consider your mind to have achieved perfect alignment with money. For, at this point, you are neither stressing in order to earn money nor are you undergoing troubles to that end. Here, it is also essential to grasp that despite having millions of rupees in your bank account, if you are still enduring troubles to earn more money, then know well that your mind is not yet aligned with money. In this scenario, you are still a victim of 'the lure of money'.

2) In case you are no longer working for money, what will you do with the money acquired through your work? Undoubtedly, you will dedicate most of the surplus money you earn towards

the welfare of others, in other words, towards charity. However, if your mind begins to soar high on new flights of fancy due to this surplus money, then know well that your mind and money were not aligned. In fact, the mind was just waiting for more money to arrive. Of course, you may see your requirements change in accordance with your increased income, but if your mind begins to draw up an ever-growing list of needs alongside your escalating income, then be certain that your mind and money were definitely not aligned. You were simply mistaken that they were aligned. Had they aligned permanently, most of the surplus money would have been spent on charity only. The very essence of alignment is that your mind is now perfectly in sync with 'money'. Thereafter, even if the treasures of the entire world fall into your lap, they wouldn't hold any significance for the mind. Instead, this 'set mind' will shower that wealth back on the world, but never on its own needs.

From the points elucidated above, you must have realised that achieving an alignment between the 'mind and money' is not a cakewalk. And it is not easy because this is a 'spiritual state' and attaining any height of spirituality is never easy. The mind can be cajoled into a temporary alignment with money, but aligning it permanently is nothing less than an accomplishment. For, it is quite common for the mind to soar on new flights of fancy with the arrival of more money. So, if you are still fulfilling your needs with the newly acquired money, then know for sure that the process is incomplete. In other words, the alignment between the mind and money is not in place yet, and this is because with soaring wealth your needs too are on a continuous rise.

Incidentally, there is another way of aligning the mind with money. The setting explained above is meant for those who have an abundance of money, but several people are no doubt spiritually inclined and psychologically powerful too. And if you are not one of them, you can become one. Indeed, I have mentioned earlier that aligning the mind with money is a 'spiritual art' and anyone can cultivate this art at any point in time. To that end, you need not wait for an abundance of money to come your way. In fact, if you so desire, you have the option to align your mind with money even before acquiring abundant wealth. You can align your 'mind' with your savings, investments, fixed income and current earnings right here, right now. If your mind aligns with your present financial situation, the alignment is complete. If your mind neither craves more nor demands anything beyond the available financial resources, then the alignment has been accomplished. Then it doesn't matter whether the money you possess is scarce or abundant.

In this case, you have instantly aligned your mind with money on the strength of your spiritual power. And that is, indeed, a wise decision because you have straightaway liberated yourself from the pressures of money. Now, comprehend the fact that even after this alignment, you are continuously working, so it will naturally lead to an increased income. In fact, your earnings will increase further, because the sense of contentment and peace you experience from having established a setting between your mind and money will invariably enhance your performance. As a result, you will attract money effortlessly. And since you had aligned your mind with lesser money initially, you can now increase your needs alongside your escalating income. For, ultimately, you have to lead a magnificent life. However, you must take care that the alignment is not disrupted in the process of increasing your needs. Ensure that the mind soars in proportion to the escalating income. And this approach of making 'alignments in installments' is truly wonderful because it instantly eliminates tensions and

> It is **the principle** of **psychology** that **ownership** never comes **without 'responsibility'**

pressures regarding money. Moreover, in the future, you will also find opportunities to fulfil newer needs that may arise on account of your rising income.

In essence, when you forge an instant alignment of this kind, your enhanced income too becomes a part of the mind-money alignment, so you will obviously not donate this surplus money to charity. You will use it only to fulfil your newer needs. And there is no harm in that! Everyone has the right to fulfil their needs with the money they have earned. Once the mind and money are aligned, you are not obliged to make charitable contributions. Those who have aligned their minds with limited money can certainly expand their needs with their escalating income. Having limited money certainly does not mean that they are condemned to suffer the pressures and tensions associated with money. Aligning their mind with money, they can instantly rid themselves of such pressures and stress. In a similar vein, aligning the mind with limited money also does not imply that one must refrain from increasing one's needs. In my opinion, this is the best form of alignment because it can be forged instantly and one can also expand one's needs alongside the escalating income. However, in this process, there are two things to keep in mind. First, your needs should expand only in proportion to the escalating income, and second, once the alignment is in place, you should work solely for the joy you derive from it. If you are working for money even after your mind and money have been aligned, then know well that you have failed to achieve even this alignment. What you are assuming to be a temporary alignment between your mind and money is nothing but a misconception.

Well, aligning the mind with increasing income is a temporary method to shield oneself from the assault of money. However, even such an alignment will be considered foolproof only when the needs stop expanding alongside the escalating income. In other words, it is only when you begin to engage in charity with the surplus money that comes your way that you can consider your mind to have achieved a permanent alignment with money. Comprehend clearly that 'engaging in charity' is the only evidence of your victory over money. Charity itself signifies that you have now become immune to all the impacts and influences of money. The very fact that you are engaging in charity implies that the scarcity of money is no longer troubling you. If you are making donations, it means that you are no longer swayed by the lure of money. Indeed, those who are lured by money are only interested in increasing their bank balance, not engaging in charity. To put it simply, the ability to engage in charity is the sole evidence of the fact that you have triumphed over the nuisance of money. You must also grasp clearly that charity driven by fear or greed cannot be called charity in the true sense of the word. If the intention behind engaging in charity is to acquire fame, respect or wealth, then this kind of charity is certainly no proof of an alignment between the mind and money; nor can the charity done to attain heaven or appease God be considered as proof of an alignment between the mind and money. The alignment of the mind with money is a pure spiritual state whereby charity is done only with a genuine and pure intention to help others.

To sum it up, the primary goal of life should be to align the mind with money, and forging this alignment is indeed an art.

Most importantly, one must become adept at this art as soon as possible. For, sorrows, worries, frustrations and conflicts exist in life mainly due to a lack of setting between the mind and money. Once a seamless alignment between the mind and money is established, all troubles and problems will be eradicated. So, I hope you will align your mind with money as soon as possible and begin to lead a magnificent life. I am confident, from this day onwards, all your endeavours and actions will be directed solely towards achieving this alignment. And if you pursue this goal with unwavering determination, there will come a day when your mind and money will undoubtedly be aligned. Then onwards, your joy of living will soar to an altogether different level. In fact, you don't even need to wait for another day to do this. For, I have already disclosed the technique of temporarily aligning the mind with money. If you wish, you can adopt this formula and align your mind with money today itself. Of course, you can align them permanently when an opportunity arises in the future. But no matter what, strive to earn with the sole purpose of aligning your mind with money. Endeavouring to earn money for any other purpose will only compel you to suffer the nuisance of money. I hope you will take this matter seriously and implement it in your life at the earliest.

Indubitably, money is the supreme necessity of life. The more money you possess, the wider is the range of needs you can fulfil. And surely, there is nothing wrong with fulfilling needs and leading a magnificent life. Now, all this is true, but the question arises: how does one acquire money? Honestly speaking, 'How to earn money' is the biggest question in today's times. For, is there a single person today who does not aspire to earn as much money as possible? But the question is, how many can claim to earn the kind of 'money' that keeps pace with their soaring dreams? A mere handful! Barring these few, the rest are struggling to earn even the bare minimum to sustain themselves. The question is, when everyone aspires to earn money and are also working hard towards it, where does the problem lie? Why has earning money become as arduous a task as finding God? Even after taking great pains to earn money, why isn't anyone able to attract money?

Honestly speaking, it is this 'why' that holds the answers to all the problems of the present era. There is no denying the fact that money is the foremost and biggest necessity of the present-day human being. And it is so because the purpose of life is to live magnificently, and this purpose cannot be fulfilled without money. So, the fact of the matter is, money is indispensable and everyone wants it, come what may. However, the problem is, earning money is not a walk in the park, which further leads to the question: are there any set principles for earning money? Generally speaking, working hard, applying intelligence and so on are considered the key factors to earning money, but then, everyone is already engaged in this endeavour, putting their heart and soul into it. But despite this, the reality is, they are not able to attract the required amount of money. In other words, mere hard work and application of intelligence do not seem to guarantee the desired amount of money.

To sum it up, both hard work and intelligence may be essential, but they are clearly not sufficient. Similarly, academic degrees are not proving to be very helpful either. It is also true that harbouring a desire or need for money is not attracting it in any way. In a nutshell, earning money is a sore point with everyone, but even so, money is not flowing in effortlessly. And it is verily this scarcity of money that is unnecessarily stripping everyone of their joy of living. Otherwise, who doesn't wish to laugh and sing, make merry, soar to dizzying heights and live life to the fullest? But in the absence of money, how can one experience the joys of life with ease?

In such a scenario, the question arises: how does one acquire a substantial amount of wealth? Is there a science to it? Is there a formula for earning money? Of course, there is! To that end, you only need to grasp that all visible and invisible entities possess their own psychology. And psychology means that every entity exhibits its own unique behaviour. Similarly, money too possesses a peculiar behaviour and is no exception to this truth. This implies that money will not behave according to your whims. It possesses its own unique psychology and will behave in accordance with that alone.

In other words, toiling hard, acquiring academic degrees, applying intellect, nursing desires and weaving grand dreams are all so-called formulas invented by human beings. But why would money adhere to your formulas? Water is formed when hydrogen combines with oxygen—this is verily the formula for water. Now, if you invent a brand-new formula which claims to create water from a combination of nitrogen and ammonia, do you think you'd be able to create water? In other words, would water accept your formula? Similarly, money will not behave as per the formulas created by you, and this is precisely the reason

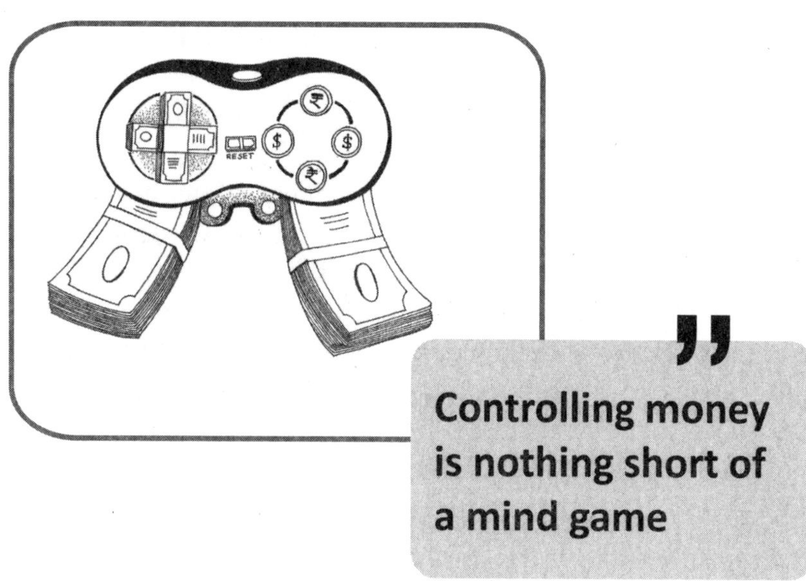

> **Controlling money is nothing short of a mind game**

why earning money has become challenging. Everyone is trying to impose their way of thinking on money, that is, everyone is trying to devise their own formulas for earning money, and as a result, money is upset with everyone. The truth is, people do not lack the talent or will to work hard as much as they feel a persistent lack of money. Money has woven such a spell that despite working hard and possessing talent, it does not readily gravitate towards anyone. And all these problems are occurring because of the inability to comprehend the psychological behaviour of money. But regardless, money remains everyone's basic necessity. Therefore, let me now directly dive into its psychological behaviour and address questions like: What does money like? What does it dislike? What attracts money and what offends it? What causes money to trouble you and what makes it shower its beneficence on you? So, let us delve deeper into exploring the psychological behaviour of money. And in this context, I will first explain a few behavioural traits of money which you must keep in mind.

Stop Chasing Money

The most prominent psychological aspect of money is that it abhors anyone chasing after it. That is why, money often eludes those who chase it or are extremely desperate to earn it, irrespective of how hard they work or strive to move heaven and earth! I have already mentioned that money's behaviour is quite similar to that of women. Just as women get offended if you chase them incessantly, so does money. And whether it is money or women, people tend to commit the same mistake in both cases!

Well, you must now comprehend why money gets offended when someone chases after it or why it scurries away when one becomes desperate to acquire it. What is the psychological reason behind it? Well, the psychological reason is quite simple—every form of desperation compels you to commit mistakes. And this is verily a psychological truth that I am stating. You too must have experienced several instances wherein desperation has compelled you to act foolishly. You too must have surely faced the detrimental effects of desperation. This implies, neither should you chase after money nor show a desperation to earn it. Otherwise, in your foolishness, you might end up depleting the money in your possession instead of augmenting it.

So, if you genuinely wish to increase your income, learn to relax when dealing with money matters. Maintain a "Take it Easy" policy and never become desperate to earn money. I hope you have now thoroughly comprehended the detrimental effects of desperation. If you find yourself overly desperate to earn money, focus immediately on alleviating that sense of desperation. Relax a little. Otherwise, you are bound to lose your mental balance along with your money. For, desperation will drive you to commit such foolishness that money will forever run away from you. Therefore, instead of showing desperation for money, focus on living a good life with whatever money you possess currently. Rest assured, this relaxed attitude will attract money towards you, because in a relaxed state of mind, the chances of making erroneous decisions become nil. Etch this fact in your mind that all erroneous decisions stem from desperation alone. More often than not, it is only desperate people who end up depleting their wealth. Why don't you comprehend that the very psychology of desperation is to drive a person to commit errors?! When you show extreme desperation, be it for money or anything else, you will surely lose it one day. Here, I am outlining the most profound psychological principles, so kindly take maximum advantage of them at every juncture of life.

Fulfil Needs First

Agreed, one must not chase after money and also avoid being desperate to earn money. But one still has to earn well, right? So, how can one ensure this? Well, the only recourse humans have is to work. If you expect money to flow in without expending any effort, I'm sorry to say you are deluded. Therefore, one has no alternative other than to work. However, the problem is, as long as you 'work' to fulfil your needs, you will never be able to amass substantial wealth. This is the supreme law of money. And this is because, sooner or later, needs will give rise to desperation, and this desperation, no matter how minor, will cloud your judgement. An even bigger truth is, the desperation to fulfil one's needs often turns an individual into a 'labourer'. Putting everything aside, he finds himself trapped in a loop, blinded by his relentless pursuit of money. Generally, such people work assiduously to make ends meet, and the fact is, a vast majority of people find themselves trapped in this category, struggling to meet life's basic needs even after slogging all month long. Indeed, food, clothing and shelter are the fundamental needs of life, so one has to fulfil these at any cost. Hence, it is justifiable for people to feel desperate to make ends meet. The predicament is no doubt challenging, but you must understand that the initial phase of life is anyway fraught with challenges. However, one must break free from this phase as soon as possible, for, the desperation for money is bound to hinder progress.

In short, this is a vicious cycle. Failure to meet life's basic needs naturally triggers a desperation to earn money, and it is a psychological truth that once desperation takes hold, it impedes progress. So, what is the solution? To put it simply, earning money is similar to flying an airplane. The onus is on the pilot to take the aircraft up to a certain altitude. Once the airplane reaches a particular altitude, the rest of the flight can be completed smoothly on autopilot. The same is the case with money. Every individual has to earn the money required to fulfil basic needs. And this task in itself is not easy, for, it involves undergoing tremendous hardships. This is because whenever you are working to earn money, you are inevitably gripped by desperation, which is the very reason why money eludes you. For, every desperation that grips you disturbs the mind, making you anxious, irritable and frustrated. Thereafter, such a disturbed mind keeps committing errors and is unable to perform efficiently. Thus, know for certain that the root cause of all these problems is desperation.

Therefore, do whatever it takes to ensure that you triumph over desperation. By working hard and applying intelligence, strive to earn the kind of money that enables you to establish a reasonable alignment between your mind and money as quickly as possible. This endeavour on your part will ultimately help you break free from the desperation to earn money. In this context, comprehend another point that this is possible only when you refrain from increasing your needs along with your expanding wealth. This alone will weaken the desperation in your mind to earn money. And once the desperation to earn money subsides, you won't need to look back. For, once the needs are fulfilled, one begins to work simply for the pleasure one derives from it. This greatly alleviates the pressure to earn money or work assiduously. In the absence of pressure, the intellect operates with remarkable efficiency and one finds oneself in a relaxed state of mind. Needless to say, such a person also leverages opportunities effectively. Making progress then becomes effortless for him as he is no longer chasing money. And as a result, money naturally starts gravitating towards him.

In essence, struggles will persist in your life as long as your basic purpose of working is to fulfil your needs. The day your income reaches a stage whereby you no longer feel the pressure to fulfil needs, money will start chasing you. Rest assured, from that day onwards, money's behaviour towards you will change. To sum it up, all money-related struggles persist only till the time one is fulfilling one's basic needs. Having said that, there are some people whose needs are never fulfilled and whose minds are habituated to craving "more and more". Their desperation never wanes, and as a result, they are never able to make strides in life. Consequently, toiling hard and receiving ordinary results becomes their destiny. Remaining mired in stress, worry and frustration becomes a part of their nature. So, kindly curb the habit of whining and lamenting about your needs. A far better approach is to work sincerely and fulfil your basic needs as quickly as possible. Eliminate the 'desperation to earn money' from your life as swiftly as possible. Rest assured, this approach will guarantee your progress. Indeed, an extreme desperation to earn money has driven even some of the richest people to commit grave errors, ultimately making them bankrupt. Hence, as quickly as possible, liberate yourself from the desperation to earn money; thereafter, just watch how money comes chasing after you.

In short, the primary focus of your life should be to reach a stage whereby you 'stop working in order to fulfil needs'. Kick-start your career with this very mindset. The initial phase of a career is anyway marked by exuberant, youthful enthusiasm, so all you have to do is keep that flame burning till you triumph over the desperation to earn money. Work hard and apply your intelligence to the fullest. Don't stop until you have triumphed over your needs. Whatever efforts you have to put in, do it regardless. Set a target to reach this stage as quickly as possible. Strive to take the airplane of your life as quickly as possible to a level whereby it begins to cruise in 'auto-mode'. Then, sit back and watch money chase after you. For, you have now reached a stage where you are no longer working to fulfil your needs, and that is precisely what money approves of.

Leverage the Fervour of Youth

Although money is the supreme necessity of life, most people are still not able to attract the required money—and this is the biggest challenge in today's life. It is verily the scarcity of money that has distressed the world at large. Despite working hard, a sufficient amount of money seems elusive and this harsh reality confronts everyone on a daily basis. Especially when it comes to earning money in the initial stages, it is certainly not easy. It requires one to undergo arduous struggles and endure considerable hardships, making the entire process excruciating. However, there is absolutely no need to feel disheartened. I have explained earlier that money behaves quite disdainfully in the early stages of life. Despite your relentless efforts, it remains totally unyielding. The bottom-line is, one's needs are unlimited while the available money is limited, and this is verily every person's story in the initial stages. Everyone is compelled to endure the cold behaviour of money at the outset of their career. And you are no exception to this. Therefore, you must not become despondent and put down your weapons, and neither should you resort to dishonest means to earn money.

Basically, you embark on your career brimming with exuberance and the fervour of youth; and as I have already explained, you are compelled to endure the cold behaviour of money only till the time you achieve a reasonable alignment between your mind and money. Having said that, achieving this alignment is far from easy, as everyone desires a good life. Therefore, in the initial phase, you are bound to have a thousand needs, while

> "**Money** is like a **beautiful woman**; life **without** either of them is **dull** and **boring**. But living with either of them is **not** a **breeze** either

the money in hand is a mere fifty. The story of even the most successful people is no different from this. Regardless of who it is, in the nascent stage of one's career, there inevitably exists a huge gap between one's needs in life and the available income. So, the question arises: in such a scenario, how does one align their mind with money? However, one still has to, because in the absence of such an alignment, everything will go awry. There are clear-cut examples of several people who have notched up tremendous success by surmounting this challenging phase of their career. It is only because the vast majority of people are unable to reach the stage where they can align their mind with money that the problem is not getting resolved. As a result, they grapple with their needs lifelong, struggling till their last breath.

Well, no matter what, you have to undergo the journey of aligning your mind with money and emerge victorious at the end of it. In the initial stage, there will certainly be a drastic gap between your needs and the available income, but with hard work, dedication and intelligence, you must plunge headlong into this endeavour. Strive to align your mind with money on both fronts—on one hand, increase your income from fifty to five hundred, and on the other, reason with your mind and reduce your needs from thousand to five hundred. Achieving this alignment may take a few years, but it must be done at any cost. And for this purpose, move heaven and earth if you have to, during the initial phase. A person is anyway in the prime of youth in the initial phase of earning money, therefore there is no dearth of energy in this phase. So, make a firm resolve and endeavour relentlessly to align your mind with money. Your efforts should not cease till the time this alignment is established. If you wish to lead a magnificent life, you will have to put in at least this much effort in your youth. The maxim that wisdom and laborious work applied in one's youth alone make one flourish in old age, is not at all unfounded. So, why shy away from pouring your heart and soul into your work while you're still young?!

Well, once your mind and money are aligned, take a pause. Savour the joy that this alignment brings into your life. For, a perfect alignment of the mind and money means being able to sleep peacefully at night—in other words—scoring a victory over the tension and pressure created by money. And this triumph is a monumental accomplishment, for, you are now engaged in work that will fulfil your needs throughout your life. Quite possibly, you have now accumulated enough wealth to lead a comfortable life too. So, allow yourself to enjoy this feeling of tranquillity. Do not unnecessarily burden yourself with the pressure of earning more money. When your needs are being met, why fret over accumulating more money? I would even go so far as to say that even if you were to live your entire life in this state, there is nothing wrong with it! Because, to live without the pressure and tension caused by money is, after all, the primary objective of life. Reaching this goal is no mean feat; in fact, from this point onwards, you are free from the compulsion of pursuing money desperately. At this juncture, you will be engaging in work for the pleasure you derive out of it, and in exchange, money will flow to you naturally. This is precisely why it is crucial to attain psychological victory over the desperation for money. The one who has triumphed over the desperation for money has conquered money itself! And you must achieve this victory. In short, even if you have to sweat it out or burn the midnight oil, you must not stop until your mind is aligned with money. Ensure that the energy and fervour of youth does not wane till the time this alignment is achieved. I sincerely hope that you will not disappoint me.

Comprehend What Your Income Is Primarily Based On

Surely, everyone desires the maximum amount of money possible. Having said that, it is also certain that money is not raining down from the skies for people to catch and fill their pockets with. Neither is money growing in the soil for them to harvest and hoard in their coffers. Had that been the case, one would not have faced so many hardships regarding money. The challenge with money is that it needs to be acquired, in other words, it needs to be earned. And when you have to earn it, there must be some or the other basis for earning money—in other words—a psychological base underlying the earning of money. Surely, you have been earning for many years now, so answer this question: what is the primary basis of earning money? Since you are engaged in this activity for so long, you should ideally be aware of the basis of earning money. Unfortunately, very few people have an inkling about the primary basis of earning money. Well, haven't I reiterated time and again that the ignorance of psychology is the most unfortunate reality of this world!

Be that as it may, but the question remains: how can one expect positive outcomes when one is totally ignorant of the 'basis' of earning money? Evidently, one does not acquire money just by working hard or wishing for it. Therefore, it is crucial for a person to be fully aware of the primary basis of earning money. Grasp well that the primary basis of earning money is 'exchange, transaction or mutual engagement'. It is impossible to earn money without an exchange, transaction or mutual engagement. For, money is neither showering down from the skies nor is it sprouting from the ground. Hence, if you want to earn money, it is imperative to enter into some sort of mutual engagement or transaction. And whom does one engage or transact with? Obviously, with other people. Even if you wish to plant a tree, you will need to procure seeds from one person and manure from another. Moreover, when the tree bears fruit, you will have to sell it to someone, in other words, engage in another transaction. Extending this logic to other spheres, I need not explain how many people one needs to engage with when running an office or a factory.

Comprehend well that earning money is impossible without engaging with people. In other words, the primary basis of earning money is mutual engagement. Surprisingly, even after years of relentless toil, not many people are aware of this psychological truth. Truly, such abject ignorance of spirituality and psychology is beyond my comprehension, especially considering the fact that life cannot be enriched without these two! Well, for now, let us return to the main topic. And in that context, there is no need to explain that the more money you wish to earn, the more transactions you will need to engage in. For instance, a factory may have ten employees or even a million. Needless to say, the factory with a million employees is a bigger business, and this is because its scale of engagement is also extensive. This factory purchases raw materials from a larger number of people and also supplies finished goods to a greater number of people. The sad part is, even this simple psychological truth is often overlooked; and honestly speaking, earning money has become challenging only because of the ignorance of these small psychological truths.

Well, it is now clear that mutual engagement is the primary basis of earning money. The pursuit of higher earnings invariably requires engaging with a larger number of people. And the direct implication of both these points is that earning money is directly dependent on 'engaging with people'. Flawless engagements will be beneficial, while engagements gone wrong can prove to be detrimental. In other words, if the engagement goes awry,

"It is a **psychological truth** that every form of **desperation** compels you to **commit mistakes**

then one might even lose money instead of earning it! This also implies that an increasing number of positive and value-creating engagements increase one's income. In essence, the entire game of earning money revolves around 'mutual engagements', and surely, this matter does not require any further clarity.

Well, the unfortunate truth remains that while everyone aspires to earn money, most people are clueless about this 'psychological basis' of earning money. It is like jumping into battle without the faintest idea about how to wield a weapon! Imagine, if you neither have the foggiest idea about weapons nor how to wield them, how can you ever win a war? And now, it is perfectly clear that the sole 'weapon' for earning money is 'mutual engagement'. And if one aspires to earn money, one must have a thorough comprehension of the psychology of mutual engagement. Without it, earning money is always going to be a challenge. If I were to state this fact as a principle—the better the quality of mutual engagement, the greater will be the ease of earning money. This is a simple and clear-cut formula for earning money.

Now that we know that earning money requires engaging with people, it becomes necessary to comprehend the psychology of people with regard to money. And this psychology is absolutely clear—nobody wishes to lose money. In fact, everyone aims to earn 'money' when engaging with others. And this is an irrefutable psychological truth, with no exception whatsoever. Always bear in mind that no one is ever engaging in any transaction to incur losses. Therefore, I shall now directly delve into the key principles of mutual engagement.

i) Be Loyal to Your Organisation

There is obviously no need to spell out that when you are employed with an organisation, be it an office, factory or anything else, you have entered into a mutual engagement with it. Mutual engagement means a give-and-take or an exchange, which implies that you will seek something from the organisation, while the latter will expect something from you in return. And what will the organisation expect from you? Undoubtedly, it will seek your commitment and contribution to protect its interests. This is precisely what the management will expect from you, and obviously, the management's engagement with you will be based on this very premise. Indeed, no organisation will appoint a person to incur losses. And if you wish to make progress, you will have to respect this basis of mutual engagement. If your salary is one lakh rupees, the management will definitely expect a benefit worth three to five lakh rupees from you. On your part, you too will have to ensure the same; otherwise, the mutual engagement between you and the management will see a quick end.

Incidentally, the most beautiful principle about mutual engagement was conveyed by Jesus Christ. And if you genuinely want smooth and effortless earnings, always keep in mind this spiritual principle imparted by Christ. While outlining this principle, Christ had stated, "In the welfare of others lies your own." And indeed, based on this principle, when you are engaged in work, you must wholeheartedly focus only on the organisation's interests. And towards that end, pour your heart and soul into your efforts. For, your progress within the organisation will be directly linked to the extent of your contribution benefitting the organisation. Irrespective of the kind of management, the gains accrued from their employees is the sole criterion of their engagement with them. Hence, never think on the lines of "I'm only concerned with my salary." Refrain from shirking work or being dishonest in your work; otherwise, you run the risk of a decreased remuneration and may even be terminated from the job.

Essentially, adhere to the 'spiritual principles of mutual engagement' given by Christ and you will make rapid progress. Having said this, no principle is ever one-sided, and the principle of mutual engagement definitely applies to the management as well. They too must take good care of their employees and colleagues, and ensure that the remuneration given to their employees is in accordance with their merits. The management must partake in the joys of their employees and stand by them in their difficult times as well. If they fail to do this, they might end up losing competent employees. This can also spark a revolt within the organisation and even culminate in a lockdown of the organisation. To sum it up, in order to acquire an impressive amount of money, both the management and the employees must faithfully abide by Christ's prescribed principles of mutual engagement. Needless to say, those who defy these principles will fall behind in life.

ii) Engage in Deals Keeping Everyone's Interests in Mind

Indubitably, every person interacts or engages with others keeping their own interest in mind. And this is a natural psychological principle of engagement. Therefore, whenever you engage in any deal or interaction, prioritise the benefit of all parties involved. At this point, I would like to reiterate that you must never disregard Christ's spiritual principles of mutual engagement, be it in a major business deal or everyday transactions. You must always pay attention to the benefit of the other person to a reasonable extent. I am not suggesting that you are obligated to ensure undue or impractical benefits for others, but you must certainly be mindful that a reasonable benefit accrues to them. If ten individuals are part of a deal, it is imperative to consider the interests of all ten. The very essence of a deal is that it should be a 'win-win situation'. If even one party is incurring a loss, it can never be deemed a good 'deal'. Comprehend clearly that a deal which does not ensure everyone's benefit is not a deal at all. For, surely, even the party that is incurring losses is also engaging in the deal with the hope to gain something from it. But if the party incurs losses, they will definitely not keep quiet about it, and as a result, the deal will be needlessly marred by disputes. So, why get embroiled in such complications? A deal is that which benefits all the involved parties. And when you consistently engage in such deals with great care and caution, you will acquire an enviable reputation for engaging in fair deals. The primary principle of engaging in a deal is—the person you deal with once should deal with you repeatedly. More importantly, he should return with ten others in tow. For, it is only then that you will make progress. Focussing only on one's own benefit while remaining totally unconcerned with that of others goes against the principles of mutual engagement. And those who violate the principles of mutual engagement will, sooner or later, face the closure of their business.

Frankly speaking, most people are not abiding by this principle of mutual engagement, as they are invariably looking for short-term gains. And surprisingly, such people usually believe themselves to be smarter than others. But let me state clearly that they are actually foolish, because such individuals consider selfishness and short-term gains as the ladder to progress. They may be engaging in deals with ten people currently, but in the near future, they will be hard-pressed to find even two people willing to deal with them. On the other hand, those who are concerned about everyone's benefit will always have a multitude of people queuing up to engage in deals with them. It goes without saying that in life, progress is contingent upon deals, that is, mutual engagements and transactions. In fact, the more deals you strike, the greater will be your progress. And you will be able to strike more deals only when they are being conducted smoothly and flawlessly. Moreover, a deal will be conducted smoothly only when you adhere to the principles of mutual engagement provided by Christ, that is, when everyone's interests are being safeguarded. I have provided you a hint and you are no doubt intelligent. Therefore, I hope you will soon bring about the necessary changes in your behaviour and swiftly embark on the path of progress.

iii) Interactions Must Be Smooth

Everyone engages in deals and transactions to earn money and there are no two ways about it. However, in addition to earning money, everyone also wants their deals to be executed smoothly, without a hitch. No one welcomes a deal that creates stress; and at the very least, no one wishes to deal again with a person who causes the stress. And this is a significant loss, because if the number of deals decreases, engagements and transactions will come to a standstill, in which case how will you make progress? Therefore, if you wish to make progress, you must execute every deal seamlessly. Of course, you must approach every deal with due deliberation, but once you strike a deal, ensure that it is executed flawlessly. Even if the deal falls flat, do not shy away from it. Profits and losses are an integral part of every deal, but what truly matters is the seamless execution of every deal you have entered into. Anyone who strikes a deal with you even once should feel relaxed about it. He should not undergo stress, nor should he harbour any grievance about the deal he has entered into. Etch it in your mind that the greater the number of deals you execute seamlessly, the greater will be the number of people satisfied with you. And it is only then that they will continue to deal with you repeatedly. Besides, they will also refer you to others, which will naturally ensure your progress. For, 'mutual engagement' is the very foundation of earning money. The greater the magnitude and number of deals one engages in, the greater will be one's progress. And I need not re-emphasise that only those who execute their deals smoothly will be able to engage in more deals.

This essentially means that if engaging in deals with you is resulting in any kind of stress or loss, then no one will deal with you ever again. In such a scenario, forget about making progress, your business itself could face closure. If you are employed, your job may be placed at a risk if the management receives recurring complaints about you. The laws applicable for a job and business do not differ much from each other. Progress in both these areas will be assured only for those who execute their transactions smoothly, who are dependable and steadfast in their commitment, and who evoke a desire in others to deal with them repeatedly.

The crux of the matter is, merely desiring progress will not make it happen. If you truly wish to progress, you must learn to respect the 'spiritual principles of mutual engagement' in every deal. When even some of the greatest stars of Hollywood and Bollywood have fallen from grace due to their lack of punctuality and concern for the producer's gains and losses, of what consequence are you? The spiritual principle of mutual engagement does not discriminate on the basis of one's status; it ruthlessly topples anyone who so much as even dares to violate it. It does not differentiate between a job and a business either. Therefore, it is imperative that every person engaged in a deal with you must be satisfied under all circumstances. Being an intelligent person, you must have surely grasped the hint I have given you.

iv) Close Deals Quickly

It is absolutely clear that the greater the number and magnitude of deals you execute, the greater will be your progress. And when is it possible to execute more and more deals? It is only possible when you are closing deals quickly. Let's suppose the management has assigned you a task and you manage to complete it in a month. But someone else executes the same task in just ten days, which means that by the time you conclude one deal, the other individual would have already concluded three. Going by the principles of mutual engagement, it is clear that the management seeks profit, so tell me, in the example stated here, who is securing greater gains for the management? Undoubtedly, it is the person who has concluded three deals. So, who amongst the two has a greater chance of making progress? Obviously, it is the one who has concluded three deals. The lesson worth learning from the above-stated example is that 'perfection and speed' are essential for every deal. For, only then will you be able to conclude a greater number of deals, and only then will you make progress.

The same principle applies to business deals, for, even in the case of such deals, the criteria to successfully conclude a greater number of deals remains the same—speed and perfection. Because, in order to make progress, one has to execute the maximum number of deals possible. And needless to say, both speed and perfection are key to accomplishing this goal. Therefore, if you want to make progress, focus on speed and perfection. As soon as you strike a deal, focus on closing it as quickly as possible with perfection. Money is earned only upon closing a deal, not by merely striking one. The greater the number of deals concluded smoothly with perfection, the greater will be your progress.

So, while it is true that shirking work will yield nothing, merely working laboriously will not lead to a significant outcome either. An efficacious outcome can be expected solely on the basis of concluding the maximum number of deals with perfection. Therefore, endeavour relentlessly to enhance your 'speed and perfection' on a daily basis. This is the only task you need to focus on. Merely wishing, demanding or scrambling around will not yield anything. Therefore, start working immediately in the direction indicated here. Rest assured, with every enhancement in your speed and perfection, your progress will become increasingly certain.

Indeed, this point needs to be emphasised strongly because most people are ignorant of the true psychology of earning money. Good education, talent, hard work and so on are generally given top priority, but no one notices that even highly talented people are struggling simply because they are totally unaware of the psychology of mutual engagement. But progress is directly linked to exchanges that create excellent value. Whether it is a job or a business, speed and perfection hold utmost significance when it comes to making deals. After striking a deal, leaving the other party in the lurch by resorting to delaying tactics, making excuses, manipulating, distorting facts, constantly changing the deal's concluding dates, and so on and so forth are some of the biggest impediments on the path of progress. And it is due to these tendencies that extremely talented people lag behind in the race of life, despite having the potential for success. Therefore, be cautious if you too possess any of these habits. For, all such behavioural patterns go against the principles of mutual engagement. This kind of conduct will not be tolerated whether you are engaged in a job, business or even freelance work. In short, you must refrain from becoming your own enemy. Adhere to the principles of mutual engagement under all circumstances, else you won't even realise how callously you will be tossed away in the race of life.

v) A Rogue Will Always Remain A Rogue

Regardless of the kind of deal you engage in, the other party must certainly benefit from it. Otherwise, there are bound to arise not one but a multitude of complications. Disruptions like disputes and delays in receiving payments occur only when the other party is incurring a loss. A deal is considered to have concluded smoothly only when the other party benefits from it. Tricks such as deceiving or fooling someone do not work for too long. Now, the main point is, although the other party must definitely benefit from the deal, you should certainly gain from it too. You should not cause detriment to others, but you must certainly receive what you rightfully deserve. And you have to protect your own interests, for, that is the principle of mutual engagement. Hence, you will have to always ensure your own benefit too. The principle of mutual engagement states that everyone should benefit, and of course, you too are included in 'everyone'. And towards that end, it is imperative to take certain precautions.

In short, you must earn money and ensure your progress, but not by becoming blind to everything else in the process. Desperation should not lead you to disregard the basic principles. Everyone is aware that dealing with rogues and unprofessional and dishonest people only leads to losses. However, despite this awareness, people who are desperate to earn money still engage in deals with them; and sooner or later, they find themselves trapped. However, you must never commit this error. You should not wait for your turn to be cheated. You must realise that a rogue will always remain a 'rogue'. Do not nurse the false belief that just because a person has cheated someone else, it does not concern you in any way. The realisation that he is a cheater should be enough to raise your guard. Thereafter, you must not entertain the thought that at least he has not deceived you yet. You must certainly not grant him the opportunity to rob you. Someone who can cheat one person can do so with others too. Therefore, as soon as you identify the cheaters, delete them from the list of people you want to engage in deals with. You should never engage in any kind of deal with rogues; this is a straightforward principle of mutual engagement. For, dealing with cheaters will very likely prove costly for you. Indeed, I fail to comprehend how desperate a person can be that he breaches the very principles of mutual engagement! I have already explained that both greed and desperation inevitably spell doom. Money must be earned, but not by breaching the basic principles. It is

> “**Money** is **loyal** only if you **procure joys** in exchange for it

imperative to engage in multiple deals in order to earn money, but you must never grant rogues the opportunity to rob you of your hard-earned money. If you deal with such people, you will only end up worse off. And I have anyway been saying that you too are engaging in deals only to earn money, so you are the one who must safeguard your interests. And towards that end, you must never engage in deals with cheaters and rogues.

Another point worth grasping in this context is that if engaging in deals with certain people makes you anxious, ensure that you steer clear of them too. Earning money is a must, but one should not harbour stress unnecessarily. Why bother engaging in deals with those who cannot execute them smoothly? This will only cause you undue stress, which will further lead you to make more erroneous decisions. In short, you must widen the sphere of your interactions in order to make progress, but only with thorough professionals while your own conduct in dealing should also embody integrity and fairness; this is the simple and straightforward method to earn money. A more detailed explanation than this is surely not necessary for intelligent people like you.

(vi) Talent is Essential to Venture into Any Field

Undoubtedly, everyone wishes to earn money, but no one wants to pay heed to its psychology. But how on earth can you expect this to work? If you wish to earn money, you will have to respect the psychology of money. Otherwise, all the hard work you put in to earn money will yield no results. And this is precisely what the majority of people are experiencing. Why don't you comprehend the simple fact that you have to put in eight to ten hours of work on a daily basis? And when you are engaged in work, it should obviously yield optimum results. You must never be foolish enough to end up in a situation where you work hard but see no positive results. Therefore, it is better to thoroughly grasp the psychology of money before embarking on a career. If you have already commenced your career, begin to implement the understanding of money's psychology in your life from today itself. For, it is only then that your hard work will yield fruitful results. This is precisely why I am placing such strong emphasis on you grasping the psychology of money.

Well, let me now reveal another aspect of money's psychology, and that is, money is subservient to talent. It, therefore, becomes imperative that you venture only into a line of work which is aligned with your talent and knowledge. This point deserves special attention because most people tend to overlook the significance of this aspect of money's psychology. Rushing headlong into the pursuit of money just because you are old enough to earn money is not the right approach. Blindly venturing into any field only because it is necessary to earn is ill-advised. Similarly, jumping headlong into a field based on others' advice, hearsay or by emulating others will also lead to trouble. For, money respects 'talent' alone!

Therefore, grasp well without any confusion that earning money requires advance preparation. Plunging into a random line of work to try your hand at it without preparing yourself adequately is sheer foolishness. Why don't you comprehend that earning money is based on mutual engagement, and verily, decision-making and communication are integral aspects of such an engagement! This being the case, if you yourself lack knowledge about something, how will you make informed decisions and communicate effectively? If you fail to grasp even this simple logic, how will you ever make progress? It is no wonder then that most people continue to toil hard without any fruitful results, and this simply cannot be tolerated. I have also stated earlier that money is earned through mutual engagement and the principles of mutual engagement cannot be breached. To reiterate, the principle of mutual engagement states that only a seamless interaction yields positive outcomes. And if you wish to see a thriving and flourishing world, you will have to advocate this principle of mutual engagement to as many people as possible.

At present, the key point is, you should venture only into a field where your talent lies. And talent certainly doesn't grow on trees for you to pluck it! Irrespective of the field you are talented in, you need to prepare in advance in order to develop the talent. Even if you possess innate talent, you will still need to hone it. For instance, even if one is blessed with a melodious voice, efforts need to be made to enhance and nurture it. Therefore, the first step, in all situations, is to cultivate and nurture your talent, while the second step is to dive headlong into earning money. Those who take the plunge without any preparation inevitably trip and fall flat on their face. For, money respects talent alone and this is verily its psychology. Wishful thinking on your part will not alter money's psychology. The same principle applies to those who switch their field of work, for, even in this case, one needs to prepare in advance to develop one's talent. Before venturing into a new field, it is crucial to first acquire basic knowledge about it. At the very least, your knowledge of the field should be enough for you to make informed decisions and communicate effectively. This is necessary because earning money is directly contingent upon seamless interactions, and in order to execute smooth deals, it is crucial to make sound decisions and engage in proper communication. And it is impossible to do this without possessing the requisite knowledge of the domain. Bear in mind, taking a plunge into unfamiliar territory with no preparation will turn out to be a futile exercise. Therefore, whether you wish to embark on a new career or are considering changing your line of work itself, it is not beneficial to undertake such endeavours without developing your talent in the chosen field.

In essence, it is the 'master of a domain' who always stands to gain the most. For, he can conduct all kinds of dealings with utmost proficiency. Just think about the magnitude of decisions and communication required to accomplish a task—without these, you cannot conclude even a single deal. And one need not explain how easy it is for a master to navigate all of this. Therefore, instead of showing haste in commencing any task, kindly pay close attention to comprehending the intricacies of that task. For, money recognises neither your compulsions nor the fanciful flights of your mind. It recognises your talent alone. Your income recognises only seamless dealings. Progress salutes only the 'master' of a domain. Similarly, deals do not recognise your dreams or your mind's flights of fancy. They recognise only your decision-making and communication skills. Even otherwise, half-baked knowledge and so-called talent always prove to be dangerous. And even more dangerous is the common misconception that one is talented! Pay special attention to this last point, for, many people lack talent and yet consider themselves masters in their respective fields. I caution you that the fate of such people is the worst.

In short, don't ever invest in any business or choose a job based on half-baked knowledge. If you wish to earn a substantial amount of money, ensure thorough preparation before starting any venture. This preparation in itself is the true education, more significant than any other form of learning. Therefore, before investing in any business, it would be wise to gain practical experience by first taking up employment in that field. Indeed, you must first grasp the intricacies of that business. If you hastily rush into a business, you will never be able to conduct seamless deals. On the contrary, this will drive money away from you. I am stating this because countless people face financial ruin every other day by starting a business based solely on hearsay and half-baked information. Therefore, kindly do not breach the fundamental principle of mutual engagement. Ensure that the field you choose and the amount of work you put in allow you to conclude deals seamlessly. Otherwise, you are bound to incur losses. In fact, it is far better to derive enjoyment from such money rather than squander it by incurring losses.

In essence, there are only two conventional methods to earn money: take up employment or start your own business. The key point is, whether you choose to be employed or take up a business, the psychology of money applies to both. Money will only respect talent and salute the master alone. So, possessing innate talent in the line of work you wish to build a career in is imperative. Seen from this perspective, no other training in the world is as useful as the one that helps develop one's talent. And talent is not something that can be developed overnight. Agreed, earning becomes a compulsion for almost everyone after a certain age; and even if it is not a compulsion, it is verily the norm of life. Moreover, earning money is not a cakewalk—in other words, one cannot earn money by simply wishing to earn. You need to first select a field in which you wish to work. And the sooner you select that field, the better it is for you, because after choosing the field of work, you need to invest time to develop your talent in that field. However, it is at this juncture that people are often confounded. Even after having passed their prime, they remain confused about their field of work. In fact, some people are so intelligent that they keep contemplating about venturing into ever-new domains! In a similar vein, some people find themselves confused about whether they want to take up a job or venture into a business. Well, these aren't commendable traits for sure! When it comes to your line of work, it must be selected promptly and decisively. Likewise, when it comes to determining whether to pursue employment or start a business, one must arrive at a decision as soon as possible. For, how will you know what skill to develop if you haven't decided on anything? And if you plunge into a venture without possessing the skill for it, you will end up falling flat on your face. Surely, in these modern times, these are not matters that require reiteration.

In essence, before embarking on any endeavour to earn money, it is essential to prepare in advance. And this preparation can very well take three to five years. If one aspires to pursue a career as a doctor, engineer or IPS officer, the preparation may take longer. Whatever be the goal, grasp well that whether it is a job or a business, nothing significant can be accomplished without preparation. For, without talent, money will not accord you respect. Therefore, if you wish to begin earning once you reach the age of twenty, it is imperative to decisively choose your profession by the time you are fifteen. Moreover, investing these five years in

"**Money** has woven such an **illusion** that despite **working hard** and **possessing talent,** one is **unable** to **attract** it easily

honing your talent in your chosen field is also crucial. In short, your career should necessarily commence on the basis of talent, for, only then will you achieve the desired progress. And kindly refrain from trying to change this principle. If you genuinely desire progress, bring about the required changes within yourself.

It is because most people plunge into their chosen line of work without any preparation that they end up toiling ceaselessly. So, if you wish to ensure your progress, become a master first and then take the leap towards earning money. Instead of trying to be a jack-of-all-trades, endeavour to be a 'master of one', for, this is the era of 'masters'. Comprehend well, it is only a master who can conduct deals and engagements seamlessly; and money fully abides by the psychology of mutual engagement. Now, since we are on the subject, comprehend one more thing—in the present age, switching professions frequently is not that easy. For, becoming a master in any line of work takes three to five years. I'm sure you must have grasped what I'm hinting at. In fact, you must be knowing several people who keep changing the signboard of their shop frequently. If you still haven't grasped this point, pay close attention to the consequences such people are facing. Well, after this explanation, I hope you will commence your career with 'advance preparation' and that too in such a spectacular manner that progress will be compelled to bow at your feet.

Essentially, I am only reiterating the truth that there is no other way to achieve significant progress than this. Therefore, etch it in your mind that in the present era, money salutes the 'master' alone. Regardless of the field of work a master operates in, money keeps following him, never leaving his side. So, if you truly desire progress, never forget that money loves masters. Also, observe that it is only the masters who are ruling the roost.

Moreover, note that those who are kick-starting their professions with inadequate preparation are falling flat on their faces on a daily basis. This is because there is no match to the smoothness and efficacy with which a master engages with others. Why don't you comprehend that in this day and age, everyone is in a tearing hurry?! Everyone wants to earn money as quickly as possible. And to earn quickly, it is imperative that deals are concluded promptly, and that too, with smoothness and perfection, without any stress or tension. And this is only possible when dealing with a master. This is the very reason why, when a master demands ten times the money from the market, everyone is more than willing to pay his price. A heart surgery is performed by both, a doctor possessing average skills as well as a specialist who is the master in his field. An average lawyer fights a case and so does a master in the field of law. And everyone is aware of the fees the masters charge for their services! This is precisely why masters, irrespective of their field, are ruling the roost. Be it doctors, engineers, architects, artists, scientists or entrepreneurs, whoever is a master in his line of work is undoubtedly at the top. Therefore, first focus on becoming a master in your field. Comprehend well that if a master is employed even by a company, he receives the same respect as the boss of the company.

The crux of the matter is simple: to become a 'master' in a specific field should be the primary goal of your life. Even if you are deprived of the opportunity to become a master and are compelled to start your career under some compulsion, remain focussed on the goal of eventually attaining mastery in that field of work. You may be working as an accountant in a firm, but keep honing your skills in maintaining accounts, as this will ensure your continued progress. Grasp the fact that your current job as an accountant is nothing but an opportunity to become a master

“**Money** respects **‘talent’** alone

in your field. Hence, consider a job too as a business and treat it like one. After all, employment is a kind of business too. Whatever work you are engaged in can be compared to wares sold in your personal shop. All you have to do is continue performing every task wholeheartedly. Whenever an opportunity presents itself, continue to enhance your knowledge about your work while progressively honing your skills. Keep doing this and one day, you will inevitably become the master in that field of work. And that day, your 'shop'—which is your work—will hold tremendous value, because your ever-improving grip on your work will continue to enhance your skills of mutual engagement, and you will make progress in proportion to that. Remember, money can do everything but it can never disrespect the 'principles of mutual engagement' stated by Christ. Those who abide by the principles of mutual engagement will surely earn respect from money sooner or later. All in all, do not treat your work as just work; instead, consider it a game. And just as you keep striving to notch up higher and higher scores in a game, remain ever eager to acquire new learnings and hone your skills in your line of work. Follow this path and you will accomplish your goal.

Finally, let me state one more point: only a person for whom work is not a burden can become a master. For, a person who finds his work burdensome will never learn anything new in his line of work. Also, grasp another thing—let’s suppose you aspire to build a career in the field of dance and you are even training for it. However, I urge you to first become a master in the field of dance and only then embark on a career in that profession. A delay of one to two years is better than taking the plunge with insufficient groundwork. To state an analogy, trying to deliver a baby prematurely will only result in a child with a weak constitution. Of course, if starting a career is a compulsion, then that's a different matter altogether. But even then, keep striving to become a master in the field of your interest along with pursuing your career.

The most significant point in this discussion is, the sooner you comprehend your life and its compulsions, the better off you will be. For, without earning money, sustaining oneself is impossible. To earn money, one has to work in a specific field. And your work will yield the best outcome only when you possess the talent in that field. Developing talent is bound to take time; therefore, it is imperative to promptly gain clarity about the profession you wish to pursue and the exact time to commence your career. Pay heed to these minute details and they will surely ease the process of earning money. I am confident that you will respect the 'psychology of money and mutual engagement' and thereby make great strides in life.

Everyone aspires to make progress and they most certainly should. And I need not reiterate that there exists only one basis for progress and that is consistently expanding the scope of your deals and engagements. Progress is impossible without widening the sphere of mutual engagements. It is an established principle that as a person progresses, their deals and mutual engagements burgeon as well. Therefore, if you want to make progress, you will have to continuously expand your mutual engagements too. This is the only way to make progress; the reason being, if you want to progress in business, setting up new departments as well as increasing your engagement with new people will become necessary. Of course, these are all points that we have assimilated already, but the crucial point you must comprehend next is—who are the kind of people that get the opportunities to make progress? In this context, grasp clearly that the opportunity to progress falls into the lap of only those who are conducting their deals seamlessly, whether in a job or a business.

In this regard, there are two points worth comprehending. First, if you desire progress, you will have to expand your sphere of engagements. There is no alternative to progress apart from this. Second, only those individuals will receive the opportunity to expand the sphere of engagements whose present engagements are smooth. Therefore, if you desire progress, ensure that your current engagements are seamless. Those who engage in flawed deals should not even think about progress. This is a straightforward hint I have provided. You can think about progress at a later juncture, but you must first focus on ensuring that your current engagements are conducted seamlessly. These points may seem trivial, but the outcomes they yield are bound to be spectacular, for, these are established principles of mutual

Anyone who has set out to earn is essentially selling himself as a 'product'

engagement. Hence, kindly treat every point mentioned here with utmost gravity.

Well, let us now turn our attention to the people whose current engagements are seamless. Such individuals will undoubtedly receive opportunities to make progress, and it is also certain that their growth and advancement will be based on increasing the number of new engagements. I'm sure all these points are crystal clear and you have grasped them thoroughly as well. But at this juncture, let me caution you that even if the opportunity for progress is available to you, do not ever become blinded by the all-consuming desire for advancement. Be mindful that advancement will require new engagements, and initiating new engagements means starting afresh. And if you are not capable of handling these new engagements, refrain from plunging into them in haste. For, those who, in their greed for progress, leap into such engagements without the required competence to execute those engagements, make a mess and end up in a terrible predicament. This is because, in the absence of capability, the engagement loses the quality of seamlessness; and the moment this quality is lost, losses become inevitable.

I am explaining a crucial point here, so assimilate it well. A human being's foremost priority should always be to stand firmly wherever he is at present, and only then should he contemplate forging ahead. Hence, your primary focus should only be on executing your current engagements seamlessly. Until all current engagements are executed efficaciously, one must not even entertain the thought of making progress. Otherwise, you might end up compromising your current position too. Interestingly, the individuals whose current engagements are being executed seamlessly do not even need to nurse the desire of making progress. This is a significant hint I have provided; if you are wise enough, you will be able to gauge the futility of desire and ambition from this hint itself. The people whose current engagements are executed seamlessly will find progress knocking on their door of its own accord. For, a person whose present engagements are being executed seamlessly will invariably find himself being sought-after by other people too for the purpose of engaging in deals and engagements. And burgeoning deals are the sole measure of progress, be it of any kind. In such a scenario, why would someone who is executing his engagements seamlessly hanker after progress?

To sum it up, those who are managing their present engagements seamlessly will undoubtedly encounter opportunities for progress. However, they too must be mindful not to jump blindly into the pursuit of progress. They ought to remember that to achieve progress, they will have to engage in new deals. To give you an analogy, a river grows and expands only when it begins to engage with ever-new stretches of land. The sun too will have to cast its rays towards newer horizons in a quest to expand. I always state the ultimate principle and speak only of the paramount truth; that is why I explain matters solely with the support of the supreme principles of Nature. In any case, it is impossible to arrive at any solution without taking recourse to Nature's ultimate principles. Although this book is not about the Laws of Nature, if you adopt even a few principles I am sharing here, you will find your whole life transformed. For, principles are immutable, so wherever you apply them, they will continue to yield results automatically. You can be certain that if you adhere to the boundaries set by principles, you will never go wrong. Indeed, all the mishaps in life are occurring only because of disregarding principles.

Well, the key point is, the individuals whose current engagements are being executed seamlessly will automatically find opportunities to progress. Therefore, instead of harbouring desires or nursing ambitions, first focus on executing all ongoing deals smoothly. Your primary focus should not be on anything else apart from this. The day all your current deals begin to be executed seamlessly, opportunities for further progress will automatically present themselves to you. And when those opportunities arise, do not forget that to make progress, you will have to expand the scope of your engagements. This applies not just to you—even Nature's creations such as rivers and the sun have to expand their sphere of engagement in order to progress. Therefore, observe caution at this point. If you become excessively greedy or ambitious, you might fall into trouble at this juncture. Hence, comprehend the truth that new development requires initiating new engagements, so refrain from plunging into any venture blinded by the desire for progress. Before taking any step

> "The **thought** that '**money** is **scarce**' is less of your own and more of a **notion planted** by **money**

towards new advancement, first carefully assess whether you possess the ability to conclude new deals and engagements seamlessly. Always remember, money will never alter its principle of 'respecting talent' just because you have received an opportunity for progress. Therefore, you must surely make progress and that too, phenomenal progress, but with every milestone you achieve, continue to honour the principles of mutual engagement. Never disregard the principles of engagement, else your situation could do a volte-face. In short, if you take any step towards development without the ability to seamlessly execute your new engagements, you will only invite the possibility of your plans backfiring. It is only out of care and concern for you that I am cautioning you about this matter.

Grasp with absolute clarity that your income is directly related to the principles of mutual engagement, and the very essence of a principle is—the moment you breach it, you will be caught in a bind. Therefore, if you desire progress, adopt 'the principle of mutual engagement' as the core mantra for all your work. And the principle of mutual engagement states that every deal and engagement should be managed seamlessly; and the seamless execution of deals and engagements requires 'talent'. So, even if an opportunity for progress presents itself, first carefully assess your talent. Proceed forward only when you are sure that you possess the ability to manage new deals seamlessly. Otherwise, focus on enhancing your abilities first and then think about making progress. This single measure on your part will ensure that going forward, nothing will stop you. This is because, you have decided that wherever you stand, you will stand firmly.

The bottom-line is, with every expansion in business, you must also focus on enhancing your 'capabilities'. For, every growing business definitely requires new technical, financial, legal and market-related knowledge. And enhancing your capabilities is imperative to acquire knowledge in all these areas. Therefore, first develop those skills and then take the leap. Now, this is all about regular people dealing with regular circumstances. However, many people are sharp-minded and such individuals do not need to wait endlessly. For, it is also true that if you want to expand your business at a rapid pace, you cannot master every aspect at the same speed with which your business is growing. In such a scenario, it is not necessary for you to be a master of everything. In other words, if you are exceptionally sharp, you need not wait to become a master every time you wish to climb the next rung of progress. For, the key is to honour the principles of mutual engagement. Your target should be to ensure that even the new deals are conducted seamlessly. And towards that end, instead of becoming a master in several fields yourself, you can collaborate with masters in their fields, ranging from technical, financial to legal. But even then, you must never forget that the business is yours, and it is your money which is at stake. Here, grasp clearly that I am not in any way discouraging you from collaborating with experts nor am I urging you to put the brakes on your progress. All I wish to state is that while you should definitely collaborate with experts, you must refrain from becoming totally dependent on them. Therefore, even if you do not possess complete knowledge, having at least the basic knowledge of everything is absolutely essential. In a nutshell, those who possess the 'ability to quickly acquire basic knowledge' can progress rapidly, even without becoming the masters of every domain.

All I wish to say is, it would certainly please me if you make great strides and become the most successful person in the world. However, in pursuit of this, if you plummet from the sky to the ground, we will both be equally disappointed. This is the only reason I am pointing out the areas where you need to observe caution. So, if you are truly fast and sharp, then waiting each time to become a master in order to make further progress is inessential for you. You can certainly ensure your progress by collaborating with experts. All I am trying to caution you is that while collaborating with experts, you must never forget that it is your life and your business that will be put at risk. Hence, before every new phase of expansion, you must acquire adequate basic knowledge to arrive at the 'right decision' after receiving the expert's advice. Indeed, it is imperative for those desirous of rapid progress to possess at least this ability. For, experts may offer suggestions, but it is you who must take the final decision. The day experts begin to take decisions, you can be certain that the countdown to your doom has begun. And in order to make informed decisions, possessing basic knowledge is vital. Adopt these principles, and thereafter, irrespective of the growth your business witnesses or the extent of progress you achieve, you will never go wrong.

In essence, you must surely make progress, and that too, by leaps and bounds, but staying within the confines of the principles of mutual engagement. And what do the principles of mutual engagement state—a consistent execution of seamless deals. And this is only possible when you have absolute command over all your engagements. And a complete control over your engagements is possible only when you possess the basic knowledge regarding the deals you engage in. In a nutshell, aspire for progress unreservedly, but stay within the confines of your capabilities. Do not engage in expansion beyond the sphere of your capabilities. Surpass successful icons such as Bill Gates; that you definitely must. However, bear in mind that it is impossible to achieve this without honing your capabilities. Hence, continue to enhance your skills and keep making progress. Those who engage in adventures without enhancing their capabilities stumble and fall flat on their face, and I certainly do not wish for you to plummet from the sky to the ground. So, if you too want to avoid this situation, then pay heed to every warning issued by me with all due seriousness.

Whether you are an employee or an entrepreneur, your sole objective is to earn 'money'. And, needless to say, the onus is on you to earn this money. And who are you? To be honest, all the people who venture out to earn money are a 'product' in themselves. Just like salt, rice, sofa, table and cars are products, the human being is also a product in himself. And you are well aware that each product in the market comes with a price tag. Food grains, furniture and vehicles all have their individual price in the market, determined solely on the basis of their utility. And I need not underline the fact that the greater the utility of the product, the more expensive it will be. And as I have mentioned earlier, since every person is a product, the money market assigns a distinct price to each individual as well. That is precisely why every individual's earning varies, in other words, there is no uniformity in income. Everyone is engaged in eight to ten hours of work daily, yet there is a yawning gap between the incomes of every individual.

Have you ever wondered why this is so? When everyone is working for eight to ten hours daily, why does such a disparity exist between their incomes? Well, this is because every person in this world is a product. Comprehend clearly that anyone who has set out to earn is essentially selling himself. The language I have used here may sound harsh and inappropriate, but this is the undeniable truth. In the money market, everyone is invariably selling themselves for eight to ten hours. In this time span, they follow the wishes of the one who remunerates them. Whether it is a man of wealth or a labourer, there are no exceptions to this reality. This is precisely the course of action for an illiterate labourer from a village and even the wealthiest person in the world. The individual paying the remuneration is the only one who calls the shots and decides the tasks to be accomplished during those eight to ten hours by the person who has set out to earn the remuneration. Therefore, you must never harbour any confusion about the fact that you are, indeed, a product.

Now that it has been established that you are a product, naturally, all the laws pertaining to a product apply to you. That being the case, tell me, which products sell at higher prices? Undoubtedly, the ones that are useful, well-marketed, rare and belonging to top brands. These are the very products that command a good price in the market. Ideally, this hint should suffice for you to grasp the crux of the matter. Nevertheless, let me elaborate. And, in this context, I'm sure it is clear to you that you are a product, and in order to earn money, you have set out to sell yourself in the market for eight to ten hours. And in this duration of eight to ten hours, the price that the money market sets for you will verily be your income. Therefore, your only duty is to continuously refine yourself as much as possible. The more you refine yourself, the more you will find your value increasing in the market. This is a simple and straightforward principle.

Actually, these are simple facts that should be crystal clear to anyone who

> **'Perfection** and **speed'** are key to a **successful deal**, for only then will you be able to close **more deals** and make **great strides**

has set out to earn money. However, the problem is, although everyone aspires to earn the maximum amount of money possible, the knowledge of the psychology of money eludes them. That is why people set out to sell the product—in other words—themselves in the market without adequately preparing, refining and perfecting themselves. Without enhancing and refining the 'product', they simply launch themselves in the market. Imagine if someone were to introduce a car in the market without brakes, accelerator and a trunk—what would happen? Naturally, the car will not sell, and even in the remote possibility that it does, it will be promptly returned to the seller. This is precisely what is transpiring all around. All the products are heading out in the morning to earn, only to return almost empty-handed by evening.

In short, grasp clearly that you are a product and have entered the money market to sell yourself. And your goal is clear—to sell your product at the best possible price. However, merely thinking and desiring on your part will not fetch the product a high price. If you wish to sell the product at a reasonably high price, you will have to focus on the quality of your product. You will have to perfect the product; and the product I am talking about is you. At this point, let me also make it clear that refinement or enhancement doesn't mean dressing up, grooming or applying makeup. It is especially important to make this clear to all the ladies! Well, jokes apart, let us return to the main point. And the key point is, the higher the price you wish to fetch for your eight to ten hours of work, the more you will have to refine yourself. There is no other strategy to fetch yourself a higher income from those eight to ten hours of work than this.

Now, the question arises, how does one refine oneself? So, first try to hone your skills as optimally as possible in the field or domain that you want to work in. Additionally, learn a variety of tasks related to your chosen field. Most importantly, never forget that irrespective of the kind of work you are engaged in, seamless engagement and clarity in communication are crucial for undertaking every task. In the absence of these two, no matter how much you refine yourself, it will fail to yield an efficacious outcome. As I have mentioned before, you are a product, and in the market, only a useful product fetches a relatively higher price. And, in this context, comprehend clearly that a product is considered useful only when it possesses talent, engages seamlessly in its dealings, and communicates with clarity. A lack of even one of these qualities can very well diminish the value of the product.

In essence, you are a product and you will command a higher price for yourself only when you prove your utility in the money market. And utility cannot be proved without refining oneself. It is worth noting that the market is teeming with discerning experts, one better than the other. So, if you are not able to sell yourself in the market, then the flaw invariably lies within you. Otherwise, well-refined products are purchased overnight at premium prices. Whether they are engaged in a job or a business, people do make progress overnight. Therefore, if the product is not fetching the right price, then surely the defect lies in the product itself. Do not point fingers at the experts in the market. Indeed, there exist countless people who keep lamenting that they possess talent but the world does not value them. However, that is not true. The market is teeming with experts who can evaluate absolutely everything under the sun. Hence, instead of nursing such absurd notions, it is far better to focus on refining the product. Never forget that the more useful you make the product, the higher the price it will continue to fetch in the market. This is verily the norm of conducting deals in the money market. And I have already elaborated upon the various ways to

> Not only does **money** possess **hands** and **feet** but also a **brain** of its own

make the product, that is, yourself, more valuable.

Additionally, do remember to focus on a few other aspects. In the present era, even the best product requires marketing—not false or manipulated marketing tactics—but genuine and professional marketing. In other words, you must learn to market yourself professionally. In the case of business, it is your customers, and if it is employment, then it is the management, but in either case, you must master the art of showcasing your true utility to them. Quite often, even the products that are exceptional in all respects fail to make a mark due to ineffective marketing. But you must ensure that you do not allow this to happen to you.

Alright, let us comprehend one final point regarding this subject. It is clear to everyone that those desirous of progress must respect all the principles of mutual engagement. And since you are a product, you will have to definitely respect all the principles of engagement related to a product. In this regard, we have already discussed most of them, so just grasp one last point. You must refrain from selling the product for a price that does not justify its utility. In other words, do not get caught in the complicacy of demanding more than what you are worth. Otherwise, you will lose even that which is your worth. Therefore, do not engage in such pointless endeavours. Essentially, you must neither engage in false or manipulative practices to inflate the product's value, nor harbour a desire to obtain more than your true worth. As I have mentioned earlier, the market is anyway teeming with astute experts. So, any sort of manipulation is short-lived. In fact, those engaging in such endeavours are quickly ousted from the market. Just imagine, what would happen if you attempt to sell a regular car that runs on the road as a 'flying car'? You are intelligent and I'm sure you must have grasped the hint I have provided. Therefore, your focus should only be on ensuring that the product fetches the right price. For, this is verily the psychological principle of mutual engagement. In short, you must not undertake futile endeavours to manipulate and sell the product at an exorbitant price, but you definitely need to ensure that the product is sold at the right price. Moreover, whether it is a job or a business, if you fail to fetch the right price for the product even after a prolonged wait, then you simply need to find new customers for the product. Being mindful of all these aspects will ensure that you lead a smooth and splendid life.

Money is, indeed, the paramount necessity of life. And the more money one possesses, the greater is the possibility of leading a magnificent life. And verily, one of the direct paths to earning a substantial amount of money is becoming an entrepreneur. However, it is also crucial to comprehend that entrepreneurship is not an adventure that can be undertaken on a whim. It is not the same as acting on an impulse to try out paragliding while you are vacationing at a hill station. Enjoying an adventure at a hill station is a one-time fun activity, the cost of which is already known to you. However, if you take a plunge into becoming an entrepreneur deeming it to be an adventure, then this endeavour could put your very life at stake. There is no harm in desiring progress, but taking missteps in the pursuit of progress can prove to be dangerous. I am not in the habit of sharing senseless motivational advice just for the sake of boosting morale. While such words may sound encouraging, they are actually precursors to grave consequences. Therefore, I will never egg you on and say, "Become an entrepreneur, what are you waiting for?" Neither will I say, "Forge ahead, your destination is awaiting you!" I only speak what is psychologically correct. And the psychologically correct advice is—progress must be pursued. For that purpose, one should also keep one's eyes and ears open. And undoubtedly, being an entrepreneur eases the path to progress. However, it is imperative to understand that entrepreneurship is not a surefire way to achieve progress, for, it can very well lead to losses too. What I wish to convey is, before quitting a decent job and taking a leap into entrepreneurship, one must first assess one's capabilities. And in case the capabilities seem lacking, one must focus on developing them first. The bottom-line is, you must forge ahead only when you are equipped to reach your destination.

Indubitably, progress is the law of life. So, you should not only progress, but progress by leaps and bounds. And towards that end, if the opportunity presents itself, you must become an entrepreneur too. However, I want to caution you that for this purpose, you must first prepare yourself thoroughly and then forge ahead. Admittedly, one's aspirations can be fulfilled only in this lifetime; in other words, this is the only opportunity available to fulfil one's dreams. So, one must surely pursue progress and live a splendid life, but bear in mind that one must not embark on a suicidal path towards that end. All in all, comprehend well that one needs to adopt a balanced approach when it comes to entrepreneurship. I have explained repeatedly that the entire game of life is psychological. If the mind is prepared, then nothing is impossible to accomplish. What I am trying to elucidate is that if one has to embark on the journey of becoming an entrepreneur, it is essential to first prepare the 'mind' for entrepreneurship. And to prepare the mind, it is crucial to first comprehend the fundamental difference between being employed and being an entrepreneur. We are all well aware that in order to live, everyone has to work—there is simply no other alternative. The option of leading a grand life without lifting a finger does not exist in Nature. And there are only two types of work—you can either take up a job or become an entrepreneur. And bear in mind, there is a vast difference between the two. The most prominent difference is with respect to responsibilities. In a job, your responsibilities are limited to your assigned tasks, whereas as an entrepreneur, you are responsible for everyone working for you. Another significant difference is that as an employee, you have to follow instructions, whereas as an entrepreneur, the onus is on you to give instructions to all the people working for you about 'what activities or tasks they need to undertake'.

All in all, becoming an entrepreneur can increase the scope of your responsibilities manifold. Therefore, till the time your mind is not completely prepared to shoulder this responsibility, kindly put aside the thought of embarking on the adventure of entrepreneurship. Besides, preparing the mind is not difficult at all; a few days of contemplation will suffice for its preparation. Therefore, do not think that I am dampening your spirits; I am merely assisting you in preparing your mind towards becoming an entrepreneur.

Now, even if your mind is ready to shoulder the responsibility of becoming an entrepreneur, you must avoid committing haste. As I have mentioned earlier, entrepreneurship cannot be compared to a paragliding adventure undertaken at a hill station merely on a whim. So, once your mind is prepared to take on the responsibility, ensure that it acknowledges the fact that a job will bring with it a steady income on a monthly basis, but entrepreneurship leads to the uncertainty of both profits and losses. Thus, it is absolutely crucial to prepare your mind for these fluctuations in earnings as well. Otherwise, a weak mind will be alarmed and beat a hasty retreat at the first sign of highs and lows and this will prove to be even more detrimental. Because finding a job all over again and working as an employee will certainly not be a breeze. Hence, it is imperative to prepare the mind for the vagaries and vicissitudes of business. And in the event of a setback, it is also essential to prepare the mind to endure a temporary period of hardships. Once a person mentally prepares himself for these vagaries, he will not scramble away in fear of these uncertainties; instead he will stand resolute in the face of changing circumstances. And in today's competitive age, standing resolute is crucial for achieving success, especially because in these times, every big fish will go to any length to gobble up the smaller ones. This is precisely why mental preparation to stand resolute in the face of highs and lows is absolutely essential before embarking on any entrepreneurial adventure.

Now, the person whose mind is prepared to shoulder responsibility and also remain steadfast through these vagaries is undoubtedly fully prepared to become an entrepreneur. However, you must comprehend that if you aim to become an entrepreneur, you must be a successful one. Hence, I will re-emphasise that before taking any significant step, you must make the following additional preparations. For, a delay of a couple of years in taking the leap is acceptable, but you must venture forth only after thorough preparation. Indeed, if you have decided to take the plunge, then reaching the destination is an absolute must. There is no point in falling, stumbling or going astray halfway through the journey. Most importantly, you should never feel compelled to retrace your steps and hunt for a job again. Therefore, take your time but ensure that you take a firm step forward. And towards that end, keep the following key points in mind. Thereafter, rest assured that nothing can stop you from becoming a successful entrepreneur.

Expert Knowledge of the Field is a Must

Becoming an entrepreneur cannot be compared to winning a lottery that just about anyone can win. This is, in fact, a reward for competence. Therefore, ensure that whichever field you want to try your hand in, you are first well acquainted with its intricacies. Indubitably, you venture into business to generate profits, and how to generate 'profit' is a profound secret of every business. And it is this trade secret that generates income, not the business. For instance, you will never see every pharmaceutical company making a profit. Only the one who has grasped the trade secret of the pharmaceutical industry can generate earnings from it. Therefore, before embarking on the adventure of entrepreneurship, if you so desire, you can work as an employee in your chosen field to learn the ropes and the business secrets of that particular field. But do not take the leap blindly without doing so.

Management Skills Must be Exceptional

I would, in fact, urge you not to rush into becoming an entrepreneur. First, prepare and test your mind and brain adequately. Comprehend clearly that becoming an entrepreneur and a successful one at that is nothing short of a battle. And just like all the other battles of life, this battle is also psychological. Therefore, victory in this battle is assured only for those who psychologically prepare themselves in advance. So, if you aspire to become an entrepreneur, begin to train yourself psychologically from today itself. Don't worry if you need to invest a year or two in this training, but you should enter the battlefield only when you are in a psychological position to win effortlessly. And possessing robust management skills is of paramount importance for becoming a successful entrepreneur. This is because an entrepreneur has to manage countless aspects of his enterprise, and management is a game that is entirely psychological. A manager's work demands mental composure under all circumstances; indeed, a restless mind will never be able to manage any task efficaciously. Therefore, before daring to undertake any venture, be sure to acquire the skills that will aid you to calmly manage everything. If you wish, you can begin by managing various tasks at home and in the office. Bear in mind that practical knowledge always holds more weightage than any academic 'degree'. All in all, take a step towards becoming an entrepreneur only when you can trust your 'management skills'. Otherwise, you are bound to stumble even before you begin. For, when you are not able to manage anything, you can be certain that your business will fold up in no time.

Knowledge of Accounts & Legal Matters is Essential

Becoming an entrepreneur is a huge responsibility. Paying salaries to your employees on time is your primary obligation. Apart from this, there are numerous other transactions that need to be handled. One has to deal with seemingly endless taxation issues as well. So, naturally, the question arises: why would you choose to become an entrepreneur and grapple with all these challenges? Undoubtedly, to earn money. That being the case, gaining absolute control over your finances is crucial as well, and that is impossible without a grasp of the knowledge of accounts and legalities. Quite often, a lack of or inadequate knowledge in either of these domains spells disaster for businesses. Therefore, it is always advisable to gain experience in accounts and legal matters before taking the plunge.

In conclusion, life is an opportunity to progress, but you must ensure that you never fall flat on your face in the pursuit of progress. Besides, every endeavour in life is psychological in nature, and entrepreneurship is no exception to this. Therefore, you must surely become an entrepreneur, but take the step only after a thorough and complete psychological preparation. And once you take the plunge, immerse yourself in it completely. Work relentlessly towards that end; burn the midnight oil, if you have to. Then, rest assured that no one can stop you from becoming a successful entrepreneur. And for this journey, my best wishes are with you.

From our discussion so far, you must have already gained a thorough understanding of money's behaviour. Now, grasp an additional point. More often than not, people harbour the misconception that money flows in because human beings have decided to earn it. But nothing could be further from the truth. In fact, it is money that decides who it wants to shower its beneficence on, and it harbours no confusion in this regard. This is why it flows generously where it chooses to, and where it decides not to go, it makes one desperate for every single penny of it. I'm sure everyone is aware of this reality of money. This is precisely why those who possess money bask in its abundance, while those who don't have it are reduced to shedding tears of frustration. So, comprehend clearly that it is money that determines who it is going to flow to and who will remain deprived of it, and it harbours no confusion in this regard.

This leads to the question: is earning money beyond the control of human beings? If money is the one deciding who it wants to go to, then what role does a human being play in earning it? Well, undoubtedly, it is the human being who has to engage in work to earn money, so he definitely has a role to play—which is to work. What I am trying to explain is, if the human being's actions correspond with the psychology of money, then everything moves smoothly; otherwise, money becomes upset with him. This essentially means that to engage in work is within man's control, but it is 'money' that decides the outcome of that work. For, money will respond only when its psychology is being respected whilst one is engaged in work. And this fact is of paramount importance, so etch it in your mind. It is because of ignoring this fact that the efforts made by the majority are failing to yield the desired results.

In short, according respect to every aspect of the psychology of money is imperative if one desires the best

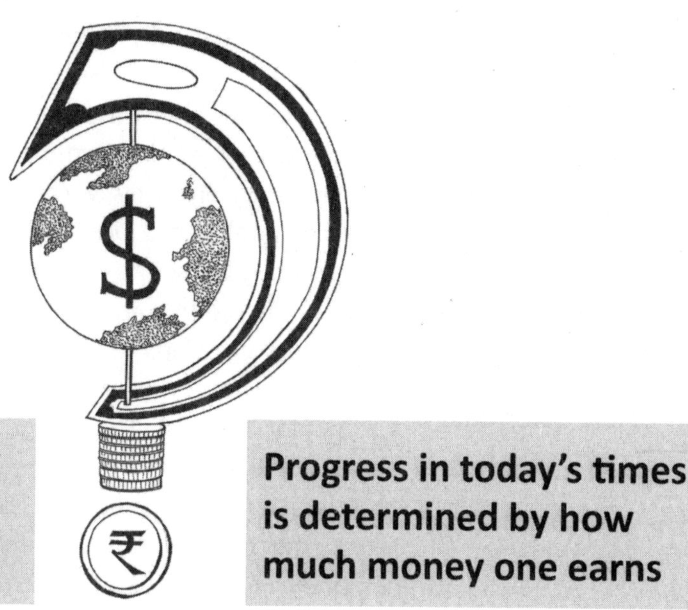

Progress in today's times is determined by how much money one earns

outcome. Now, even though I have already explained what the psychology of money is, I shall nonetheless revisit it briefly. The foremost aspect of money's psychology is that it flees when you chase it desperately. Therefore, as soon as possible, try to reach a stage whereby chasing money becomes inessential and you break free from all kinds of desperation to earn it. Next, align your mind with money as quickly as possible, for, it is only then that money's attention will be drawn towards you. These are the two fundamental conditions for earning a substantial amount of money, and I am confident that you will achieve both these goals very soon. Those who fulfil these two conditions must also grasp another principle of money—money has a soft corner for certain characteristics of human beings, and those who possess such traits find money chasing after them day and night. Neither do these people need to wish for money nor plan to acquire it, as

“

‘Money’ will lead you on **misadventures,** bringing **adverse consequences** in its wake

money automatically gravitates towards them.

Hence, do not assume that money will abide by the rules formulated by you. This is precisely why working hard or applying intelligence does not guarantee an income. It is also the reason why money remains elusive in spite of nursing desires or formulating plans to acquire it. Tell me honestly, is there anyone who isn't yearning for money or devising plans and strategies to earn as much money as possible? For that matter, even academic degrees or extra smartness does not guarantee that you will be able to attract money. For, these are assumptions made by humans and money does not care for human assumptions. It has its own mindset and psychology besides possessing its own distinct style as well. This is precisely why it flows in abundance towards those it chooses; and needless to say, it flows only towards those it prefers. Moreover, let me reiterate that in order to win favour with money, it is imperative to align one's mind with money. Only then will money chase you; until then, it will remain aloof and distant.

As far as money is concerned, everyone is well aware that whomsoever money chooses to shower its beneficence on, receives it in abundance. It is certain that such an immeasurable amount of 'money' cannot be earned merely through hard work, planning or wishing for it. Whoever possesses money in great abundance has acquired it only because money itself has chosen to flow to them. Comprehend this difference clearly: such a person has not desired money, on the contrary, it is money that has chosen him. And you too can be one of them. But how can you ensure that? Well, you simply need to develop the qualities that money admires. To help you with this, I shall now reveal all those qualities that money finds irresistible. However, bear in mind that these qualities will prove to be useful only after your 'mind and money are aligned'. As long as your mind is struggling for 'money', money will continue to keep you at arm's length. Until such time, even these special qualities will not be able to help you attract money in abundance. Alright, let me now share the key characteristics that money deeply admires.

Work Purely for the Joy of It

Money quickly gravitates towards those who work solely for their enjoyment. Working for one's pleasure and enjoyment means that the person is no longer working for money. However, take note that those who have inherited immense wealth and are engaged in work just for the fun of it do not fall into this category; their work, in fact, will be considered a 'pastime'. Such individuals, on the contrary, will end up losing their fortune. Similarly, those who have received assistance from their kith and kin or others to establish themselves do not fall into this category either. The individuals I am referring to are exclusively those intrepid souls who have aligned their mind and money after earning it on their own steam and are now working purely for the joy of it. Money will gravitate towards such people and it is only these 'self-made' people who have made a mark in history. Of course, there are some who scale up their inherited family businesses, taking them to new heights on the strength of their diligence, but they never fall into the category of those who create something out of nothing. We are, in fact, discussing those people who have toiled relentlessly to make ends meet. We are talking about those who aspire to make progress on their own merits. And such individuals must swiftly reach the stage whereby they begin to work only for the joy they experience rather than for money. Another point to keep in mind is that you will be able to derive enjoyment only from work that is to your liking. Therefore, recognising where your interest and talent lie and thereafter working in that field is an irrevocable prerequisite to be able to work joyfully. In essence, money gravitates towards those who work for the pleasure it begets. However, you must never forget that only those whose minds are aligned with money can engage in work solely for enjoyment. And even after having established this alignment, it is imperative that the field of work is as per their liking. Only those who fulfil these two conditions will be able to work for pleasure. And I promise, once they do so, money will naturally gravitate towards them.

Nurture Creativity

Creativity is money's biggest weakness! And understand well that creativity encompasses not just painting, music, literature, acting and other art forms, but also ingenious businesses, innovations, pioneering styles and thinking outside the box. Everything ranging from new management techniques to new approaches to marketing is nothing but creativity. And money is readily attracted to those who are creative. Therefore, you must try to be innovative in your thoughts and actions. Do not be afraid to try out something new. Very often, one encounters initial jolts when embarking on innovative endeavours, but so what? Money, after all, showers its abundance upon those who dare to tread uncharted routes. But, of course, those who indulge in creative pursuits as a pastime do not fall under this category. In essence, peruse the history of humankind and you'd see that money has showered its blessings exclusively on creative people.

Money is a Slave to Bravehearts

Money wholeheartedly showers its benevolence upon courageous individuals. So, what is courage? It is undoubtedly the boldness to engage in novel and ambitious endeavours. However, bear in mind that this courage should not stem from greed. You must also never forget that every form of greed is an arch-enemy of money. Therefore, never mistake greed and courage to be the same. Courage implies prudently taking calculated risks when an opportunity presents itself; while prudence is the first quality a person loses when shackled by greed. Greed is nothing but a type of desperation, which is why calculations made riding on greed-driven courage often go wrong. This is also why acts of courage driven by greed often backfire. In short, money is bowled over by the courageous, but greed or desperation is definitely not courage. Therefore, kindly do not squander away all that you possess by mistaking your greed for courage.

Now, comprehend one additional point in this regard. Courage is not only about risking your money. Staking your life for your passion is courage too. Persevering in your efforts despite all hardships is also courage. Moreover, continually endeavouring to pick oneself up and rise even after falling over and over again is courage. And money inevitably salutes all kinds of courageous people. I may have conveyed this point only through hints but I have stated it with utmost profundity. Therefore, grasp the profundity of this matter and become a truly courageous person. Rest assured, money is eagerly waiting to welcome you with open arms.

Money Salutes Vision & Intelligence

Vision means clear insight, and intelligence means thorough comprehension. Those who can see clearly and comprehend thoroughly do not ever need to expend much effort to earn money. However, even towards achieving a positive outcome with the help of your vision and intelligence, you have to first make efforts to align your 'mind with money'. Otherwise, both intelligence and vision are bound to be crushed under the weight of needs. Therefore, never forget that as long as the struggle for needs exists in life, money will continue to elude you. As long as you are gripped by the desperation to earn money, it will keep running away from you. Hence, etch it in your mind that whether an individual is courageous, creative or a true visionary, money will never favour him unless he triumphs over his needs and desperation.

Essentially, no matter how powerful a person's intelligence and vision are, if he desperately chases money, it will outsmart both his vision and intelligence. And what I am elucidating is a proven principle. You too must have surely come across numerous people whose intelligence is exceptional and vision is remarkable, yet they continue to face the hard knocks of life. Why is that so? It is simply because they fail to rise above their needs.

All in all, I have outlined four special qualities that money truly admires. But remember, while money may be enamoured by these qualities, it has certainly not taken leave of its senses. For, even in the case of people who possess these special qualities, money showers its abundance only when they have established 'a perfect setting between their mind and money'. Otherwise, despite possessing everything, they remain deprived of money's benevolence. Therefore, the foremost priority will always be to align your mind with money. Everything else follows later. Remember, without this alignment, all efforts will be rendered futile. Even intelligent and talented people are encountering setbacks only because they are not able to align their mind with money. And those who are not able to sync their mind with money remain mired in money traps. So, if you wish to acquire a substantial amount of money, then breaking free from money traps is imperative. And to evade money traps, it is essential for you to align your mind with money. Therefore, no matter which angle you perceive it from, the priority will always be to 'align your mind with money'.

To sum it up, money will not necessarily behave in accordance with the rules created by 'human beings'. Money has its own established behaviours. For instance, if you chase money, it will elude you. So, you must definitely refrain from chasing after it. This is the mistake that most people commit, as they fail to comprehend that the more they chase money, the more money will distance itself from them. Therefore, you will have to do something that compels money to chase after you. And that is an impossible feat to achieve without aligning your mind with money. So, first and foremost, you must make a determined effort to align your mind with money. Thereafter, develop within yourself any one of the four qualities that money admires. That's it! Money will gravitate towards you on its own. History bears testimony to the fact that money has showered its beneficence only when the conditions listed above have been fulfilled. And in your case too, once those conditions are met, money will surely bless you with its abundance.

Now, let us comprehend the most significant aspect of the psychology of money, which is indeed highly beneficial. The most prominent aspect of money's psychology is that it is quite 'affable'. So, if you judiciously make long-term investments, then money develops a deep 'camaraderie' with that investment, irrespective of whether you invest in shares, property or gold. The only point to keep in mind is that this companionship should last 20–50 years. In other words, you must avoid looking at this investment for a long period of time. And verily, money invested for such long periods has appreciated thousand times its value. In fact, all those who have maintained a long-term companionship with their investments have been consistently rewarded by money in the form of robust returns. In other words, money has most certainly demonstrated a deep camaraderie with such investments. If your family owns an ancestral property, you must surely be familiar with this situation. The property that your ancestors acquired for just a few thousand rupees would have appreciated to a value worth millions of rupees by now. Be it stocks or gold, money has maintained companionship in every field of investment.

Therefore, ensure that you make at least one such investment whenever an opportunity presents itself. However, keep in mind that this investment should be free from the burden of a loan or EMIs (equated monthly installments). It should be funded from your savings which you can comfortably set aside for the next 20–50 years. A single investment of this kind could secure the financial future of the next generation in your family. I am confident that if the opportunity presents itself, you will certainly make such a 'wise investment' for the long term. I am emphasising the term 'wise investment' because the selection of such an investment has to be perfect. Indeed, it is crucial to make this investment after careful consideration and consultation with an expert. You can be certain that once you make such an investment, you will always find money standing by you as a loyal, steadfast companion.

Before we move on to the next topic of discussion, let me ask you a fundamental question: is there anyone who is not aware of the fact that the human being has arrived in this world on a visa of 80–100 years? That being the case, what could be the purpose of his life other than to live splendidly and cherish sweet experiences? And to enable humans to live life in this manner, Nature has unleashed a bounty in the form of air and water, rain and rivers, mountains, snow, greenery, forests, fruits, flowers and so on. Furthermore, humans themselves have left no stone unturned in building a life of peace and comfort, right from creating sumptuous food items, delicacies and exquisite clothing to developing and nurturing various art forms. And as for science, it has helped create a treasure trove of comforts and conveniences. In other words, everyone including Nature and human beings themselves have contributed in the best possible way towards 'enabling the human being to live in peace and comfort'.

The question then arises—why are human beings so distressed? Why are they anxious and despondent? Why are they gripped by frustration and senselessness? Where does this perpetual stress and scramble in their lives stem from? If you observe closely, you will find that the root cause of all this stress is 'money'. Surely, all kinds of goods and services are abundantly available, but the prevalent system is such that everything has a price tag attached to it. And except for a select few, the majority of people do not possess sufficient money. And to top it all, there exists the human mind which refuses to obey. For that matter, would it really be called the 'mind' if it yielded? As is its wont, it is always soaring high. And to fulfil the soaring aspirations of the mind, one requires money. But the fact is, money cannot be obtained easily. Consequently, as life progresses, the chasm between the mind and money continues to widen, and if observed carefully, this widening gap is the very source of all the problems plaguing human beings.

> 'The **joys amassed** with **money**' will not only **attract more money** but also pave the way for **progress**

This leads to the question: should people live in misery, dying a little every day? Should they spend their life in distress and tension? Absolutely not! For, that would be a grave insult to the precious human life. Indeed, this cannot be allowed at any cost! So, what is the solution then? The first and obvious solution would be to ensure that everyone possesses adequate money so that no one ever feels its scarcity. However, with a population of eight hundred million people, this goal will remain unattainable. The second solution is to rein in the 'mind' and curb it from soaring high. But this goal is even more far-fetched! Besides, if the mind ceases to soar, how would a person ever be able to live? The mind is synonymous with the human being, and it is for the mind itself that the human being lives. In short, matters related to money and the mind will always remain complex.

Now, the mind will obviously refuse to be reined in. At the same time, one cannot deny that the scarcity of money will always be a reality. So, should human beings give up on their primary purpose of 'living life to the fullest'? No, absolutely not! The reality is what it is, but a way out of this seemingly impossible situation must definitely be found. And surely, there is a way. Since we have been bestowed with life as a human being, to live joyously is a must. And towards that end, all we need to do is awaken a little bit of psychological understanding within ourselves. In other words, it is crucial to learn the art of effectively tackling both money and the mind. In this context, it is worth noting that there is a vast difference between the actual scarcity of money and merely feeling that money is scarce. As a matter of fact, only twenty per cent of the world's population is genuinely grappling with the paucity of money. The rest are consumed by an unfounded sense of scarcity of money due to their psychological weakness. Otherwise, they do possess an adequate amount of money that will surely allow them to live joyfully just by aligning their mind with money. In other words, they can certainly lead a life free of the scarcity of money, a life wherein the mind does not experience any pain either.

The question then arises: why are humans unable to achieve this? Honestly speaking, this is due to the rising influence and power of money. The growing influence of money has psychologically debilitated human beings, and as a result, they are not able to 'align their mind with money' despite wanting to. All things considered, in spite of possessing sufficient money, the soaring influence of money has made life arduous for people. Due to their weak psychology, everyone has succumbed to the power of money. And this 'succumbing of their minds' to the power of money is the biggest problem that everyone is facing.

Let me elaborate this point in greater detail. Answer this: what is the biggest psychological weakness of human beings? It is that their interest lies more in showcasing their happiness rather than actually experiencing it. No one wants to appear unhappy or weak. And what is the criterion for measuring one's level of happiness? There is only one and that is by assessing how much money one possesses. In other words, if you wish to portray that you are happy, you require money to do that. It is this very influence and power of money that has caught everyone in its vice-like grip. For, in order to conceal their psychological weaknesses, everyone wants to flaunt and show off to others. And in today's times, money is an indispensable requirement if one wants to show off. However, it is impossible for everyone, all at once, to acquire sufficient money in order to impress others. So, the problem remains unresolved.

It's worth grasping that not everyone is psychologically weak. There are, indeed, some people who live with a sense of high self-esteem. Assuredly, such people live only to experience happiness, without the aim of flaunting their happiness to others. That is why they give top priority to the 'alignment of their mind and money'. And having achieved that alignment, they lead a life brimming with happiness and joy. Indeed, if they shun the idea of putting up a façade to impress everyone and avoid foolishly emulating others, then most people do not actually face such a severe shortage of money. To put it simply, it is all about living your life for yourself. And those who live for themselves are not concerned about what the world thinks of them or how it perceives them. However, there are very few people, perhaps only one among thousands, who possess such a powerful psychology, whereas the rest are only inclined to flaunt their happiness to others. And it is this penchant for showing off that has pushed everyone into a quagmire. This is the very reason I had mentioned earlier that there is a vast difference between the actual scarcity of money and the 'feeling' that money is scarce.

Alright, this was all about aligning your mind with money and living in peace. Moreover, this discussion pertained only to individuals. Let us now broaden our horizon and spare a thought for the entire world as well. After all, not everyone will find it possible to align their mind with money which leads us to the question: can we eliminate the problems engendered by money from the world despite this limitation? Is it possible to do something about it? The answer to this is a resounding "Yes!" Of course, to do so, we will have to delve deeper into psychology and acquaint ourselves with the 'psychology of problems and solutions'. And the first point you must grasp in this context is, problems and solutions are two sides of the same coin. If a problem exists, then its solution certainly exists too. A problem without a corresponding solution simply does not exist. And here, I am not just referring to money-related issues but all problems pertaining to life. Well, for now, rest assured that there is definitely a solution to every problem engendered by money as well. To that end, all we have to do is conduct a proper psychoanalysis of the problems arising from money. And, in this context, the first point you need to grasp is, there are three causes behind the problems engendered by money in this world. The first is the scarcity of money. The second is the desire in human beings to impress others, because of which everyone feels the need to possess more money than they actually require. For, one can impress others only with surplus money. And the third important cause is the unimaginable influence of money. Here, you must also grasp that in accordance with the three-dimensional theory of the universe, every problem has only three underlying causes. And by identifying these three causes, one can triumph over every problem existing in this world. The psychology of problems is certainly not the focus of this book, but the hint I have provided here will always prove useful to you.

Well, returning to our present issue—'money', it is evident that if we want solutions to money-related problems, we must delve into each of the three underlying causes one by one. We will need to grasp which of these causes can be eliminated and which cannot. So, the first cause is the scarcity of money, and clearly, it can never be eradicated. Hence, the insufficiency of money is bound to persist. It is impossible for all eight hundred million people to acquire a sufficient amount of money all at once. So, let us move on to the second cause, which is a persistent desire in people to impress others. In this regard too, it is quite evident that the human being's yearning to make an impression on others or to be perceived as notable and distinguished cannot be eliminated either. For that matter, this human desire should not be eliminated anyway, because progress would then come to a grinding halt. And progress is synonymous with human life. Just think about it—if the human being lacks the very desire to impress others, of what consequence would progress be for him?

Well, since we are discussing this topic, you must also grasp that aligning the mind with money is a path, not the destination. The goal will always be to progress; the destination will always be to lead a magnificent life. The alignment of the mind with money or being content is merely a psychological setting to ensure 'the mind remains peaceful and cheerful'. This is absolutely essential because a cheerful mind will progress effortlessly. In other words, the advice of being content is nothing but a 'psychological treatment', much like a tablet given to the mind, the primary objective of which is to ensure happiness and prosperity for human beings. Contentment simply means attaining prosperity in a joyful state of mind. For, even if one attains prosperity, whether big or small, but is still harbouring stress and tension, then it will undoubtedly be termed a bad bargain. This implies, there is no harm in wanting to make your mark over others, as progress is the primary goal of life.

Well, since advancement is the goal of life, there is absolutely no question of giving up the desire to make your

> Ask yourself if 'the **pain** you're experiencing because of **scarcity** of **money**' is **real** or **imaginary**

mark over others and attain progress. This brings us to the third cause, which is the unimaginable influence and power of money. And surely, this can be reduced with a little bit of psychological prudence. In other words, out of the three causes mentioned above, this alone is possible. And a solution can only emerge from what is possible. This is verily the principle of the psychology of solutions. When something is inherently impossible to implement, how can it offer a solution? Therefore, we have no choice but to work on the only possible option to achieve our objective. In other words, we have no alternative but to address the issue of the power and influence of money. Essentially, scaling down the power of money is the only solution to all money-related problems. For, it is impossible to eliminate the other two causes. And we have already grasped this by conducting a profound psychoanalysis of the problems engendered by money. If you wish, you can apply the same approach to find the solutions to the rest of your problems.

Well, since the only alternative is to reduce the power of money, we need to first comprehend the source which is lending money its tremendous power. It is only when we are able to discover the source of its power that we can think of reducing the power! And in this context too, it is evident that it is all of us who are collectively empowering money. And how are we doing this? Most definitely, through our needs. In other words, money is deriving its power from our needs. But in spite of this, cutting down on our needs is not the solution. For, needs alone pave the path to progress, and we certainly seek progress and advancement. Besides, we have already comprehended all these points thoroughly. So, at present, all you need to grasp is, money definitely derives its power from our needs, but not to the extent that it snowballs into a problem. Hence, there is absolutely no need to curtail our needs in order to diminish the power of money. The simple truth is, 'money is deriving its extra power' from the fact that in society and the world at large, respect and honour is bestowed only upon the wealthy. And surely, everyone yearns for respect and honour. This is precisely the reason why there is so much desperation for money all around. And it is this very desperation for acquiring respect and honour that is supplying this 'surplus power' to money. For, who doesn't crave respect and prestige? Well, for now, just comprehend that the problem can be resolved if we disconnect money from the source that lends it this 'surplus power'. This is the simplest way to diminish the power of money. In fact, this is the only solution for the entire world to liberate itself from the nuisance of money.

This is all very well, but how can one sever this connection? It is possible only by increasing our psychological understanding. In order to do this, we will need to create a world wherein wealth is no longer the criterion to bestow respect and honour; a world wherein respect and honour are based on a person's virtues, talents and work. In such a world, money will lose its power overnight. Because, when money is no longer the determining factor in receiving respect and honour, who would give it undue importance? And in such a scenario, money will be reduced to simply serving as a means to fulfil needs. Then, no one will be desperate to earn more money than is required. And in the absence of the desperation for surplus money, money will lose its extra power. As for the ordinary power that money derives from our needs, it is definitely tolerable. Besides, the amount of money required to fulfil one's needs can also be earned. Hence, this does not pose a major problem. The real issue lies in the pursuit of that extra money through which one seeks to gain respect and honour. However, when the criteria for gaining respect and honour will itself change, the extra power that money derives will also diminish on its own. For that matter, a mere piece of paper holding sway over human talent does not befit human beings at all. Importance should always be lent to the human being, not to money.

Essentially, the power of money will diminish the day the value and weightage given to human goodness surpasses that of the luxurious cars and mansions owned by scoundrels. The day when an artist is bestowed greater respect than a corrupt politician, money and its power will diminish automatically. And the day when the dedication of scientists is considered supreme, the world itself will be transformed. Then, neither will anyone chase after money nor will they lament its absence. Consequently, every person will not just find contentment in becoming a noble-minded and loving individual, an artist or a scientist, but also aspire to emulate such people. Most significantly, being happy in itself will become a matter of pride for everyone. Indeed, a day will dawn when sponsors arriving in luxurious cars will humbly wait with folded hands to honour a scooter-riding artist. And the day this transpires, the nuisance of money will disappear forever. Even more importantly, crimes will be as good as wiped out too. Indeed, when money will no longer be granted undue respect, to what extent would anyone commit wrong deeds in order to acquire it? That will be the time when everyone will quietly join the race to become artists and scientists, and just imagine how beautiful that world would turn out to be!

In short, the nuisance of money can be reined in with ease. Its power can be diminished to a considerable extent. A world teeming with good-hearted, cheerful people can very well be created. But all of this will transpire in its own time. As for you, kindly do not sit back and wait for that day to dawn. For, you have a world of your own too. Needless to say, your family, friends, acquaintances and so on form your world. And in this little world of yours, you must start giving importance to humanity instead of money. Let talent and happiness become the basis of gaining or giving respect. By doing so, at least the nuisance of money will vanish from your world, as both the pressure and the power of money will cease to exist. Thereafter, the people in your world will always remain happy and cheerful and will also fulfil the purpose of life. As for the rest of the world, it will change when it has to, but you should definitely continue to create your own little world wherein humanity and talent overpower 'money'. Accomplish this and watch all the sorrows and tensions vanish from your world. Take the lead and one day, the world will follow in your footsteps.

The entire world will be liberated from the nuisance of money in its own time; however, your own world may not be able to escape the trap of money. With the existence of a large family, numerous relatives, friends and a social circle, everyone may not be able to show prudence collectively. But even so, you must not succumb to the nuisance of money. Ensure that you choose your path wisely. You are well aware of the fact that you have arrived in this world to live out your life on a visa of 80–100 years. Hence, you must never lose sight of the purpose of life. Yes, money is indisputably the biggest source of sustenance. So, in order to earn money, you must work honestly, pouring your heart and soul into it for eight to ten hours a day. Ensure that you do not compromise on this front. Then, with the help of whatever money you earn on the basis of your honest, diligent work, align your 'mind with money' as soon as possible. However, also remember that progress is synonymous with life. Therefore, always keep your heart and mind open. Welcome every opportunity for progress that comes your way without compromising on living your life to the fullest.

In essence, just live joyously utilising the money available to you while also fulfilling your responsibilities, and even as you revel in the joy of life, continue to make progress. Irrespective of what you do, never chase after money. For, money dislikes being chased. Instead, strive to become a person that money would want to chase! And even if it doesn't, how does it really matter? Nurture little passions, work with dedication and lead a life full of zest—keep doing this and everyone will salute you one day. In fact, making you their role model, they will take inspiration from you.

This essentially means that the world will transform in its own time. Those around you will improve in their own time. But you must not wait for that day to dawn. Waste no time and ensure that you create a beautiful world of your own. Do not fall prey to the money trap and depart from this world without living this priceless human life to the fullest. Let the world be blinded to the significance of this matter; let friends and family not cooperate with you. But you must certainly live this precious human life as splendidly as possible. And consider this the greatest lesson of this book.

Based on our discussion so far, I would like to make a final request to the entire world. It is, in fact, crucial for the whole world to comprehend my message clearly; otherwise, it will be too late. We are well aware that over two hundred countries dot the globe, each with their countless beliefs and traditions that are given tremendous importance too. But the fundamental question is: what holds the greatest value? Is it traditions, beliefs or the human being himself? Undoubtedly, the human being is the most precious entity in the universe. And, traditions and beliefs, well, they keep changing with time. The only reason I am emphasising all these points is because in today's times, any belief or tradition that proves to be a hindrance in the human being's endeavour to lead a fulfilling life is totally unacceptable. Anything that obstructs human advancement cannot be accepted in this day and age. Today, everyone must collectively determine what holds the greatest value for them. Oscillating between statements such as "this is essential and that is also crucial" will no longer work.

Therefore, the entire world will have to come together and determine once and for all that the 'human being' is the most valuable entity. There is absolutely nothing that is superior to the human being, and when I say nothing, I truly mean there is nothing! So, harbour no confusion in this regard, and neither should you misbelieve nor argue that there is anything else which surpasses the value of the human being. For, in this vast universe, it is only the human being who is capable of living a complete life in the most splendid manner. So, how can anything be more significant than the human being leading such a life? If I have to state even this simple fact so emphatically, then this is definitely a sad state of affairs. The entire universe, in fact, pales in comparison to the value of a human being living his life to the fullest. The cheerful smile that adorns a human being's countenance is worth more than all the treasures of the world put together, in fact, even beyond what you have heard, known or held to be true so far. In short, it is an indisputable fact that nothing is more important than the sound of the rippling laughter of a human being and a life that is lived magnificently.

Well, it is crystal clear that a human being leading a splendid life surpasses everything else in importance. Hence, ensuring such a life for the human being should become the world's topmost priority. Therefore, whether it is the beliefs, traditions, ideologies or even the laws of the land, they should all aid the human being in living his life to the fullest. In fact, they should support human advancement. Anything that hinders human beings from leading a magnificent life or poses obstacles to human advancement should be discarded immediately. Then it doesn't matter how historically significant such customs, ethos or beliefs are. Only rules and traditions that contribute towards facilitating a meaningful and enriching life for the human being should be adhered to; everything else must be discarded right away. If you wish to see the world transformed into a beautiful paradise, then these decisions will have to be made.

Now, let us discuss the manner in which 'human beings' lead their lives. How can the present-day human being lead a happy and splendid life? This is possible only when all his practical needs are met easily. Until that happens, it is truly impossible for anyone to live peacefully. In such a scenario, it goes without saying that fulfilling the practical needs of the human being should be the world's sole priority. And until the practical needs of the entire global population of eight hundred million people are met, nothing else should take precedence. And this 'nothing else' comprises all those things that many people take pride in. This 'nothing else' also includes all those issues and matters which are creating a divide amongst human beings. 'Nothing else' literally means 'nothing else'. It includes nothing else apart from fulfilling the practical needs of human beings. And this is the most significant hint I have provided. Today, I appeal to the entire world that lending importance to anything else other than 'fulfilling the practical needs of human beings' would entail paying a heavy price. If we wish to transform the world into a beautiful paradise, then everyone must collectively embark upon this endeavour with unwavering determination. Otherwise, this world will turn into a mental asylum in no time!

Kindly comprehend that at the very least, everyone should be able to afford basic necessities such as food, clothing and shelter of a certain standard. Why should anyone have to live in anxiety even for a moment, worrying about these three fundamental needs? In this scientific age, how can one tolerate the sight of people going to sleep on an empty stomach or living without a roof over their heads? How can one expend their energies on anything else as long as the paucity of food, clothing and shelter exists? How can money be possibly frittered away elsewhere? In fact, in today's scientific era, how can only food, clothing and shelter suffice? Undoubtedly, everyone wishes to provide excellent education to their children and the best healthcare facilities for their families. Apart from that, basic comforts and amenities are necessary too. Who doesn't want to offer the world on a platter to their children? How long will the people of this world suffer the agony of the insufficiency of all these amenities? If human beings are compelled to live in such agony, then of what consequence is everything else? How can anything else be prioritised over these necessities? How can time, energy and resources be squandered on anything else?

The world of thieves is governed by just one spiritual principle—the big fish will devour the small fish

Here, once again, let me make it clear that nothing else truly means nothing else, leaving no room for exceptions. As long as everyone's fundamental needs such as food, clothing and shelter along with healthcare, education and basic comforts remain unfulfilled, shifting focus elsewhere, even momentarily, must be abstained from. Whether the world takes this as an appeal or a warning, this is what everyone will have to work towards collectively.

Now, the question is, how can all these needs of human beings be fulfilled? Well, the only solution is 'money'. These fundamental requirements of human beings can be fulfilled solely with 'money'. And money is neither raining down from the sky nor is it sprouting from the ground. Human beings have to earn it themselves. And for such a large number of people to earn sufficient money simultaneously, it is imperative to have an extremely robust economy. If viewed from this perspective, 'economy' is the true dharma (religion) and also the foremost priority of the present-day world. And the country that grasps this truth and works accordingly will flourish and its people too will thrive and live happily. Indeed, apart from a robust economy, everything else holds little relevance in the present times.

Frankly speaking, whether it is religion, society or tradition, everything should be acceptable only to the extent that it is supporting the economy. Anything that goes against supporting a country's economy should be discarded promptly. For, the human being holds utmost importance, and living a fulfilling, dignified life is the most precious thing for a human being. Obviously, money is indispensable for survival and only a 'robust economy' can provide the means to acquire 'money'. Therefore, whether it is the rules and regulations, the laws of the land, religion, beliefs or traditions, only those that support the economy should be adopted. Bear in mind, if the economy collapses, everything will be ruined. Then, no other measure will work. Therefore, countries that fanatically cling onto futile beliefs and traditions should observe extreme caution. All forms of fanaticism are toxic as they hinder both 'living a fulfilling life as well as progress'. You can be certain that only a country that liberates itself from fanaticism will flourish and thrive. As for those who have already resolved to march along the path of ruination, what can one say about them? More importantly, this is a fact that must be grasped by India as well. A massive population of 1.3 billion people is a huge responsibility and providing a meaningful life to those 1.3 billion beating hearts holds utmost importance. In other words, a massive and developing country like India simply cannot afford to focus on anything else but its 'economy'. In fact, 'economy' is the only religion in today's times. That being the case, merely talking of becoming a world leader will not make India one. If India aspires to become a world leader, it will happen only with the assistance of a soaring and thriving economy. Hence, it is imperative for India to break free from all pointless pursuits. Everyone will have to collectively direct all expenditure solely towards strengthening the economy. All frivolous expenses incurred in promulgating and nurturing useless beliefs and traditions will have to be curtailed drastically. Know well that by merely talking about being a world leader will not make anyone a world leader. The key lies in collective action. Everyone must realise that science reigns supreme in today's world. For a nation like India with a population of 1.3 billion, the annual expenditure on scientific research stands at approximately 17.7 billion USD (as per 2018-19 figures). In contrast, Switzerland, with a population of 8 million, spends 25.5 billion USD on scientific research (as per 2019 figures). I'm sure this matter needs no further elaboration and if I were to speak any more than this, it would indeed be a matter of shame for me and every other Indian.

My only request is, everyone right from individual families to nations and from nations to the entire world should collectively live with the sole purpose of strengthening the economy. Only then will we be able to truly reap the benefits of the phenomenal progress made by science. Only then will we be able to offer human beings the priceless gift of a dignified and fulfilling life. Everyone has the right to live life to the fullest and the opportunity to live magnificently must be available to all. I hope the entire world will join hands to work towards strengthening the economy, and together, we will soon transform this world into a veritable paradise.

Let me now draw your attention to another significant point. As you have been bestowed with human life, do not ever forget its significance. It is, in fact, a beautiful opportunity to live to the fullest. Remember, you have arrived in this world on a visa of just eighty years, and in these eighty years, you have to amass as many moments of joy and peace as you can. Indeed, the true value of life lies solely in garnering such moments of joy and peace, so let this alone be your topmost priority.

Indubitably, money is the primary necessity in today's times, for, neither joy nor peace can be attained without money. Moreover, one also wishes to enjoy the wonders of scientific discoveries, and to fulfil such desires, one requires a substantial amount of money. The point I wish to convey is, you must pour your heart and soul into earning the maximum amount of money possible, and towards that end, dedicate eight to ten hours to working devotedly. For, in this day and age, the greater the amount of money you possess, the more magnificently you will be able to live your life. And do I need to re-emphasise that living your life to the fullest is the very purpose of life! Therefore, do not perceive life's purpose and earning money as different from each other; they, in fact, complement each other. Hence, put in your best efforts in both these endeavours.

Well, this was one aspect of the matter. However, despite putting in the best efforts in your work, if you are still unable to earn sufficient money, do not lose heart. You have made the effort and that's the end of the matter. You have performed the action and your job is done. Never mind if the expected outcome does not materialise; it certainly does not mean that you have failed. So, you must neither nurse such defeatist thoughts nor should you allow yourself to wallow in misery. For, the ultimate significance lies not in earning money but in living life magnificently. Therefore, just live a beautiful life with whatever money is available to you. After putting in an honest day's work for eight to ten hours, do not bother about whether the money you possess is scarce or abundant. Know this—if your life abounds with joy, peace and tranquillity, it verily means that you have attained everything. Your journey into this world has been a success! To give you an example, in order to attain peace of mind, Gautam Buddha had renounced his palace and all the opulence associated with it. This implies that happiness and serenity are not necessarily found in palaces alone.

> "The **first principle** of **making** a **deal** is, the person you deal with once **should deal** with **you repeatedly**

Let me reiterate that the primary objective of life is to live magnificently. And towards that end, everyone must put in their best efforts and strive to earn the maximum amount of money possible. Of course, if the expected outcome eludes you despite your best efforts, then only should you seek peace minus the luxury of a grand palace. But the first priority should always be to live joyfully in the lap of opulence. Do not surrender without a fight like Arjuna, who tried to desert the battlefield in the epic, Mahabharata. Those who seek peace in the wilderness or the Himalayas without making earnest efforts to earn money are called escapists. Finding peace in the wilderness or the Himalayas should be the last resort. And even then, it is the final recourse for only those who have put in their best efforts to earn, for, they have performed their duties with integrity. Besides, the outcome is never in anyone's control, so never mind if the expected outcome has eluded you. You must seek peace in whatever outcome comes your way. For, the ultimate purpose of life is to live peacefully.

Lastly, you must pay heed to 'Krishna's teachings' alone. And Krishna's only message is to endeavour earnestly, irrespective of whether your efforts yield the desired outcome or not. However, those who shirk effort itself are unacceptable to Krishna. Despite being born in a dungeon, Krishna went on to scale dizzying heights of life. He became a king too and even married several princesses. A cowherd marrying princesses is, undoubtedly, a remarkable accomplishment. That's not all! Krishna also wholeheartedly pursued and fulfilled all his passions in life. Truly, in the entire history of humankind, there is no tale greater than this, of creating everything out of nothing! That is precisely why Krishna is called the 'complete avatar'. And just like him, you too must rise and soar to the skies. You too must elevate yourself to great heights. So, discard the very thought of putting down your weapons. Comprehend well that Krishna's accomplishments transformed into reality because he was a true 'man of action'. And you too have to embody the same essence. Krishna was a master of psychology as well, and it is vital for you too to gain valuable insights from his psychological power. For, your destination also lies high above in the skies! In fact, to enable you to soar high, I have penned the complete psychological biography of Krishna titled 'I am Krishna', encompassed in six volumes. Read this book if you wish to gain a comprehensive understanding of the profundity of Krishna's psychology and his entire life. The psychological biography of Krishna holds great significance because we too must lead a magnificent life just like Krishna. And for that purpose, this biography teaches us to wholeheartedly engage in action. It also imparts the lesson that one should refrain from lamenting if one's actions fail to yield the desired results. A sumptuous meal comprising 56 food items was Krishna's favourite, but he was not in the habit of lamenting on being served a frugal meal either. And you too must emulate him in all these aspects. Life is meant to be lived to the fullest, so you must live every moment with zest, irrespective of the circumstances. Strive for a palace by all means, but if all you get is a shed, live joyfully nonetheless! Consider this the most significant spiritual lesson of this book. And with this, I rest my pen thus, bringing this book to a close.

Other Bestsellers by **Deep Trivedi**

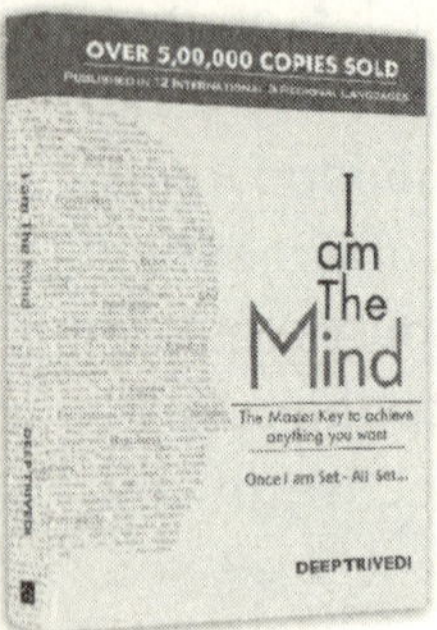

A book that not only reveals the seven minds of a human being, but also helps him experience them within, while also showing him how to awaken their powers. Essentially, this book hands you the remote control of your mind!

Written in a simple language, this book explains how and why everything is psychology. It also answers the biggest question of life - 'Is hard work and effort really necessary?' To explain this, it delves into the science and psychology behind 'Doing and Happening'.

Profound ideas are often grasped easily and imbibed instantly through the medium of stories and anecdotes. A collection of such all-time great stories, this book is a must-read for everyone and should especially be narrated to young children along with the moral of each story.

This book holds the power to completely change one's mind and life. It not only sheds light on all the important aspects of life, but also shows easy and practical ways to implement these key learnings in life.

This book proves the existence of the 'Soul' in a precise, scientific manner, grasping which a person will experience the soul within him with great ease. The book shows how the 'soul and its powers' are not illusory, and in fact can be experienced within.

'I am Gita' is the first-ever book that elucidates the essence of all 700 *shlokas* of the Bhagavad Gita along with its psychological and spiritual dimension in totality. Imparting the thrill of a story, this book will help you grasp the true essence of the Gita effortlessly.

Available in English, Hindi, Marathi & Gujarati at **www.aatmanestore.com,** all leading book stores, e-commerce sites and Deep Trivedi app in e-book and audio book format